Behavioral
Science
and
Human
Survival

Science and Behavior Books brings to
those interested in the behavioral
sciences important and timely books
produced economically in durable
vinyl covers. We solicit opinions and
ideas from our readers.

*This is an Original Edition
in vinyl covers*

Behavioral Science and Human Survival

Edited by

MILTON SCHWEBEL

New York University

for

The American Orthopsychiatric Association

and

The World Federation for Mental Health

 SCIENCE AND BEHAVIOR BOOKS, INC.

577 College Avenue, Palo Alto, California 94306

Foreword

We, who are living during the second half of the twentieth century, may consider that this period of history is unique because it is the time when we are living, a time that has a different significance for us than the past, before we were born, and the future, after we are dead. But in fact this period of history is unique for another reason: it is the unique epoch in the history of civilization when war will cease to be the means of settling great world problems, or civilization will come to an end.

During recent decades the world has been greatly changed, in all of its aspects, through the discoveries of scientists. The use of these discoveries to improve the lot of mankind has been hindered by our retention of social, political, and economic systems and attitudes that are no longer appropriate to the changed world of today.

The greatest of all changes has been the change in the methods of waging war. Nuclear explosives and vehicles for delivering them now exist in such quantity that if they were to be used in a great war most of the people on earth might be killed, the great nations might be converted into radioactive wastes, the pool of human genetic material might be subjected to irreversible change, and possibly the human race itself would cease to exist. War has ceased to be a rational means of settling disputes between nations.

Yet, despite the general recognition that these changes in the nature of the world and the significance of war have taken place, the national governments and world leaders have found it impossible to achieve the transition from the world system of the past, which has been based upon sovereign nations that resort to war to settle disputes, to the world of the future, in which all nations abandon enough of their sovereignty to permit the development of a system of world law based upon justice and morality that would take the place of war.

The problem to be solved is a tremendous one, the greatest problem that the world has ever faced. Its solution will require contributions from all sides—not just from the politicians and statesmen, and from the physical scientists and military experts, but also, and perhaps most importantly, from those scientists who make a study of man himself and of the relation of men with one another.

It is accordingly gratifying that the American Orthopsychiatric Association and the World Federation for Mental Health should have cooperated in arranging a conference of behavioral scientists to discuss issues relating to world peace, and should have collected some of the contributions to this conference in this book, Behavioral Science and Human Survival. I believe that men have enough good sense to solve the present great problem by abolishing war, replacing it by world law, and developing a world in which the resources of the earth and the fruits of labor are used for the benefit of human beings, rather than preparation for death and destruction.

Linus Pauling
Center for the Study of
Democratic Institutions
Santa Barbara, California

Contributors

EMILE BENOIT is professor of international business in the Graduate School of Business and on the staff of the School of International Affairs at Columbia University.

VIOLA W. BERNARD is professor of psychiatry and director of the Division of Community Psychiatry at Columbia University.

RAY L. BIRDWHISTELL is professor of research in anthropology, Department of Psychiatry, Temple University Medical Center, and Senior Research Scientist III at the Eastern Pennsylvania Psychiatric Institute in Philadelphia.

ELISE BOULDING is editor of the International Peace Research Newsletter.

KENNETH E. BOULDING is research director of the Center for Research on Conflict Resolution, University of Michigan.

FRANCOIS CLOUTIER is a psychiatrist who is attached to the University of Montreal and Notre Dame Hospital as a consultant, and he is the director-general of the World Federation for Mental Health.

SIBYLLE K. ESCALONA is professor of psychology in the department of psychiatry at Albert Einstein College of Medicine, Yeshiva University.

JOHAN GALTUNG, Director of the Peace Research Institute, Oslo, Norway, is head of the Section for Mathematics, Statistics and Methodology at the Institute for Social Research, University of Oslo.

NATHAN KOGAN is a senior research psychologist in the Personality Research Group at Educational Testing Service and a visiting lecturer in the Department of Psychology, Princeton University.

JUDD MARMOR is clinical professor of psychiatry, University of California at Los Angeles and president of the Academy of Psychoanalysis.

SEYMOUR MELMAN is professor of industrial engineering at Columbia University.

IDA C. MERRIAM is director of research and statistics, Social Security Administration, Department of Health, Education and Welfare.

CHARLES E. OSGOOD is professor of psychology and director of the Institute of Communications Research at the University of Illinois.

PERRY OTTENBERG is attending physician at the Institute of Pennsylvania Hospital; assistant professor, Department of Psychiatry, University of Pennsylvania, and an associate member of the Philadelphia Association for Psychoanalysis.

TALCOTT PARSONS is professor of sociology in the Department of Social Relations at Harvard University and a Fellow of the American Academy of Sociological and Economic Theory.

FRITZ REDL is Distinguished Professor of Behavioral Sciences at Wayne State University, Detroit, Michigan.

VINCENT P. ROCK is director of the Program of Policy Studies in Science and Technology at George Washington University.

MILTON SCHWEBEL is professor and chairman of the Department of Guidance and Administration at New York University's School of Education, a psychotherapist, and a consultant.

MUZAFER SHERIF is director of the Institute of Group Relations and research professor of psychology at the University of Oklahoma.

MICHAEL WALLACH is associate professor of psychology, Department of Psychology, Duke University.

BRYANT WEDGE is director of the Institute for the Study of National Behavior in Princeton, N. J.

Introduction

This book is about life. It is not filled with words about work and play, loving and mating, children and laughter, or nature and beauty. It is not about the stuff of life that the authors write but about the preservation of our lives and those of the generations that are to follow endlessly. They write about the specter that hangs over the world of man, that mushroom-shaped aftermath of a tragic decision to destroy life on our planet, about its effects on our lives, our emotions, our relationships with our fellow men, and about the social, economic and psychological factors that perpetuate conflict. And they write with the deep conviction that man, with his infinitely creative brain, has the capacity to solve the problems of survival.

Such confidence in reason is characteristic of all scientific endeavor and no less so of behavioral science. Under this heading are such fields as psychology, sociology, anthropology, psychiatry, economics, and political science—any science or branch of a science that studies the behavior of man in his physical and social environment. Behavioral scientists, including the authors of this book, are not likely to regard their efforts as futile. On the contrary, while fully aware of the dangers that confront us at this moment of history, they believe that free and open discussion within our nation and between nations is now, as ever, the best guarantor of wisdom in the relations of states and of men, the surest safeguard of peace and sanity in foreign affairs.

This volume was born in an act of faith in the value of communication among scientists and between them and the public, a faith almost as old as science itself. The papers were originally written for presentation at the annual meetings of the American Orthopsychiatric Association in Washington, D. C., March, 1963, the opening program of which was cosponsored by the World Federation for Mental Health. "Human Survival" was selected as the theme of the meetings because an organization of scientists and practitioners serving the mental health of the nation could afford to neglect the state of the world in this nuclear age only at the risk of professional ignorance and incompetence. It hardly needs saying that a dead people cannot be a mentally healthy one, nor that almost two decades of Cold War following upon the heels of a ghastly hot war were bound to leave perhaps indelible marks on human behavior.

The American Orthopsychiatric Association asked some seventy-odd behavioral scientists to address themselves to various issues related to the maintenance of peace. Several assumptions, implicit in the planning of the program, are stated here because they clearly apply to the book.

1. In the face of grave danger, man is least effective in panic or ostrich-like denial of threat and is most effective in using his intellect. Science is but a specialized form of the use of intellect wherein stringent laws are applied to heighten the objectivity and reliability of the conclusions.

2. The problems of survival are of such scope that they require a broad interdisciplinary approach. Were any one group alone to attack the problems, e. g. , psychologists, they would confront the issues in much too narrow a fashion regardless of the merits of their contribution.

3. Neither all the behavioral sciences nor all the important issues are represented. What we have are samples of the ways in which thoughtful scholars, many of them eminent in their own fields, attack some of the problems of war and peace.

4. As the first major onslaught on the problem of survival by the Association and one of the first by so large a group of behavioral scientists, it must be regarded as only a beginning.

5. The behavioral sciences cannot "solve" the world's or the nation's ills, but they can provide some insights into the causes of conflict, the processes of resolution, and the effects of continuing Cold War and intermittent crises on the health of our people.

The unity that the book possesses is achieved by virtue of the fact that the topic is survival, the authors are all behavioral scientists, and they all have confidence in man's rational processes. Beyond that, some cohesiveness is achieved by the organization of the papers into four parts, each part representing a different type of scientific approach to the problems, and each preceded by a brief introduction. The first consists of a sample of general papers on the over-all topic of survival. Here, to a large degree, the authors write as behavioral scientists far more than as specialists in particular fields. In Part II, however, which also consists of a sample of theoretical papers, the mark of the specific behavioral sciences is apparent. The nature of the papers in Part III is different from those of both preceding sections, for here empirical data drawn from controlled observations and from questionnaire studies are reported. The final section of the book, Part IV, includes an important up-to-date report on peace research activities in many parts of the world, as well as an annotated review of the published literature and other resources on peace.

Acknowledgement is made to those who planned the American Orthopsychiatric Association's program from which these papers were selected, among them the Chairmen of the Program Committee, Doctors Cynthia P. Deutsch, Edward J. Hornick and Edwin S. Kessler; to Lyle Stuart, publisher of George Seldes' The Great Quotations from which the introductory quotations were drawn; to those who lent encouragement and support in the publication of the book: Dr. Marion Langer, Executive Secretary of the Association, the two previous presidents and the incumbent, Dr. Edward D. Greenwood, Miss Gisela Konopka, and Dr. Arthur L. Benton; Dr. Leon Eisenberg, Editor of The American Journal of Orthopsychiatry; Dr. Francois Cloutier, Director, World Federation for Mental Health; to the publisher's consulting editor, Mrs. Dimmes Bishop; to my secretary, Mrs. Sally R. Santini, and especially to my wife, Mrs. Bernice Schwebel.

Milton Schwebel
Washington Square
New York, July, 1964

Contents

Part IV THE PEACE RESEARCH MOVEMENT

Part I

GENERAL PAPERS:
THE INTERDEPENDENCE OF NATIONS

Whoever undertakes to set himself up as a judge in the field of Truth and Knowledge is shipwrecked by the laughter of the gods.

Albert Einstein

The behavioral scientist does not set himself up as a judge of the truth. He chooses a problem that seems significant, considers the relevant knowledge already available, and then proceeds to ask the questions that he thinks need to be answered. He will not declare "the truth"; the answers he obtains through controlled observation and logical analysis will begin to approximate the truth in the form of solutions to the problem he wishes to solve.

His success depends on the way he conceptualizes the problem, that is, on his "theory," from which he will derive the questions he will try to answer and the assumptions he will make. The investigator who assumes that all humans are instinctively aggressive and that these inherent tendencies must be harnessed if war is to be prevented will ask fundamentally different questions from the scientist who rejects such an assumption. They cannot both be right. Obviously the questions and the research of one of them will be unfruitful.

Also, the success of the scientist depends on the stage of development of his field of science and the objectivity of the investigator himself.

These principles apply to his studies on human survival as on other matters. In fact, investigations of international conflict pose even greater problems because they have a greater urgency and this makes objectivity all the more difficult to attain. Such problems of the scientist are analyzed by sociologist Talcott Parsons in the first paper in Part I, in which he considers the special difficulties in the scientist's confrontation with international conflict. Cautioning against what might be called the fireman's emergency role whenever

1

a crisis arises, he favors giving priority to the advancement of the behavioral sciences through research and teaching, but with encouragement of research in areas in which action is urgent. He proposes two other roles, both pertaining to governmental policy-making function.

The other papers are excellent examples of the enlightened science-oriented mind coping with human problems. In his paper on unquestioned assumptions about national security, psychologist Charles E. Osgood demonstrates the importance of challenging what has long been taken for granted. In questioning these assumptions he follows the scientific tradition of looking afresh at beliefs that are widely accepted as "common sense," or passionately held as the necessary foundations of social practice.

The outcome of his analysis is to offer the possibility of greater flexibility in our attempts at reconciling differences in the world. This he achieves by indicating the inseparability of the two great powers and their unavoidable interaction. Political scientist Vincent P. Rock examines one particular form of interaction, the interdependency of the United States and the Soviet Union. Here a behavioral scientist is at work in attacking the fundamental problems of conflict and communication between the powerful antagonists; he emerges not with panaceas or grandiose solutions but with real possibilities for modest steps toward resolution of conflict, drawn from rigorous analysis of several propositions. Similarly, psychologist Morton Deutsch, in examining the military policy of stable deterrence, finds that just because there is a sensitive interaction between two powers who possess nuclear weapons, neither can achieve security except by helping to make the other more secure. He makes specific suggestions to aid in a move from "a peace of mutual terror to a peace of mutual trust."

Here, then, are the papers of a sociologist, a political scientist, and two psychologists on broad issues of survival.

The Role of the Behavioral Scientist in International Relations

————————————————————————— **TALCOTT PARSONS**

The behavioral sciences share with all other sciences an acute problem in the complicated relation between the emphasis on pure science, research and the advancement of knowledge "for its own sake," and the uses of science in the wide variety of applied fields. In some respects these pressures are becoming increasingly severe: first, because science has become of much greater practical importance than ever before, and second, because certain of the acute practical problems of our society are in part, at least, consequences of the use of science. The most salient single case is perhaps that of nuclear weapons. The recent public agitation over the uses of insecticides is another case in point.

On this general level, pertaining to all the sciences, it may be worthwhile to distinguish two aspects of the applied problem. On the one hand, the growth of scientific knowledge — different in different fields—produces possibilities of its practical use in one way or another. Some of these uses, like those in a good deal of the medical field, are so unequivocally beneficent that there is no serious problem involved in promoting them energetically. Indeed, the problem more often lies in getting people to accept benefits opened up by scientific developments when for various reasons they are reluctant to do so.[1] This, however, is by no means uniformly the case. Other developments, like that of nuclear fission, open up very serious possibilities of abuse and create dangers to a wide variety of human interests which otherwise would not be present. The matter is further complicated by the fact that very frequently the potential effect of use is not either beneficent or harmful—but, rather, that there is some complex balance of possibilities in both directions.

The problem, then, is, what is the nature of the scientist's responsibility for the uses to which the results of his work are put? For example, should the community of scientists take strong meas-

---

[1] Cf. the formidable political resistance to the fluoridation of water supplies.

ures to discourage research whose results might possibly or probably eventuate in harmful consequences? There is a school of thought which would go rather far in this direction. I think a distinction should be made between discouraging research and taking some form of responsibility for the use of knowledge, once gained. The former is almost unequivocally to be condemned. It is too difficult to know in advance what the practical consequences of lines of purely scientific investigation are likely to be. To insist on stopping this investigation because harmful uses might eventuate is to come very close to a totalitarian point of view.

With respect to responsibility for uses of knowledge already in existence, the situation is somewhat different. I do not think we can absolve ourselves from all responsibility; at the same time, neither can we assume the whole, nor even perhaps the primary responsibility. It is in the nature of the case that scientific knowledge, once arrived at and published, is a general resource available in the society. The uses to which general resources are to be put cannot be determined by one group and by them alone, but must be decided by some kind of complex decision-making process in which many groups (and individuals) are involved. Scientists should participate in this process, but should not arrogate to themselves the sole responsibility, which would carry with it also the prerogative of excluding others from the decisions. So far as ethics is concerned, there is a direct parallel between this situation and that of economic production in an impersonal market. Should the telephone company be held responsible when its lines are used to transmit messages grossly immoral in one form or another, or should the General Motors Corporation be held responsible for the use of one of their cars by gangsters in a bank robbery? There have been times when the answers to these questions would ordinarily have been "yes," but now both the doctrine of the law and our general moral sentiment is that it is quite unreasonable to impose such responsibility.

The second main facet of the problem of application is the pressure on the scientist to "do something" about distressing situations which arise in areas of practical interest and affairs in which his competence might be relevant to a solution. An example is the urgency of the practical care of sick people. It is right and proper that the practicing physician should make this care his primary responsibility. It does not follow, however, that the total social investment in the mitigation of illness and premature death through illness should be directed to training and equipping practicing physicians. That an important fraction of these resources should be diverted into research has become a fully accepted view. The very obvious point is that if a certain number of competent people, properly equipped, devote themselves to research for the future, they will advance knowledge of the causes of disease to a point at which a quite different order of control of it will become possible. It should not be forgotten that, in the meantime, a good many people will suffer and die who might have been cured or saved if the resources devoted to research had been devoted to medical practice.

Precisely because the behavioral sciences are relatively young and have not yet produced, except in a few fields, practical results of the same order of clear importance as those of the physical and biological sciences, the institutional solution of these dilemmas has not proceeded as far as in the other cases.

Above all, there is a widespread sentiment, both within the relevant professions and in a more general public, that applied professions whose members are trained in relevant fields should devote themselves to solutions of these practical problems, and that any conscientious person who has a competence in those fields should devote himself mainly to them. I suppose the outstanding current example is the problem of war and peace. There is certainly considerable feeling in many quarters that any normally conscientious social scientist whose competence might have bearing on this problem should devote himself entirely to it and should abandon all concern with research problems which cannot be expected to have a rather immediate impact in this area.

Some Special Situations of the Behavioral Sciences

There seem to be three main sets of circumstances which make these problems particularly acute for the behavioral sciences. The first is the combination of the fact that these sciences are relatively new with the fact that they have grown enough to become publicly conspicious and to arouse a great many expectations.

The rise of these disciplines to a major position in the whole system of academic status, teaching, and research is an altogether new phenomenon of the present century. Nothing like it has ever been known in human history, and indeed it has gone much further in the United States than anywhere else. This is, I think, a natural extension of the development of the older sciences. Of course, there is still a substantial lag with respect to numbers of trained personnel, positions in universities and research organizations, and financial resources. Nevertheless, psychology, sociology, and anthropology, following with some lag behind economics and political science, have in our generation attained positions which are quite unprecedented in terms of the historical background. They are now established in all of the principal universities in the country, in terms not only of undergraduate teaching but also of professional training at the graduate

level. They are included among the approved recipients of financial
support for training and research by the major fund-granting agencies,
both private foundations and, most particularly, such government
agencies as the National Science Foundation and the National Institutes
of Health.

It is only natural that, when these fields have developed a social
position of this magnitude, expectations of their performance should
rise very rapidly; furthermore, for the more general public it is only
natural that these expectations should concentrate in the field of practical benefits. As Shyrock has pointed out, it was only when, chiefly
through the development of modern bacteriology, the practical payoff of medical science became impressive that the whole complex of
medical education and research could develop to a new status in Western society.

The second set of circumstances underlying the pressure on the
behavioral sciences is a matter of the development of our modern society itself. The important point here is that we have left far behind
a traditional society in which it was presumed that processes not subject to deliberate control were the main processes involved in the
functioning of the society. Ours is a society in which collective planning at many levels has become enormously important — more important than in any previous societies. This includes the level of
government but is by no means confined to it. The very fact of the
increasing size of organizations everywhere exemplifies this. The
large modern university is a good case in point; it simply must plan
over a relatively long time span.

Together with this goes the increase of pressure to gain active
control of the situations in which we operate. I believe we are de-
creasingly willing to accept undesirable and distressing situations as
inevitable. We are continually venturing into new areas of attempted
control of behavior. If such planning and active control is to be carried out rationally, there is a tremendous demand for established
knowledge on the basis of which this can occur. The dilemma consists, then, of pressure, on the one hand, to mobilize such knowledge as is available for immediate practical urgencies and, on the
other hand, pressure to devote resources to the advancement of
knowledge.

The third focus of difficulty is the special salience of certain
particular problems requiring action. We can mention the acute
problem of race relations in the contemporary United States as well
as those of juvenile delinquency and other forms of crime. However,
the topic of this meeting is the most compelling one of our time,
namely, that of war and peace, the nature of which has itself been
heavily influenced by the application of science.

Here it should be realized that there is an important sense in which the extension of the range and area of political order is one of the factors in the instability of the new order. There is a certain disposition to treat this as an either/or problem. The United States and the Soviet Union, however, are types of sociopolitical organizations that are qualitatively different from the European nation-states of the nineteenth century. They comprise vastly larger territories and populations than did the latter. Furthermore they command, even per capita, resources both for human advancement and for destruction which are of a new dimension. Whenever there are weak points in the new social order, the stakes are larger than ever before and the possible consequences of a breakdown of order are more serious. It is not surprising that in relation to this particular problem there is a very heavy pressure on the infant behavioral sciences to try to contribute what they can to its resolution. I do not wish in any way to minimize the extreme urgency of this situation, but the way in which I have stated the problem surely suggests that the slogan "Let anybody who knows anything devote himself to no other task than using his knowledge in this field" is not one which can be accepted without qualification. What are some of the qualifications?

Some Limitations on an All-out Effort

First, I would like to mention two of the features of the purely elementary state of development of the behavioral sciences. These features greatly limit the usefulness of these sciences, but, at the same time, promise great returns if they are controlled through the application of substantial human and other resources. The first of these is the simple matter of the technical state of the behavioral sciences. This has been developing rapidly in the last generation, but from such elementary beginnings that the current state has not gone terribly far, if seen in the light of the potentialities of one or two further generations of continued development. We have had a vast accumulation of factual empirical indigestion in that technical theoretical resources probably have not kept pace in their development with the empirical. With respect to specific empirical problem areas which bring the relations of theory and factual knowledge into focus, we have a spotty situation. In other words, there is a strong imperative for devoting major resources to the internal technical development of the disciplines.

Second, the severity of the pressure for practical results is increased by a source of difficulty which is much more acute in our field than in the natural sciences. This is the sheer difficulty of attaining a requisite level of objectivity. It is in the nature of the social science enterprise that it should emerge out of intellectual orientations which are heavily ideological. In this connection, sophisticated ideology is merged with the crassest of simple partisanship.

The scientific observer and analyst is, in an almost unprecedented sense, part of the subject matter he is expected to study. To study it competently, which means objectively, requires a degree of self-discipline in objectivity and an institutional reinforcement of that self-discipline which presents a more formidable task than in any other area of science. There is always the shadow of public reactions to what we are doing which would, if they developed their full potentiality, dwarf the resistance which Darwinian theory in biology aroused in religious circles nearly a century ago. The very fact that the potentiality of such adverse reactions is present affects the fields themselves.

The problem is not a simple matter of being free of values. Quite the contrary — I think that the value-commitments of social scientists are as profound as those in any other fields. It is a matter of a particular ordering of our value attitudes and of relating our commitments to our professional scientific work to those we must hold as citizens and human beings in other respects and share with others in the nonprofessional public. The parallel to medicine seems to me quite close in this case. The obligation of medicine to help the sick is as paramount and as fully institutionalized as any obligation can be. Yet medicine, in order to develop, has had to become intimately articulated with a whole group of sciences which, however these non-medical scientists welcome and promote their practical usefulness, cannot, in the nature of the case, be primarily concerned in their immediate operations with the treatment of sick people.

Until recently, the social scientist has been particularly concerned with establishing his right to be a scientist rather than a practitioner. In any case, it is a severe dilemma. With respect to the general role of behavioral scientists in the near future, it seems to me that four different kinds of activities, which can be arranged along a spectrum, should be encouraged in some sort of balance which is difficult both to define and to attain in practice.

A Spectrum of Types of Involvements

It is in accord with the general position I have taken that first priority be given to the fundamental advancement of the behavioral science disciplines themselves. This has two primary aspects. One is research, in which I would naturally include research devoted to the development of theoretical propositions and schemes as well as to the gathering of new empirical information and the specific testing of hypotheses. The second aspect is the training of the oncoming generation of members of the profession, who will be both in the forefront of the technical developments of the fields themselves and also those who can adapt the knowledge which is available at a later stage to a variety of practical problems. This basic structure, of course, is very well known.

The next pattern, and I would put it next in priority, is the encouragement of research in problem areas where action is urgent. This research should be oriented to the understanding of the phenomena rather than to the formulation of recommendations for policy. This is clearly not necessarily incompatible with what, under the first heading above, I have called "fundamental research." Often such research is done in fields which also call for practical action. There is, however, no simple one-to-one correspondence; some fundamental scientific advances come from empirical fields which are either of no apparent importance whatever, or of only very slight practical importance. [2]

A good example of my second category is research devoted to analyzing conditions underlying the extension and maintenance of normative order. It is, for example, my conviction that much more is to be learned for international order from clear understanding of the nature and condition of development internal to politically organized societies than has tended to be assumed in the relevant circles. I would go a considerable distance in denying the absoluteness of the gulf between the two fields. I think we have been unduly influenced by the Austinian type of doctrinal sovereignty, with its suggestions that the sovereign has absolute control within his territory and that there is no border of any sort between such organized units. In fact, however, there have been many varieties of relatively stable international relations at many periods of history. These have involved various sorts of interests crosscutting the political lines, such as those of religious movements, various aspects of intellectual culture, professional associations in the sciences and elsewhere, and the very big field of international trade and the many conventions regulating it.

This means that there has also been a considerable amount of procedural consensus with respect to the conduct of these relations — not least the right of very short-run visitors but long-time residents to hold important property and other interests. Underlying all this there has been a certain amount of consensus on values in certain matters. For example, in the present situation, something approaching a world-wide consensus on the value of political autonomy has been evidenced by the drive toward independence of previously colonial societies. One can speak similarly of at least two others: namely,

---

[2]For example, Mendel's famous ratios were derived from the breeding of sweet-peas, not even important to agriculture.

the valuation of economic development, looking in the direction of levels of economic productivity approaching those of the Western societies and, closely related to this, the valuation of mass education. You will find few societies today in which the leaders would say explicitly that eighty to ninety per cent of the adult population must be illiterate.

The third type of work concerns the use of professionals in this area for research directly on policy problems. This is the sort of thing of which a great deal is done in government agencies and it provides an indispensable groundwork for intelligent decision-making. The line between it and my second category is gradual, and many of the same people are involved part of the time in one and part of the time in the other.

Finally, the fourth is the participation of behavioral scientists in the process of policy decision itself. Here possibly the least important and the least appropriate kind of participation is in the role of the final, responsible decision-makers as such — even in the middle echelons of government. I have the impression, for instance, that in the New Deal period too many economists were catapulted too soon into policy-making posts, and that this helped to provoke a reaction against the utilization of their services in government at all. There seems to be two kinds of roles which are most appropriate at this level. The first is that of some types of advisory relations to the policy-makers. This is, above all, the role of providing the latter not merely with information but with analyses of the situations involved in policy questions as they come up and indications of the probable consequences of choosing one or another among the alternatives which seem to be open. I do not think that roles of this sort absolve the expert adviser from responsibility for decisions. The old-fashioned idea that there can be a completely sharp line between line and staff is unrealistic; nevertheless, the primary decision-making responsibility should not be in the hands of the technical expert as such.

The second appropriate role is more frequently played outside the framework of government. This consists of influencing opinions in this area. It should certainly include influencing the opinions of members of the experts' own professional groups, many of whom are ill-informed and have not given serious thought to the problems in question. Of course it shades from them into wider publics. Since we are talking about the high-level technical experts, the immediate public will, in the nature of the case, consist of highly educated people, more or less intellectual. Thus their media will be semi-professional journals, such as the Scientific American, the Bulletin of the Atomic Scientists, or Daedalus. From this there is a progression to The New York Times and a variety of other media. (One would not expect such voices to be very prominent in the Hearst press.) Though this is not a mass influence, its importance should by no means be underestimated. This is one of the fields in which the line between ideological promotion of rather particular points of view and something which can be genuinely claimed to be the voice of technical opinion is especially difficult to draw. Inevitably, some of the names which are prominent in such contexts will be people regarded by most of their professional colleagues as grinders of axes and proponents of views not shared by the profession as a whole and not grounded in sufficiently solid work. These disadvantages seem to be an inevitable concomitant of getting the thinking of these disciplines before a wider public.

In conclusion, I think I may say that the case of the behavioral scientist with respect to international relations, as in other fields of practical application, is not basically different in kind from that of other scientists, but it is substantially different in degree. We live in a time when practical urgencies are perhaps more salient and more widely recognized than in almost any other time; at any rate, the demand for solutions of our problems is at an extremely high level indeed. The very fact that there is a sense in which the physical scientists may be held responsible for the danger of nuclear war tends to motivate people to look to other scientific groups for solutions of the difficulties that have arisen. The rise of the social sciences, which I have sketched, makes their members obvious targets for the demands to "do something," to provide real solutions.

We are caught in a very complex set of conflicts. We are all too well aware of the immature state of our disciplines and, therefore, of the inadequacy of the state of knowledge to give really solid policy recommendations for more than a small part of the range of urgent problems pressing in on us. Not only is the state of knowledge primitive, but the number of people trained to a point at which they can adequately command what knowledge there is or can contribute significantly to its further advancement is quite small and inadequate. This small group is subject to great demands for contributions in too many directions. It cannot possibly satisfy them all. This is a case for a particularly delicate and subtle balance. It would be my view that none of the demands which I have sketched can reasonably be altogether denied.

Partly this is because it would be incompatible with the basic canons of intellectual and academic freedom to legislate any particular direction of effort for all of the competent professional people involved. It must be left, in the last analysis, to their individual responsibility. In placing the advancement of the disciplines themselves, including their training function, as the first priority, I am motivated by a double consideration. First, if I believed that mobilizing the present resources of behavioral science had a good prospect of being the deciding factor in averting an otherwise nearly inevitable catastrophe, I would certainly be the first to be in favor of doing so. Unfortunately, considering both the state of knowledge and the exceedingly complex political conditions of getting the knowledge which exists implemented, I do not have this confidence in the crucial character of our role in the immediate future. The second factor is that if sufficient resources are devoted to the advancement of knowledge in these fields, the prospect that they will in fact be of crucial significance will be greatly improved over the present state of affairs. Indeed, it seems to me that they are sufficiently firmly grounded now so that this expectation, over a generation or two, is a one of high probability. It would be a pity to sacrifice this future prospect for much more dubious short-run gain. This is the essential focus of my case.

In this situation as a whole, finally, I think a word should be said about the strategic importance of the universities in our modern situation. The universities are the primary organizational trustees of the great intellectual traditions of the Western world. They must be the primary seedbed in which the most important new developments are cultivated. I do not wish to underestimate the contributions which can be made by various types of free-lance people outside such organizational settings or by those in research institutes, government agencies, and so on. Nevertheless, the universities seem to be the crucial node at which the most important threads of conditions of the development of these new sciences come together. The fact that the first responsibility of the university professor is the advancement of knowledge in his field and the training of his successors as professional experts in it seems to me the most important single guarantee that the balance will not tip too far in the direction of sacrificing the potential of the future to the urgencies of the present.

Questioning Some Unquestioned Assumptions
About National Security

—————————————————————— CHARLES E. OSGOOD

There are many contributions the intellectual, academic or otherwise, can make to public policy. As a professional specialist he can orient his research and scholarship toward untangling some of the admittedly complicated but critical issues underlying policy. To accomplish this he may have to relax somewhat the level of confidence he usually applies to his own work, realizing that people in government have to make decisions regardless of the certainty of the evidence at hand. He can try to inject the viewpoint of his discipline into the decision-making process. In doing so he may find, as I have, that the view of man that he and his colleagues take more or less for granted is quite novel — sometimes refreshing, sometimes threatening — to many people in government. Another role he can play is that of devil's advocate: he can make explicit some of the fundamental assumptions underlying public policy that usually remain implicit.

It is this last role I wish to play here. I want to question some assumptions about national security that usually remain unquestioned. * Precisely because they are not recognized as assumptions, open to debate, these implicit rules form the most rigid framework of national policy, and there is often resistance even to considering them. Nevertheless, they must be questioned and debated — because in this way we may open some new areas for flexibility and social innovation that we did not realize existed. Even though it may be true that some of these assumptions are questioned in private by our decision-makers, if they espouse them in public as obvious facts it really makes little difference as far as the value of publicly questioning them is concerned.

About the Nature of Political Man

Assumption 1. That national decision-making is predictable from models that assume rationality. Men can behave rationally, and

---

*The ideas expressed in this paper are the author's and do not necessarily represent those of any organization to which he belongs.

often do; men can behave irrationally, and often do. With a few exceptions, writers on national decision-making and researchers using game theory and other methods for simulating international relations have assumed that political man behaves rationally, regardless of what ordinary man may do. If our national policies are in fact based on this assumption, and it turns out to be wrong, we may be in for some grim surprises.

Psychologists are familiar with the fact that, as emotional stress increases beyond some optimum level, certain nonrational mechanisms in human thinking become more prevalent. Faced with an overwhelming threat over which he feels he has no control, the human individual typically denies the reality of the danger rather than keeping it in mind and trying to cope with it. This is particularly the case when the very language used to talk about the threatening situation is remote from his own experience — as are "megatons," "intercontinental ballistic missiles," and "fifty million casualties." The greater the stress under which he is operating, the more likely he is naively to project his own norms and values onto others; having done so, he easily condemns others as deliberately lying when they claim to see things otherwise than he does. Striving to simplify this complicated and dangerous world, he typically substitutes "psycho-logic" for logic, applying double standards of morality to the WE's and the THEY's and distorting facts in order to maintain a TV-western view of the world in which everything is absolutely black or absolutely white. Driven by exacerbated hopes and fears, he becomes prone to deciding in terms of mere possibilities rather than reasonable probabilities — like the paranoid psychotic. Under stress, his thinking and his behavior become more stereotyped; his perspective narrows to the immediately here and now; the range of alternatives he can conceive of narrows to either this or that, and thus, paradoxically, he becomes least capable of solving problems when solutions are most urgently needed.

Is all this in any way relevant? Do men become purely rational when they join in groups or become members of the decision-making elite? Or would our war-and-peace games provide a better mirror of reality if we played them under more realistic conditions of stress? I do not know the answer to this question, but I think we should find out. Robert C. North's recent analysis of decision-making in past crises, such as the build-up to World War I, clearly suggests that these irrational factors operate on leadership elites as well as the rest of us. Certainly, when such fundamental policy notions as the feasibility of "stabilized deterrence" depend upon the answer, we should try to find out whether political man is always rational — and if not, when not.

Assumption 2. That the primary motive of the opponent is aggression, not fear. Psycho-logic encourages us to believe that our motives are always defensive and theirs are always offensive. When WE arm ourselves ever more impressively, when WE conduct a new series of nuclear tests, it is because the enemy leaves us no choice. But when THEY arm themselves ever more threateningly, when THEY conduct yet another series of nuclear tests, it is because they want to destroy us and make the world over in the Communist model. Since we assume that the opponent shares our own image of ourselves as primarily peaceful in intent, we are unable to explain his behavior as being based on fear. And yet if there is anything certain in this uncertain world, it is that the Soviets are just as fearful of us as we are of them. All one need do is look objectively at the way Khrushchev justified their newest series of nuclear tests, and he will see that it matched, almost word for word, the way Kennedy justified our tests.

If both sides could fully accept the fact that their motives are symmetrical, not asymmetrical, that both are impelled primarily by fear and only secondarily by a desire to eradicate the other's way of life, I think this one insight would breathe fresh hope across the world. But is this the case? One would suppose that on a matter so critical there would be solid evidence, but instead he finds a mountain of opinion floating on a sea of ambiguity.

One difficulty with research in this area arises from what I call the relativity of credibility which, again, is a special instance of psycho-logic. Soviet communications to us are complex, diverse, and often contradictory, as are ours to them. Unfortunately, it is always easier to believe aggressive statements from an opponent (such as "We'll bury you!") than conciliatory statements (such as "We can co-exist peacefully"); this is because, psycho-logically, it is consistent for "Bad Guys" to make threats and inconsistent for them to make friends. But surely the scholar, aware of this built-in bias, can search for objective evidence on Soviet motivation — in their internal communications, in their justifications for actions, and in their actions themselves.

About the Nature of Deterrence

Assumption 3. That we must maintain military superiority. This assumption is an extension of our traditional policy of "peace through military strength" into the nuclear age. In this age, when the weapons are primarily offensive as well as incredibly destructive, and when the two polar powers are apparently committed to the same assumption, this traditional policy becomes "peace through fear of mutual annihilation." The hope is that this mutual fear of reprisal

will somehow preserve a stable, if uneasy, peace. Is this hope justified? I do not think so. It is becoming abundantly clear that the same
fear that deters also drives an arms race, and, because the arms
are essentially offensive rather than defensive, our real security
decreases as our military capabilities increase.

It is necessary to distinguish between two different philosophies
about armaments: the deterrent philosophy and the superiority philosophy. The deterrent philosophy assumes that there is some minimum
degree of retaliatory destructive capacity that is near-maximal in its
deterrent effect; we do not need more than this, as long as our intent
is to deter. It says, in effect, that to be able to destroy the opponent's
civilization once, but good, probably deters him almost as much as
to be able to do it ten or even one hundred times over. The superiority philosophy assumes that the deterrent effect on an opponent increases linearly with the ratio of our capability to his, regardless of
of the absolute level of destructiveness.

It is clear that when two opponents share the superiority philosophy, an arms race is the inevitable result. It is also clear that if
the two opponents shared the deterrent philosophy, the arms race
would peter out at some level at which the degree of potential mutual
destruction became unacceptable. What is not clear — and therefore
invites research — is how a shift from one philosophy to the other
could be accomplished. Is it possible for one party to induce a deterrent posture from the other by assuming it himself? I do not know
the answer to this question, but if the motives of the opponents are
really symmetrical, based on mutual fear, than I suspect the answer
is "yes."

Assumption 4. That an invulnerable nuclear retaliatory capability is nothing more than a deterrent. Here we have a magnificent,
and dangerous, example of the Tyranny of Words. We refer to our
capacity to deliver devastating destruction to the opponent as our
"deterrent" — a threat which, as long as he is rational, inhibits him
from attacking us. We worry about the credibility of our "deterrent"
to the opponent and about the stability of a system of mutual "deterrence." And here, caught in the grasp of a term, most strategic
thinking seems to stop. I think that the entire pattern of our strategy
might have been quite different had we gotten into the habit of calling
the same nuclear retaliatory system our "security base" instead of
our "deterrent," for it is equally both. To the extent that this system
does deter, does make an opponent cautious about aggression, then
to that extent it also provides its possessor with security.

Security for what? Security that enables us to take the initiative,
gives us room for calculated risk-taking. The problem is to utilize
the small margin for risk-taking provided by this security base in

such a way as gradually to broaden it. This can be done _if_ we emphasize the second-strike or retaliatory nature of the deterrent (and thus reduce reciprocal fears of surprise attack); _if_ we use the risk-taking potential to reduce and control international tensions rather than increase them; and _if_ we communicate this intent effectively to the opponent — which leads directly into the next assumption.

Assumption 5. That maintaining the credibility of our deterrent requires a hostile image of ourselves in the eyes of the opponent. The usual rationale goes something like this: we believe that the Soviets want to destroy us and are kept from attacking only by their fear of retaliation; the best way to convince them of our will to retaliate is to demonstrate by word and deed that we are implacably hostile; any word or deed of a conciliatory nature will be interpreted by the opponent as a sign of weakness and thus will encourage him to attack. Of course, since the opponent reasons the same way, he also behaves like an implacably hostile enemy, which confirms our expectations about him, and vice versa.

How can such a vicious, self-fulfilling cycle be interrupted and reversed? The first step, I think, is to recognize the fact that there are two types of credibility and two kinds of behavior to be deterred. Credibility Type I: The Implacably Hostile Enemy Image. A behaves in such a way as to convince B that he is unalterably hostile and is liable to attack B regardless of what B does. A creates the impression of irrationality by behaving unpredictably, by not practicing what he preaches, and generally by keeping B uncertain and anxious. B is convinced that A would attack if given an opportunity. This is the kind of credibility employed by rival gangs of teen-agers in our city slums. Credibility Type II: The Firm but Potentially Cooperative Image. A behaves in such a way as to convince B that he is potentially cooperative and will only attack if B breaks certain prescribed rules. A creates the impression of rationality by behaving predictably, by making his words and deeds consistent with each other, and generally by making B feel less threatened. B is convinced that A would attack under the prescribed conditions but not otherwise (since, after all, A is rational and predictable and always does what he says he will do). This is the kind of credibility a wise father tries to create; it is the kind of credibility that police officers have found to be most effective in deterring criminal behavior as well as in encouraging socially constructive behavior.

What kinds of behavior on the part of the Soviet Union do we wish to deter? Behavior Type A: All-out Nuclear or Conventional Attack. We want to deter the Soviets from launching a full-scale nuclear attack — which because of the obvious advantage of first-strike, would necessarily be a surprise attack that would make Pearl Harbor look like a tea party in slow motion. We also want to deter the Communists from starting the type of large-scale conventional attack that would probably, because of its locus and significance, escalate into all-out nuclear war. Behavior Type B: Limited and Sublimited Aggression. We would like to deter the Communists from all use of aggression and force as means to their ends, and this includes limited actions like the Korean War as well as the constant guerrilla nibbling around the perimeter of the non-Communist world. It seems perfectly obvious that to employ Credibility Type I (implacable hostile image) as a means of deterring both Behaviors Type A and B creates a highly volatile and dangerous international environment. It is one in which the likelihood of unintended war is high, because accidents, miscalculations, and errors of judgment are much more likely to be interpreted as having deliberate aggressive intent when mutual hostile images exist. The extreme of this posture was John Foster Dulles' concept of massive retaliation, which might be likened to a man's threatening to use dynamite to get rid of the mice in his house! It also seems fairly obvious that to use Credibility Type II (firm but potentially cooperative image) to deter Behavior Type A (all-out attack), while relying on conventional, non-nuclear means to deter Behavior Type A (all-out attack), while relying on conventional, non-nuclear means to deter Behavior Type B (limited and sublimited aggression), would maximize stability and encourage a general easing of tensions. The problem, of course, is how. How can we create in Soviet eyes the image of a nation that is potentially cooperative and yet firm in its resolve to resist aggression? To answer this question we must inquire into some other assumptions.

About the Nature of Nonviolent Alternatives

Assumption 6. That prior commitment from both sides is necessary before either can undertake any tension-reducing action. The traditional nonviolent means of resolving conflict between groups is negotiation. If successful, both sides proceed to act as agreed, each feeling secure in the prior commitment from the other. This procedure appeals to the legal mind, but it is not the only means of resolving human conflicts. As a matter of fact, in most sub-national forms of conflict (e. g., marriage relations, parent-child relations, intra-committee relations, and intra-government relations) negotiated agreement is neither the most frequent nor the most effective means. Nevertheless, nations seem to operate on the assumption that prior commitment from the opponent is an absolute prerequisite for any tension-reducing action; otherwise it might be perceived as a sign of weakness. In effect, each side is providing the other with a veto over its own freedom of initiative in this direction.

Let me begin my advocacy of the converse by questioning the notion that prior commitment really guarantees that an agreement will be kept. Even though a formal agreement does carry the weights of private morality and public opinion, when these are put in balance with a nation's "vital interests," the commitment is usually evaded in some way. Capacity for rationalization at the level of the nation-state is unbounded. At least, this seems to be the lesson of history. But, more than this, the prospects for even achieving prior commitments of any significance in the present atmosphere of tension and distrust seem very remote. This is another lesson of history.

Once the assumption that prior commitment is a prerequisite is questioned, an array of new strategies appears. The arms race itself provides a model for one kind of interdependent behavior between nations that does not require prior commitment. We do not wait for agreements with the Soviets before producing a new weapons system or conducting a new series of tests; we do it on our own initiative. But the fact that we have done it creates pressures on the Soviets to reciprocate by making further tests and developing more effective weapons systems of their own. In other words, in an arms race a kind of post commitment (the reciprocation) is substituted for prior commitment.

Can the notion of post commitment be substituted for the requirement of prior commitment in formulating a type of conflict-resolving behavior? I think it can. This notion is the essence of a policy proposal I have elaborated in some detail elsewhere, [1] bearing the complicated but accurately descriptive title, Graduated and Reciprocated Initiative in Tension-reduction.

The essence of the idea is that this country should take the initiative by unilaterally executing steps of a tension-reducing and controlling nature across a broad spectrum (e.g., cultural, economic, diplomatic, and scientific actions as well as arms control, disengagement, and disarmament). These steps would be designed, executed, and communicated about in such a way as to maximize the pressure upon the opponent to reciprocate with tension-reducing steps of his own. Such reciprocation would constitute the post commitment that makes it possible for the process to continue and develop momentum. Each side would graduate its own actions in terms of its own evaluation of what the other side has been doing, and each would maintain adequate national security by retaining capacity to deliver unacceptably devastating nuclear retaliation should it be taken advantage of in any serious way. This deterrent is the security base which makes such graduated risk-taking possible. By combining (a)

[1] Osgood, C.E., An Alternative to War or Surrender, Urbana, Ill., Illinois Press, 1962.

persistent tension-reducing steps across the global board with (b) firm resistance to encroachments, wherever they may occur, we should be able to create and maintain the kind of credibility (Type II) required for maintaining security without provocation.

Assumption 7. That inspection is prerequisite to any disarmament. Inspection has assumed the proportions of a sacred cow on both sides of the fence. Since the Soviets are the weaker contestant in a strictly military sense, but have a closed and controlled society, secrecy about military missile and production sites becomes a primary defense for them and is perhaps feasible. As the stronger contestant in a military sense, the main danger perceived by the U.S. is that of being duped and then subjected to surprise attack after honestly disarming. Of course, "fool-proof" inspection is technically and humanly impossible in any case, yet psycho-logic dictates that if THEY can cheat, then, being evil and always seeking an advantage, THEY will cheat. Is there any way out of this impasse?

First, let us look at some of the points on which the Americans and Soviets agree. (a) They agree roughly on the phased ordering of disarmament, beginning with nuclear weapons and ending with a world disarmed except for national forces of sufficient strength to maintain internal order. (b) They agree that the greater the degree of disarmament achieved, the more intensive must be the degree of inspection, the argument here being that in a largely disarmed world, the possessor of even a few nuclear weapons would be able to blackmail his opponent into submission. (c) They agree that inspection and regulation must be by "the other" rather than by "the self," although here the Soviet position is not as clear as the American.

What about the "nuclears first, popguns last" order of disarmament? This order is consistent with public concern, but it may be inconsistent with the political and psychological realities of our present world situation. The nuclear powers see their security as resting primarily in the deterrence provided by their ultimate weapons, and when mutual tensions are high it is difficult to imagine them seriously negotiating these weapons. A "popguns first, nuclears last" ordering of disarmament would begin with actions of a nonmilitary nature designed to reduce the atmosphere of tension; it would proceed to political and military adjustments designed to disengage the opponents and neutralize the regions between them; it would then move into negotiated agreements to reduce conventional forces and transfer policing authority and power to international bodies; and it would finally proceed to the dismantling of the nuclear deterrent systems themselves, by negotiation in a much less tense atmosphere. Note that retaining nuclear retaliatory capabilities until late in the process provides the degree of security which permits limited risk-taking in the early phases.

What about the need felt for inspection? It seems likely that it is inversely related to mutual trust. We feel no need to inspect Canada for concealed nuclear weapons, although they could be there in large numbers and prepared for use against us. We trust the Canadians. If this inverse relation holds, then techniques which increase mutual trust can be substituted for techniques of inspection in maintaining equal degrees of felt security. Furthermore, it seems hardly conceivable that mutual disarmament steps could be taken without increasing mutual trust. Therefore, rather than requiring legions of inspectors crawling over the globe, an increasingly disarmed world should demand less and less inspection.

I will make the further assertion, as a basis for debate and research, that "self-regulation" is psychologically more acceptable and more stable than "other-regulation." As every parent, teacher, employer, or leader soon discovers, often to his deep dismay, distrust breeds counter-distrust and is the rationalization for cheating. If the same rule applies to international relations, as I suspect it does, then in a fundamental sense insistence on "other" inspection is self-defeating. It maintains the very mutual distrust it is supposed to alleviate, and it encourages evasion.

But what if the Russians really are not trustworthy? (Or, for that matter, what if we are not?) I submit that, even if this were the case, retaining invulnerable nuclear second-strike capability makes it possible for both sides to take limited disarmament risks without requiring any more direct inspection than present techniques permit. Rather than insisting on "other" inspection, we could take the initiative in providing demonstrations of our own internal compliance, thereby setting powerful precedents for the opponent to follow. Would the Soviet communal ethic support "self-regulation" as effectively as the Western individual ethic would, once the commitment to disarm had been accepted? This is yet another important area for research.

Questioning these assumptions about national security has revealed their interlocking nature. It has also, I think, directed attention toward some pivotal issues of policy to which behavioral and social science research could contribute significantly. Advocacy of the converse has enlivened some fresh alternatives. If, like ourselves, our opponent behaves irrationally under stress and is motivated more by fear than by aggression, then a deterrent weapons philosophy offers us more security in the long run than a weapons superiority philosophy. If we fully committed ourselves to a deterrent philosophy and used our deterrent as a security base from which to take calculated risks in the interest of tension-reduction, thereby creating belief in our being firm but potentially cooperative, we should be able to get out of the inspection-disarmament dilemma and take the initiative in moving gradually toward a more peaceful world.

Conflict and Interdependence:
The Soviet-American Case

_____ VINCENT P. ROCK

Interdependence between the United States and the Soviet Union exists. The task facing the people and leaders of both countries is to manage and direct its enlargement so as to control conflict. The outline for a strategy of interdependence which follows does not pretend to offer the solution to the conflict. Rather, it should be viewed as an exploration of a hypothesis. How can the foundation be laid for controlling the conflict? What will be the contribution of a complex web of interdependence between the two nations to restraint on the use of force? Will it open the way to new and diverse forms of unity? Is it possible to achieve? What talents and resources are required?

Unity, an ancient concept, has gained new meaning and significance in the twentieth century. States and political movements have made world unity the objective of their action. Such aspirations are not new. What is new is that in the twentieth century the advance of science and technology — of communications and weaponry and many other fields of human endeavor — has made the goal appear a material possibility and indeed a necessity. Increasing numbers of men have found it feasible to cast their mind's eye upon the objective of unity and to commit themselves to work for its achievement.

The main obstacles to unity are three. First, the changed conditions created by the advance of science and technology are unevenly distributed and, in many respects, still insufficient for the easy acknowledgment of a world civilization. Not only are the sciences of nature far more advanced than those whose subject is man, but the fruits of technology are still mainly limited to the United States, Europe, and now the Soviet Union. Second, the institutions, and particularly the modern industrial state, which provided the principal framework within which past progress has been achieved, represent not only a building block for the future, but an obstacle to further progress. The solidarity of the peoples of each nation-state is a great step forward in the advance of mankind, but the state itself is a mixed blessing in achieving a wider sense of solidarity. Third, the growing specialization of skills, interrelation of functions, and numbers of associations which accompany technological advance require a kind of solidarity which accepts diversity and operates by consent rather than the unity of hierarchy resting on coercion. Much remains to be learned by many about what this implies for the world's political organization.

The twentieth century is as equally characterized by the failure of restraint as by the search for unity. Indeed, the interest in the latter stems in considerable part from the former. Two world wars, innumerable violent revolutions, and a steady increase in the capital investment in arms suggest that something fundamental may be awry. Statesmen have historically been concerned with either preventing or managing the consequences of change; technological accomplishments have opened the possibility of directing and managing certain important aspects of change itself so as to enhance and reinforce restraint. Technology, if it is directed to the task, can create the conditions for interdependence of interest which will contribute to restraint. At the end of the climb to interdependence may well be found the unity with diversity which the shrunken globe demands.

Unity, Restraint, and Interdependence signify different ways of looking at the world community. They are also the products of certain kinds of human activity and not of others. Each has certain virtues and limitations when looked at in the context of Soviet-American relations. They are, in a real sense, complementary approaches — just as love, threats, and work may all be part of the relationship of individuals.

Often, it may appear less costly and more prudent to seek to block change than to manage it, let alone bring it about. Yet, it is evident that a vast redirection of resources toward new purposes will have to occur before the United States and the Soviet Union can establish a viable relationship. Control of conflict will remain precarious as long as the ratio of negative to positive allocations of state resources for managing their relationship remains in the ratio of ten thousand to one.

Conflicts of purpose give rise to tension between states. Tensions are increased by the capacity of states to resort to force in order to seek to resolve conflicts. Thus the control of tension requires that incompatible purposes be eliminated, modified, or reduced in relative importance, both by the creation of common interests and by the restraint of force which aggravates tension. In short, conflict has to be controlled if tensions are to be controlled. Successful control of conflict depends upon the creation of an environment in which such control is in the interest of the main adversaries.

The emphasis in this paper is on the creation of new purposes and of an international environment in which they may be pursued. The suggestions are tentative. A substantial program of research, development, and experimentation will be required to elaborate, perfect, and test each element of the strategy.

The conceptual basis for the approach which follows is relatively simple. It views international society as a single, imperfect, but rapidly developing system. It is a system in which control over force is diffused in the hands of the nation-state. Control of conflict in this system requires an offsetting, cross-national diffusion of power and self-evident interests. Two areas are of paramount importance: first, positive constructive endeavors and enterprises; second, arrangements for restraint on the use of force. Positive action is needed to reshape the goals of men and nations. Restraint on the use of force is essential to provide time.

Survival is one interest shared in common by the United States and the Soviet Union. Since the survival of each is in the hands of the other, neither is sure of what is necessary for it to survive. Interaction between the two exists in the fields of weapons, science, communications, and politics. Survival requires the control of conflict. But progress involves conflicts in values.

Within the nation-state conflict is controlled and progress is permitted when force is concentrated but power is diffused. A primary problem in all states is to control conflict while permitting satisfaction of the changing values and purposes of the individual. In this process a balance must be struck between the needs of the individual and the needs of society. Two methods have been found useful. Since neither is infallible, they are frequently used to reinforce each other. The first is to devise common purposes of continuing value. The second is the employment of force.

Domestic tranquillity requires that the existence of force be continually complemented by efforts to sustain and expand the validity of common purposes. In the long run, a necessary condition is that the population as a whole share in common and satisfying experiences.

Since, internally, force is concentrated in the hands of the state, restraint on its arbitrary use represents a continuing problem. This can be met when influence over the affairs of the individual is diffused among a multitude of organizations, each serving particular functional or geographical interests. He thus retains the freedom to associate himself with one or another group. These groups, in turn, represent varying elements of power which must be taken into account in the actions of the state.

Many proposals for the establishment of world peace have emphasized the need for common purposes and some form of world "police" force. Yet progress toward the control of international conflict has not been rapid. Two main obstacles stand in the way of control of conflict on the world scene. First, force in the international system, in contrast with that in the internal affairs of the state, is diffused among the different nations and no path appears open at present for its just concentration. Second, cross-national purposes and structures for the diffusion of power are inadequate to engage the interests of any substantial body of men.

The absence of salient and important cross-national purposes and action in almost all fields makes progress in the field of arms more difficult. Existence of such purposes, and programs for achieving them, would provide a positive incentive for actions to reduce reliance on military force. Security based on arms control, as well as on arms, involves uncertainties and risks. The creation of positive interests which would profit from restraint of arms may be required to tip the balance. Otherwise, the known danger may be preferred to the unknown. Moreover, any system of arms control will almost inevitably involve the creation of a third system of social and political arrangements, tied to the two nations but in some respects different from either. Since arms control is a most sensitive area, constructive experience in other fields less intimately connected with security would be valuable. Finally, the engagement in peaceful endeavors in cross-national structures will help to reshape the distinct historical and industrial experiences which make common understanding of the interaction of the two sides difficult.

Interdependence, as an approach, emphasizes the need to work simultaneously and on a broad front on the two main obstacles to the control of conflict. On the one hand, there must be an intensive and steadily widening exploration and experimentation with the whole array of measures which may restrain or reduce the role of force. On the other hand, there must be an even more substantial commitment of resources and talent to the development of enterprises of understanding and action which will provide common experience for citizens of the two sides.

Obviously, the present relationship between the United States and the Soviet Union is anything but consciously planned interdependence. It consists of vast areas of conflict, other areas of competition, and still others of limited tacit or explicit cooperation or common action. In Berlin, the two states are deeply involved in conflict. In the United Arab Republic, they are in competition. In Laos, they have cooperated in attempting a new arrangement to reduce conflict in that area. Conflict among states, as among individuals, stems from incompatible purposes. Yet most state purposes are mixed.

The purposes of a nation emerge from the totality of its experience, past and present, internal and external. In seeking to cultivate cross-national action in the field of arms or any other area, the differences which result from the unique experience of each state can be ignored only at the risk of frustration or failure. Equally important, similar experience provides the ground on which common action in the mutual interest may be built. Emphasis on differences may be prudent to avoid surprise, but the identification of areas of common development is essential for the creation of constructive enterprise.

The task of understanding the totality of Soviet and American experience which provides the opportunity for and establishes the present limits of common action is a large one, which has nowhere been systematically attempted. It is beyond the scope of the present paper. Clearly, however, there are three great clusters of experience which are relevant to the management and enlargement of a viable interdependence between the two societies. First are the general but germane historical experiences of each nation. Second are their common experiences with industrialization. Third are their experiences with each other directly and in other areas of the world.

The different historical experiences of the two are an important factor in their very different perceptions of what is necessary and equitable in many situations. Two examples must serve to illustrate the point. They are not by any means intended to encompass the range of diversity.

The Soviet Union, located in the center of the great Eurasian land mass, has suffered numerous invasions. As a consequence, it has come to see its security vitally involved in the establishment of friendly or subservient buffer areas all around its periphery. The United States, in contrast, located half a world away from the centers of conflict, has in the twentieth century twice found itself involved in world wars on foreign soil. Experience seems to have shown that its security is best protected by prompt military action in distant lands; hence, it has developed a worldwide system of bases and political influence.

Americans came to the New World in search of freedom of either ideas or opportunity. They undertook to settle and develop a virtually unpopulated continent. The task put a premium on individual initiative and enterprise. Governmental authority, in a sense, followed rather than preceded the creation of communities. In the realm of ideas, America borrowed first from the intellectual ferment that produced the French Revolution, but in time the substance of the democratic system was derived from the English liberal tradition. The American Revolution was a revolt against England, but only in a very limited way against European culture.

Russia, in contrast, has a history of centralized authoritarian government reaching back for centuries. It is a land, at least in its western parts, long since settled with highly organized communities.

The modernization of the Soviet Union has been pre-eminently an undertaking of the state, which for the first time freed and organized
the energies of the people for a vast constructive effort. The central
ideas guiding the undertaking represent both a protest against nineteenth century Eupropean culture and a defense against the continuing
threat from Europe. The writings of Marx represented a devastating
critique of Europe as he knew it. The organizing genius of Lenin provided a means of defense against the West. Out of the Russian experience and the ideas and myths orginating with these men rose a new
authoritarian state dedicated to the creation of an advanced industrial
society.

The purpose in stressing the different historical experience of
the two nations is to underline the scope and complexity of the task
of creating a viable interdependence between them. The differences
in history not only make for a difference in world outlook but differences in outlook in the daily life and style of living at all levels of
society. An appreciation of the entire range of differences as well as
a search for similarities will be essential in seeking stability in the
relationships of the two.

Among those who have been optimistic about the possibilities
of eventually getting along with the Soviet Union, reliance is often
placed on the benign effects of the increase in the standard of living
expected to result from further industrialization.

These expectations about the role of industrialization in mitigating the conflict between the Soviet Union and the United States
may be justified by events, but the effect is not inevitable. As the
Soviet standard of living rises, it is said, the Russian people will be
less interested in foreign adventures. They will have less to gain and
more to lose. Moreover, as the people become more satisfied with
life, the state will have less need for maintaining tight control over
their actions. In addition, as industrialization takes place the increase in education and specialization will multiply the number of
group objectives, and may open the way for a greater diversity of
cross-national contacts and undertakings. Three points need to be
made about this optimistic vista.

First, for the present and for some years to come, the differences in the level and maturity of industrialization in the Soviet Union
and the United States will remain substantial. In these circumstances,
the ability and inclination of the United States to "keep the pressure
on" the Soviet Union may have the cumulative effect of offsetting the
benign effect of hard-won affluence. At the same time, it is undeni-
able that industrialization does open new possibilities for constructive action between the two societies.

Second, in the absence of intervening common action, the belief that the Soviet Union will somehow accept Western values after

a long period of continuing conflict and advancing industrialization is, so far as can be seen, without adequate foundation. In the full power and vigor of a successful, isolated development, it is equally reasonable to believe it might simply assert more vehemently its exclusive formula for organizing the world.

Third, while the past has made for differences in outlook and the present industrialization opens the possibility for growing similarities in values, the future outcome will be critically dependent on the experiences of the Soviet Union and the United States with each other.

The alternative, for which time may be still available, is, first, to devise and invest in areas which will provide understanding and common action in order that, as the "enemy" grows stronger, the common interest will prevail over parochial, even though continental, purposes; and, second, to seek by a variety of approaches to restrain and limit the means and occasions of violent conflict.

The Importance of the Individual

In these tasks each individual has a part to play. Purpose is central in the life of man, acting alone or as a member of a state. He has a capability for setting goals for himself. Intimately connected with this ability is man's pervasive inclination to attach values to all aspects of his experience in life. From this, two principles emerge for the control of conflict. First, there must be a continuing and vigorous search for common purposes, or common interests, as they are referred to in foreign relations. One's own purposes or those of the adversary may have to be dealt with as fixed in order to act, but it is essential to realize that the very action will alter in some degree the values and purposes on both sides.

Second, the infinitely varied capability of man to attach values to life's experiences requires that his opinion of what is needed or acceptable, threatening or rewarding, must be recognized as an important reality. Thus, for example, the worth and reliability of deterrence or interdependence or any other approach to interstate relations is closely related to the extent to which it serves purposes of value and the extent to which opinions can actually be known.

Man, however, does not live apart from his environment. His purposes and his values are shaped by his experiences. As his environment is modified, he changes. What he considers valuable will shift depending upon the tasks he undertakes and the means he uses to accomplish them — in a word, upon his experience. At the same time no man comes to a new task without an infinitely varied series of purposes and values generated from previous experience.

The infinite possibilities inherent in this view of man in action account for the uncertainties of social prediction. They also suggest that whenever men interact with one another it can be expected that they will find conflicts of purpose and even disagreements over the best means of achieving what appear to be common goals. It is exactly in this infinite capacity of man for attaching values to experience and thus of giving an infinite variety of meanings to experience that are to be found the origins of the plurality of causes of conflict. It also helps to explain why no state has found an absolutely certain way to control conflict or any way at all to eliminate it completely. Yet the role of experience in shaping men's values provides the opportunity for mitigating conflict and directing men's energies to new and constructive purposes.

Jean Monet, the architect of the European Common Market, summed up the practical man's understanding of the potentialities of new experience when he said, "Men change their minds because of the conditions in which they are placed, which are different from the conditions of the past."

The Limitations of Coexistence

In their struggles with each other the two great powers have sought to substitute "coexistence" and the "cold war" for a hot war. These moves represent progress in that they signify a recognition on both sides of the costs and futility of nuclear war. Neither is sufficiently adaptive to the world environment being created by science and technology to give great promise of avoiding catastrophe in the long run. Military interdependence between the United States and the Soviet Union exists and is recognized. Both admit the power of nuclear weapons and the desirability of avoiding war. Yet war is not seen as certain and its costs are not wholly and vividly visualized. For the leaders and people on both sides, working within the existing state structures to enhance power and influence is widely accepted as adequate.

Interdependence also exists because of scientific and technical advances in communications, transportation, and many other fields outside the military. These advances permit and facilitate a world-wide political conflict. While both sides wish to avoid general war, the world-wide competition for power and influence continues.

Therefore, the conditions necessary for the control of conflict are not only those which pertain directly to the management of military forces, but those of the whole environment in which the competition is taking place. New conditions, situations, and structures must be created to ensure common restraint on military force and to open the possibility of a future which both may live to enjoy. Interdependence exists; the Soviet and the American are confronted with the mutual task of making it a constructive force in the world.

The Soviet Union has proposed coexistence as the basis for relationships of the East and the West. The limitation of coexistence is that, while it recognizes interdependence in strategic nuclear weapons, it seeks to deny the need or reality of interdependence in other areas. Coexistence often conjures up an image of the two adversaries pursuing parallel paths until one, the West, collapses from its own contradictions. Coexistence seeks to keep alive an exclusive vision of unity. By inference, it denies the reality or vitality of the society of two-thirds of mankind. At the same time it maintains that the Soviet Union retains the right to support wars to reshape new nations. Coexistence is designed to permit the Soviet Union to pursue its self-selected tasks, including that of expanding communism, without taking undue risks. In this approach there is a constant tendency to underestimate the effect of its action on the West. Even as it seeks to undermine "capitalism," it strengthens the forces in the West inclined toward more extreme forms of conflict.

Despite these fundamental limitations, the idea of coexistence represents a movement in the right direction toward facing the consequences of the nuclear armed world. The long run importance of the shift for Soviet society is easy to underestimate in the West. It is hard for Americans to appreciate the emotion of the Russian lady who told the American scientist at a cocktail party, "It has been difficult for a Marxist to accept even peaceful coexistence; it meant giving up a lot that one had come to believe." To admit the possibility that we exist together is to open the possibility that our fates may be interdependent. If they are indeed interdependent, working together as well as competitively will be necessary to manage and shape them.

It is in just this respect that coexistence, as presently interpreted by the Soviet state, is most deficient. At best, the Soviet view of a joint endeavor is a collaboration at arm's length. Often it is designed to provide an advantage to the Soviet Union without taking sufficiently into account the need for a comparable advantage for the United States. Even when mutual agreements have been arrived at, as is the case in the exchange program, Soviet participants often seem to be driven to exploit every opportunity in a deprived and shortsighted way to gain an added advantage. In part this may be an "underdog" response stemming from the recent hardships and poverty of Soviet society. But since the Soviet Union is now a powerful nation and soon to be an affluent one, it may be possible for the Soviets to learn to identify the cumulative mutual advantages to be gained from restraint, cooperation, or common endeavors.

Criteria for the Implementation of a Strategy of Interdependence

Control of conflict in the international system is a process which must be learned. Identification and cultivation of common purposes are necessary. Survival is such a common purpose, but in the midst of the myriad of other aspirations and goals of both sides it may be inadvertently sacrificed. Therefore, it is essential to create a web of subordinate purposes which serve the interests of both sides. How to achieve this must be learned gradually by experience. Thus a Strategy of Interdependence requires a whole range of action from which the two sides learn by experience the scope of restraint which must be developed and the areas of endeavor which bring mutual reward. The entire relationship of the two powers must be dealt with, not merely one or another element of their interaction. Neither disarmament nor cultural exchanges, neither military power nor economic influence can be sufficient. They must be handled and used in proper proportion. The goal is experienced by both sides, which contributes in a significant way to the control of conflict. To be effective the experience must meet five criteria.

First, experience must contribute to the convergence of values and purposes in the two societies.

Second, experience must be germane to the present stage of development or interrelationship of the two sides.

Third, experience must be material to the control of conflict — that is, it must contribute to the restraint of force or the cross-national diffusion of power.

Fourth, experience must be sufficient across the entire breadth of the relationship. Thus, resources for the conduct of positive programs must be in balance with expenditures for the creation of instruments of force.

Fifth, experience must be cumulative. New and expanded cross-national arrangements and organizations within which transactions can gain a momentum of their own will be required

Convergence of Values

The prospects for the growth of constructive interdependence between the two nations find encouragement in some of the individual transactions which have taken place in fields in which the two states have permitted contacts. For five years now exchange of individuals, groups, exhibits, and cultural material has been taking place on a reciprocal basis between the two nations under agreements carefully negotiated by their governments. Meetings and travel have also been arranged on the initiative of citizens of the two countries. From farming to fiction, from science to art, interested individuals have managed to make more of the occasion than their States, bent on competitive coexistence or the cold war, had intended.

In these engagements of Russian and American citizens, achievement of common action for a common purpose appears to conform to a kind of "law of inverse relevance." The more remote the field of action, the more distinct the symbols of communication from the polemics of the confrontation between the United States and the Soviet Union—the more likely the success of the joint undertaking. Thus the fields of music and art have provided some of the finest examples of the possibility of cross-national action.

The possibilities inherent in all fields for satisfying achievement resulting from common action for a common purpose may be illustrated by an example from the field of art. Yuri Faier, the mountainous Soviet conductor of the Bolshoi Ballet, met recently with the American orchestra which he was to lead through the Ballet's tour of the United States. Mr. Faier is nearly blind, and excitement was lent to the occasion by the hope raised by several American specialists that a major portion of his sight might be restored by a surgical operation. But the business of the day was strictly musical. As he was led to the podium, Mr. Faier called out the name of the first cellist, and when he arose, seized him with one arm and pounded his back with the other. They were old friends and had worked together on Mr. Faier's previous visit. Several other musicians also got bear hugs.

Mr. Faier then removed his coat and went to work. The first number was <u>Spartacus.</u> Mr. Faier beat time and the orchestra played smoothly until there was a false entrance by the trumpets. Mr. Faier looked pained. He shouted in Russian. From then on it was any good conductor rehearsing any good orchestra, with the usual give and take between maestro and musicians. At the end of the first part of the rehearsal, Mr. Faier bowed to the brass section and said, "Das ist gut." A murmur of approval went through the orchestra. Flushed with linguistic success, Mr. Faier started calling out some numbers in the score in English. A trumpet player, not to be outdone, commented "Horosho," meaning "good," when he reached an understanding with Mr. Faier about a mix-up in six measures. "Très bien," said Mr. Faier to him. Later, conductor, orchestra, and dance troupe teamed up to put on a series of reportedly sterling performances. The lesson must not be lost. A common purpose, give and take among the participants, respect for the skills each brings to the task, developing friendship, and the sense of excitement and satisfaction that results from positive accomplishment are important. But, as an eminent American musician pointed out, "For decades Americans revered the great German composers of the eighteenth and nineteenth centuries — yet this had no relevance to the two wars

with Germany in this century. " Ballet music is unlikely to be deci-
sively material to the control of conflict.

Germane to the Present Stage of Development

Some forms of cultural exchange are, of course, very germane to the development of relationships of the United States and the
Soviet Union. When these occur, often at the initiative of individuals,
the official response of one or the other state is likely to be ambiguous or resistant to the free development of the cross-national transactions of its citizens.

The experience of Professor H. J. Berman of the Harvard
Law School, while visiting lecturer at Moscow University, illustrates the point. Soviet law has in the past few years been undergoing
substantial rehabilitation. Increasing emphasis has been placed on
protecting the rights of the Soviet citizen. Efforts have been made to
carry out these changes without interfering unduly with the power of
the state in Soviet society. Law, as a consequence, is pertinent to
the present stage of Soviet development. During his stay in Moscow,
Professor Berman began a series of twelve lectures on American
law at the University. Early lectures were crowded, but attendance
began to drop off and students told Mr. Berman informally that they
were being criticized in some quarters for being too interest in the
course. In order to avoid getting the students into trouble, Professor
Berman felt it necessary to halt the series after the seventh lecture.
The opportunity given Professor Berman to deliver the lectures represents the workings of coexistence. The inability of the students to
continue to attend them suggests a lack of acceptance of the minimum
kind of interdependence that is required for survival in the nuclear
age.

Agriculture is a field highly germane to the Soviet-American
confrontation. The United States has much to offer and the Soviet
Union a great deal to learn. The Soviet Union is desperately trying
to increase the quantity and efficiency of its agricultural production.
From many points of view the U. S. interest would be served if the
Soviet Union solved its agricultural problem and got the millions of
surplus people off the farms and into the cities. In a minimum way,
perhaps largely owing to the efforts of a single individual, the United
States has accepted the desirability of Soviet agricultural progress.

Up to the present time, United States expressions of interest
in the progress of Soviet agriculture have rested largely with Mr.
Roswell Garst. The official exchange program has accepted a small
but significant number of Soviet technicians who have come to the
United States to learn better methods of farming. Some American agricultural experts have gone to the Soviet Union; but, if one can judge

from their comments, more for the purpose of finding out what was wrong than with any thought of helping to correct it. Agriculture is indeed relevant. It might even be of great material importance if the United States were willing to help and the Soviet Union were willing to accept. For such transactions to meet the criterion of sufficiency, they might well have to be on a scale, both materially and technically, at present undreamed of on either side.

In building a viable interdependence it is as important to seek for fields in which we can ask the Soviet Union for help as it is to identify areas in which we are ahead. Electric power, in modest degree, has been suggested as such an area, although it has nothing like the significance to our present stage of development that agriculture has to the Soviet Union. Still, at least in certain regions and types of power, the Soviet might make a contribution — or so Secretary Udall appears to think. The Secretary recently returned from a tour of the Soviet electric power developments. On his return, he pointed out that the Soviet Union is one of the leading countries in the development of water power and Americans have "much to learn" from Soviet specialists in this field.

On further investigation, power may not turn out to be significantly applicable to our development, but at the moment the possibility stands. It is of particular interest because it would represent a positive contribution from the Soviet Union. Another indication that technical gains for the United States may be possible is suggested by the fact that the President of General Electric International was recently in Moscow negotiating for manufacturing arrangements for certain Soviet technical products. Still, such initiatives represent only a trickle of effort at present. They will have to approach the dimensions of a stream before they become obviously material to the control of conflict.

Material to the Control of Conflict

Experience which contributes to restraint on the use of force and to the creation of cross-national increments of power are the two key elements in this criterion. Normally, one thinks of arms control, reduction, or elimination as most relevant to the restraint of force. In the long run this is undoubtedly correct. Face-to-face negotiations by representatives of the two powers, the experience of the last fifteen years suggests, is at best only one of many relevant forms of experience for achieving progress. At the level of discussion, the Pugwash meetings of American and Soviet scientists and government advisers represent a remarkable and fruitful innovation of a technical-policy character. On issues as complex as armament a vast exchange of information and ideas is required before either side is prepared for "negotiation" in the conventional sense. On the whole, premature "negotiations" are counterproductive.

The recent Cuban "quarantine" represents another kind of experience contributing to the restraint on the use of force. While it is too early to foresee the ultimate outcome, and while only a little learning is possible from each crisis no matter how grave, the lessons of the most recent one may be significant. The Soviet Union has learned that the geographic expansion of strategic forces will be resisted and that there are dangers inherent in attempting it. The American people have learned somewhat more about the threat posed to the Soviet Union by their overseas bases. Both may have learned that it may be prudent to consider the acceptance of non-exclusive forms of political competition. Other areas of the world have probably learned something about the dangers as well as the prestige of missile bases. Resistance to the expansion of force, as well as the search for means to regularize its control, are both part of the experience necessary to its restraint.

The hazards of resistance are, of course, substantial; thus in the intervals between "crises," experience and action which contribute to cross-national understanding and endeavors may be of great value. Cultural exchanges, as has been suggested, can play a useful role, but much more is needed in the way of great common endeavors. Space is a prime field for such activity. The modest program of cooperation between the Soviet Union and the United States hardly represents more than cultural contact supplemented by an exchange of statistics. Bolder visions are necessary if space is to play a material role in the control of conflict rather than representing merely another dimension for its conduct. Agriculture has already been mentioned as possibly making a material contribution. A scientific breakthrough which would open the possibility of large-scale weather control represents the most compelling possibility. The point is that action must eventuate in a significant improvement in the restraint on force or in the creation of cross-national power elements if it is to be <u>material.</u>

Sufficient — Equal to the Purpose

The balance of the entire range of interaction will play a major role in the ability of the United States and the Soviet Union to control conflict. The balance in their transactions will be significantly affected by the size and composition of the allocation each makes for national power purposes and for the control of conflict. At the present time there is an overwhelming reliance on military force as a method of restraint and also as a means of settling conflict. The single-minded reliance on military force is reflected in the allocation of resources and talent for the various modes of interaction between the two adversaries. In the United States, for every dollar spent for the development of interaction which seeks to devise and implement common actions, a thousand dollars are spent for competitive purposes and ten thousand dollars for purposes of preparing for conflict. The disproportion is probably even more extreme for the Soviet Union. States will use the instruments available when they are confronted with incompatible purposes; thus the present allocation of resources seems likely to contribute to the cumulative possibilities of armed conflict however much, in the short run, it may appear necessary to prevent aggression. Substantial resources will be required to shift the emphasis in the Soviet-American confrontation from conflict to one in which experiences of mutual gain predominate.

The tendency of the United States is to seek small changes in the hope that they may have cumulative effects. This is necessary but unlikely to produce the desired results in the absence of substantial investment in programs designed specifically for constructive cross-national purposes. Moreover, even significant efforts in one area are likely to be frustrated unless there is an effort along the entire front of interaction with the Soviet Union. Since there is no single cause of conflict, points of friction must be tackled more or less simultaneously if success is to be achieved. Just as in the military area, when it is judged impossible to imagine the exact situation which will require force, investments are made along a broad front, so also in the case of constructive investments, when the exact opportunity for their use cannot be wholly envisaged, a similar large-scale effort is needed. While in the military field systematic planning and investment have been generally accepted, a similar approach has rarely been the basis for action on other fronts. Little progress in the nonmilitary fields can be expected until a policy of systematic planning, action, and investment is adopted.

Government investment alone will not be sufficient; other avenues of interaction must be opened. For example, the channels of trade must again be opened. This will require a shift in present U. S. policies. At the present time, even though there is a large and growing trade between the Soviet Union and Western Europe and an even larger volume of trade between Eastern and Western Europe, the United States continues to limit its trade with the Soviet Union to the very minimum. U. S. trade with the Soviets has been restricted for a variety of reasons. Yet without trade, without Soviet exposure to live, public-spirited U. S. businessmen, and without the opportunity for these men gradually to acquire a first-hand understanding of both the limitations and strengths of the Soviet economy, all other measures may be insufficient. The strength of the two societies lies in great part in their industrial establishments and those who manage the enterprises. In many respects their occupations provide a parallel experience which is extra-political. Unless they in some degree come to appreciate their mutual experience, other measures for the control of conflict may not suffice.

The scope of present exchange programs is noteworthy, but alone they are unlikely to do more than open the door to an opportunity. In the past few months there have been visits of representatives or citizens from the two countries, displaying their talents, competing, talking, seeking new knowledge, and even occasionally engaging in common undertakings in a wide range of fields. In advertising, agriculture, electric power, journalism, law, literature, music, meteorology, sports, space, science, and other fields, travelers have found common interests with their opposite numbers on the soil of the adversary. Moreover, tens of thousands of books and other publications move each year between the two nations and find their way into the hands of the scientists, scholars, and students in the universities and centers of research. American movies, limited in number, are each seen, on the average, by one hundred million Soviet citizens. A good beginning has been made at correcting stereotypes, advancing common understanding, and identifying common interests of specialized groups, yet, despite the range of activity, significant constructive action remains for the future. The door is ajar, but plans to capitalize on the opportunity are for the most part missing. Individuals either lack adequate resources, or, if they have them, await the lead of government. Conflict and the gaining of national advantage at the expense of the other remain the dominant mode of thought. Specific suggestions are made and sometimes explored, but they come to nought in the absence of an approach to interdependence on a broad front. Trade, public investment, increased resources for arms control, and political settlements are all essential parts of a coherent and sufficient effort.

Cumulative Creation of Structure

The Strategy of Interdependence envisages a step-by-step approach, but on a broad front, to the creation of conditions in which the United States and the Soviet Union will find it in their self-evident interest to work together both constructively and for the restraint of the use of force. Such a result will be impossible to achieve if transactions of importance are limited to heads of state and the diplomatic corps. Planning is needed which will mark out broad areas of approved interaction in which both government officials and private individuals are encouraged to take the initiative in devising constructive tasks with their Soviet counterparts. What seems to be required is for the government to come to believe it can achieve increased influence over events by reducing somewhat its direct control over instruments. The desirable form of organization for the creation of viable interdependence appears to be in a certain sense acephalous. Initially, not so much the cooperation of heads of state is needed, since they must continue to stand guard over each nation's security, as the acquiescence in the common action of others. Constructive interaction of many others is needed, not alone for conversation and understanding, but in order to devise meaningful common tasks and arrangements.

A kind of acephalous organization is essential because mutual action requires a degree of inventiveness and initiative not present in normal state relations, largely confined as they are to questions of national security and power. Interdependence requires the invention of new ways of thinking about "the enemy." Area by area, it requires the application of domestic norms to "alien" groups. New models of competition and of common action must be developed. Neither checkers, chess, nor chicken, which are the most widespread present models of the interaction with the Soviet Union, will suffice. A whole variety of "non-zero sum games" which involve an increasing number of individuals on each side of the contest will be required. Such an effort will, as has been stressed, demand substantial resources and at this point the state must play a positive role and, of course, have appropriate controls.

The experience of joint effort cannot spring full-grown from the brow of Zeus. At least two levels of action will be required to generate and implement the development of common rules, procedures, or codes of competition for common enterprises in the mutual interests of both sides. At each of the two levels there are likely to be both psychological and structural obstacles to be overcome before the new conditions can be created. Each step in the process must be sufficiently limited that it does not represent a major shift in the power of either state in its relationships with the other. At the same time, if the total effort is finally to succeed in creating significantly different conditions and thus changing men's minds, it must be carried out on the broadest possible front. Somewhere along the spectrum of transactions, a movement forward must be taking place at all times.

At the first level of action, each sector of the front need be manned by only a few individuals. Indeed it probably must be, since only a few individuals capable of the initiative required are likely to be found on either side. These few men in each main field of human endeavor face a demanding task. First, in the absence of nuclear war, they must by an act of imagination anticipate the consequences of the present course. Second, they must visualize the changes required and possible in their area of competence. Third, they must commit themselves to the task of devising the new conditions and structure which will permit their fellow men to see where their new self-interest lies. Fourth, they must identify and learn to know their opposite numbers in the other camp. Fifth, jointly, they must find a permissible structure in which a steady exchange of views can take place. Finally, from this exchange there must emerge step-by-step proposals which will create the conditions of common action within which a far larger number of talented but perhaps less creative men will find it gradually possible to change their views of what is valuable.

At the first level there is no substitute for the creative few who, by a leap of imagination, see the new conditions which must be brought into being if man is to adapt to his increasingly interdependent environment. But this is not enough; practical step-by-step measures must be devised which can be taken by common men, whether at the top or just beginning the climb. Once this is done, the task at the second level is to provide the new structure with adequate resources and manpower and, to a large extent, to let common experience work its effect on men's purposes and methods.

Arms control, space, communications, weather, industry, trade, social sciences, and other areas are all in urgent need of such an approach. Not detailed, formal, arm's-length agreements between impermeable states are required, but men facing common tasks and seeking to create a common structure of action. There is no single cure for conflict. Physicists and psychologists, physicians and politicians, are all likely to make a more constructive contribution if they work from their own areas of knowledge, seeking to forge the links of common action rather than seeking to devise general cures for the whole spectrum of conflict.

Two countervailing outlooks are necessary for the success of these efforts. First, there must be an appreciation of the fundamental nature of political power, which is no more than the ability to persuade others to work for one's own objectives. In a modern state it need not be, and frequently is not, exercised through the bureaucracy or other organs of the state. A scientist who conceives a Geophysical Year and arouses his colleagues throughout the world to see it carried through is engaging in constructive political action beyond the scope of all but the most powerful statesmen. Each man of talent, whether in science, business, or government, has some potential for political action which will contribute to the control of conflict. Together, their efforts can be sufficient. Anything less may not be adequate for survival.

Second, it is necessary to guard against overoptimism, although in a man's particular field of competence it may be hardly necessary to stress the point. In his own field a man knows the intractable nature of the problems, the difficulties of progress, and the never-ending character of the task. Time is always needed. In the control of conflict, a substantial period of time will be required for the myriad efforts to be initiated, planned, accepted, and implemented. Perhaps a decade or more will be required before a cumulative momentum is created. The moral is clear. It is necessary to begin at once, but also to guard against overoptimism about early results. In the meantime, force will continue to be our major reliance and war our continuing hazard.

Some Considerations Relevant to National Policy

_____ MORTON DEUTSCH

Peace is currently maintained by a delicate balance of terror. The delicacy of the balance has justifiably alarmed many of those who are aware of the awesome destructive power of nuclear weapons. A common response of intellectuals, military strategists, and statesmen alike to this alarm has been to focus their attention upon the problem of making the balance steadier and more durable. The interest in "arms control" and in the concept of "stable deterrence" reflects this focus. Although efforts to reduce the military insecurities of East and West are obviously laudable, I believe that the current emphasis on methods of stabilizing the mutual terror should be viewed as, at best, dealing with stopgap measures. The "hostile peace" of stabilized mutual terror and of institutionalized mutual suspicion is intrinsically vulnerable to the social and psychological maladies that breed in an atmosphere of tension and suspicion. We must begin to find roads to a peace rooted in mutual interests and mutual respect.

Thus, the basic theme of my paper* centers on the question: How do we move from a peace of mutual terror to a peace of mutual trust? This question proliferates into many other, related questions, e. g. : What should our military policy be; what steps can we take to strengthen existing elements of international order; how can mutual suspicions be reduced; how can we learn to communicate with one another more effectively; what nonviolent techniques for resolving international conflicts can be developed; how can the problems of a disarmed world be coped with? These are some of the difficult questions to which the social sciences must address themselves if civilization is to survive. Here, I cannot hope to do more than deal with some limited aspects of our military and international policy. For a fuller discussion of these matters see Wright, Evan, and Deutsch's book on the prevention of World War III (1).

*Reprinted from _The Journal of Social Issues_, Vol. XVII, No. 3, pp. 57–68.

Let me indicate in a brief, summary fashion some of the basic psychological assumptions which come from theoretical and experimental research that I have been doing on interpersonal trust and suspicion and interpersonal bargaining (2, 3, 4, 5, 6, 7).

1. There are social situations which do not allow the possibility of "rational" behavior so long as the conditions for mutual trust do not exist. I believe our current international situation is a situation of this kind. A characteristic symptom of such "nonrational situations" is that any attempt on the part of any individual or nation to increase its own welfare or security (without regard to the security or welfare of others) is self-defeating. Thus, for example, if the Soviet Union attempts to increase its security by taking over Berlin, it will decrease its real security by increasing the likelihood of nuclear war. In such situations the only way that individuals or nations can avoid being trapped in a mutually reinforcing, self-defeating cycle is to attempt to change the situation so that a basis of mutual trust can develop.

2. Mutual trust is most likely to occur when people are positively oriented to each other's welfare—i. e., when each has a stake in the other's doing well rather than poorly. Unfortunately, the East and West, at present, appear to have a stake in each other's defects and difficulties rather than in each other's welfare. Thus the Communists gloat over our racial problems and our unemployment, and we do likewise over their agriculture failures and their lack of civil liberties.

3. To induce a mutual welfare orientation in another, you have to demonstrate toward the other that your own behavior is based upon such a premise, and that he cannot improve his welfare by violation of it.

4. Another person is likely to be convinced that your behavior is guided by a mutual welfare orientation (i. e., is more likely to be trusting) as a function of such factors as: the amount and frequency of the benefits he receives from your behavior; the confidence he has that your behavior has no other purpose than to provide mutual benefit. The other is more likely to perceive that your behavior is not guided by ulterior purpose if it does not result in disproportionate gain or loss for yourself and if your behavior is not seen to be determined by weakness, insanity, or inanity.

5. Another person is less likely to violate a mutual welfare orientation (i. e., is more likely to be trustworthy) if he can trust you; if he knows what you consider to be a violation; and if he knows that you will neither condone a violation nor use an apparent one as an excuse for destructive retaliation but will, instead, attempt to restore cooperation without allowing yourself to be, or remain, disadvantaged by it.

6. Mutual trust can occur even under circumstances in which the parties involved are unconcerned with each other's welfare. The presence of third parties who are "neutral" or who are valued in the same way (either favorably or unfavorably) may enable the development of limited forms of mutual trust. Thus, neutral nations, if they were sufficiently united and uncommitted, might facilitate communication or mediate conflicts between the East and West.

Military Policy

I shall discuss briefly two concepts: military superiority and stable deterrence.

Military Superiority

A public opinion poll would, undoubtedly, show that most Americans accept the traditional view that the security of the United States would be enhanced if we had a clear-cut military superiority over the Soviet Union. However, in the age of hydrogen bombs and missiles, the quest for military superiority is dangerous, provocative, and enhances the possibility of war. The basic axiom of military doctrine for both the United States and the Soviet Union in the missile age must be the recognition that military actions should only be taken which increase the military security of both sides; military actions which give a military superiority to one side or the other should be avoided. We should recognize that we have a positive interest in the other side's military security as well as in our own. The military forces of both sides should be viewed as having the common primary aim of preventing either side (one's own or the other side) from starting a deliberate or accidental war. Possibly, periodic meetings of military leaders from East and West might foster the mutual awareness of common concerns.

The assumption here, as I see it, is very simple: neither the United States nor the Soviet Union will allow itself to be intimidated by the other on a vital matter. If one side envisages that the other may achieve a temporary military superiority, it may be frightened into rash actions to prevent this from occurring. If one side feels it has achieved a temporary military superiority, it may be emboldened to attempt to intimidate the other before the seesaw shifts its balance. We must recognize that just as military inferiority is dangerous, so is military "superiority"; we neither want to tempt nor frighten a potential enemy into military action.

Stable Deterrence

The recognition that none of the participants in a nuclear war is likely to be victorious has led to the concept of stable deterrence through a balance of mutual terror. The essential idea is that if each side has a nuclear retaliatory capacity which has a high degree of invulnerability (i.e., a capacity to inflict "unacceptable damage" on the other side which is unlikely to be destroyed by a surprise attack), neither side would dare to initiate a nuclear war against the other.

The proponents of the theory of stable deterrence have made a very valuable analysis of the delicacy of the present balance of terror and have presented important suggestions for making the balance steadier. However, some of the sources of instability are inherent even in "stable deterrents;" others inhere in the atmosphere of tension and suspicion of the present "hostile peace." These latter sources of instability lead even some proponents of the doctrine of stable deterrence to neglect the mutuality of interest of both sides (i.e., that the weapons systems of the Soviet Union as well as those of the United States be equally invulnerable to surprise attack) which is implicit in the doctrine; it leads others who are not fully aware of the implications of the theory of stable deterrence to support such unstabilizing viewpoints as the doctrine of "massive retaliation" and the doctrine of "instantaneous, automatic retaliation."

Below, we examine some of the assumptions involved in the concept of "stable deterrence" and indicate some of the instabilities which plague it. A stable balance of terror implies (at the minimum): (a) the mutual invulnerability of nuclear weapons systems; (b) the mutual vulnerability of civilian populations; (c) rational, responsible control over the use of the weapons system, including the ability to prevent accident, misunderstanding, insanity, or local decision as the basis for use of the weapons; (d) an unnervous self-confidence in the face of potential attack or of an undeliberate attack. Moreover, for the "balance of terror" to serve as a deterrent to an attack, it is implied that: (e) the threat of retaliation is credible to the potential attacker; (f) the threat is unprovocative (i.e., does not stimulate what it is attempting to deter) and is appropriate rather than unjust; (g) the potential attacker is neither masochistic (i.e., is not self-destructive) nor irrational (e.g., has grandiose delusions of invulnerability); (h) the attacker can be correctly identified. In addition, any doctrine which is concerned with stability should provide some compensating mechanism to restore stability when it is threatened or disrupted, e.g., to prevent a vicious spiral of mutual misunderstandings about whether a deliberate attack is taking place.

Let us now consider the implicit assumptions we have listed

above to see how likely they are to be realized and to see if some
assumptions don't inherently conflict with others.

1. Mutual invulnerability of weapon systems. As Herman
Kahn (8) has pointed out, if the present level of expenditure on research relating to military weapons continues, one can be reasonably
certain that new, surprising weapons will be developed. Weapons
which are now considered to be relatively invulnerable will become
relatively vulnerable. Recognition of this possibility has led military
theorists to the view that it would be dangerous to "place all their
eggs in one basket"—i.e., to rely on one weapon system (e.g., the
Polaris submarine) rather than upon a mixture of different weapons
systems. However, without an effective agreement to limit and control weapons development, one may expect that, sooner or later, unpredictable research developments will make the balance of mutual
terror teeter to one side or the other. Pessimistically, one may even
say that an agreement which limits and controls weapons and their
development, even if "fully-inspected," might not prevent an imbalance from developing unless the agreement expresses or produces
the intention not to violate it. This is possible because the technology
of inspection evasion could, under some circumstances, develop more
rapidly than the technology of detecting incipient evasions.

2. Mutual vulnerability of populations. The "balance of terror"
doctrine not only assumes that the nuclear weapons are mutually invulnerable but also that they are mutually effective. Anything which
one-sidedly limits the destructiveness of the other side's weapons
disturbs the balance. Thus, if one side begins to develop a large-
scale civil defense program, the other side may feel that it will lose
its ability to deter an attack since its retaliation will not be so fear-
some. Yet, it is evident that there are strong pressures for a unilateral development of civil defense. Some of these pressures, oddly
enough, originate in strong proponents of the doctrine of stable deterrence: they warn of the dangerous implications for world peace
were the Soviet Union to initiate unilaterally a civil defense program
against nuclear attack, but advocate that we do so unilaterally (9).
Perhaps their recommendations are based upon the assumption that
Soviet Union has already initiated such a program; if so, this basis
for our action should be clearly stated. My criticism here is not of
defensive measures (whether they be anti-missile or civil defense)
per se but rather of measures which are not mutual in orientation.

3. Rational, responsible control of the decision to use the
weapons. One of the greatest sources of instability arises from the
possibility that one side or the other will use nuclear weapons with-

out having made a responsible decision to use them or will use them because of misinformation or misunderstanding concerning the other side. The fact is that the facilities for gathering and processing information, the communication network, the governmental decision-making apparatus, and the military command and control techniques required to make a quick decision to use nuclear weapons are extremely complex. It is very unlikely that any nation has the capabilities necessary to make such a decision, which would not, in all likelihood, be regretted after the fact. Moreover, there is always the possibility that the decision to use the bomb would be made by an irresponsible local unit—by a "mischievous" missile squad, a "grandiose" bomber crew, a "paranoid" submarine crew—which could carry out its own decision. As a social psychologist, I do not minimize the possibility of something which may be described as "collective madness" in times of acute international crisis. For reports of some studies of social behavior in situations of stress see Maccoby, Newcomb, and Hartley (10).

4. <u>Nervousness, the need to respond quickly because of the fear that one will lose either the desire or ability to respond, enhances the likelihood that a response will be triggered off by an insufficient stimulus and thus makes for instability</u>. The proponents of "stable deterrence," of course, strongly oppose reliance on retaliatory forces which would be destroyed if not used quickly. Some of the "nervousness" in military circles arises, however, from the fear of loss of a desire to retaliate if deterrence has failed.

5. <u>For a military threat of retaliation to deter, it must, at the minimum, have some credibility</u>. The doctrine of massive nuclear retaliation in relation to non-nuclear aggressions lost much of its credibility after the Soviet Union acquired nuclear weapons systems. Of course, both the Soviet Union and the United States, in contemplating the use of conventional military weapons, also have to contemplate the dangerous possibility that a conventional war, out of its own dynamism, will mushroom into a nuclear war. However, neither we nor our Allies now believe that we would initiate an all-out nuclear war unless the facts showed we were in danger of all-out devastation ourselves (8).

The implication of the foregoing is that, in the present situation, the threat of massive retaliation is itself largely deterred by the counterthreat of massive retaliation: deterrence is deterred. In a similar manner, one can argue that if one side has launched a surprise attack but has failed to wipe out the other side's nuclear striking force and has not done intolerable damage to its civilian population, the attacked nation would be deterred from a massive retaliation directed at their opponent's civilian population because of fear of counter-retaliation directed at its own population. Possibly thoughts such as those advanced in the preceding sentence have led to the doctrine of instant, automatic massive retaliation in relation to any nuclear attack: a doctrine seriously advanced by high-ranking military leaders to insure the "credibility" of the threat. It is not necessary to dwell upon the great moral and physical dangers of being "nervous" and overready to kill one hundred million or more people. Apart from the dangerous provocation and lack of control implicit in the concept of immediate and automatic retaliation, if attack and counterattack by missiles are not separated in time, how could the survivors know who started the war?

If we take the theory of stable deterrence seriously, the doctrine of retaliatory response to a nuclear attack should be a doctrine calling for an unanxious, deliberate, delayed response which permits the nuclear aggressor to be identified unambiguously before the world and before its own people. Such a doctrine might encompass the threat of limited retaliation (of no more than an eye for an eye) to induce the people of the aggressor nation to overthrow their government and to surrender to the United Nations. The threat of limited retaliation in relation to limited aggression, in addition to being more justifiable (i. e., less provocative) and less likely to result in unlimited catastrophe, is also probably more credible than the threat of massive retaliation in relation to limited destruction.

6. An effective threat does not provoke the events which it is trying to deter. Psychologists, sociologists, and psychiatrists, who have long been concerned with the prevention and control of antisocial behavior, would undoubtedly agree that one of the great dangers in the threat of force (in a "get tough" policy) is that it often incites the behavior it is attempting to prevent. There are several common reasons that threats provoke rather than deter: (a) the threat of using force is perceived to be an expression of an underlying intent to injure, rather than of self-defense (e. g., if a military leader boasts of his nation's ability to destroy an attacker, the statement is more likely to be seen as aggressive "rocket-rattling" than as peaceful in prupose; (b) the threat of force is perceived to be an attempt unjustly to restrain actions in which the threatened party feels entitled to engage; (c) the threatened party has a desire to be a "martyr" or to be punished; (d) the threatener is perceived to be bluffing; and (e) the threatener is perceived to be so irresponsible or incompetent that he can not control the use or nonuse of this threatened force and, hence, the only way to control him is to destroy his capacity to threaten.

If we examine our recent and current policies to see whether they provoke or deter, we must conclude that some of our policies are not unprovocative. The placement of vulnerable nuclear weapons and missiles in Europe and the use of vulnerable overseas bases by bombers carrying nuclear weapons are highly provocative, because the weapons and bases would not survive a nuclear attack, and, hence, could not be used as a retaliatory force: their only feasible use is to initiate attack. Brinkmanship, the reliance on the perceived possibility that limited conflicts (e. g. , over Berlin and Quemoy) might escalate to all-out nuclear war as a means of deterring limited war, and the search for information which would make the other side's retaliatory force vulnerable to surprise attack are two examples of provocative policy. To be sure, military provocativeness is not limited to one side.

7. <u>The theory of stable deterrence assumes that the potential attacker is rational, in the economic sense that he will not attack if the unexpected gain resulting from the attack is smaller than the expected loss and if the expected loss from not attacking is less than that from attacking</u>. Moreover, it assumes that the potential retaliator has a reasonably accurate conception of the nature of the potential attacker's complex system of values and nonvalues. Both assumptions seem to be rather dubious. Behavior, particularly in a time of high tension and crisis, is more likely to be determined by anxiety, stereotypes, self-esteem defensive maneuvers, and social conformity pressures than by simple rational estimates of "economic" gain and loss. Furthermore, there is little evidence to suggest that the Russians really understand us (or themselves) or that we understand them (or ourselves); certainly the Voice of America's conception of the Soviets is rejected by the Soviet citizens as is <u>Pravda's</u> conception of America rejected by us (11).

8. <u>The theory of stable deterrence is a two-country theory</u>. No one appears to have been able to think through what happens when nuclear weapons become a "N-country" problem. That is, the diffusion of nuclear weapons creates extremely complex problems for such concepts as stability and deterrence, problems which have not been solved. What would represent a stable distribution of nuclear weapons? Whom to deter?

The point of my discussion of the theory of stable deterrence is: the notion that invulnerable nuclear weapons, in themselves, produce stability is a dangerously misleading notion. They do not. Stability depends also on many other considerations. Do not misunderstand me, however; my view is that if nuclear weapons are to be maintained, it is better that these weapons be invulnerable to surprise attack.

Let me summarize my discussion of military policy by stating that: the central point which we must grasp is that there is no rational solution possible to our problems of security in a nonrational world except to make the world more rational. We are in a type of international situation which is similar to that of a panicky crowd in a theater where there is a fire. By attempting to achieve individual safety without regard for the safety of others, a person enhances the danger for all. In such a situation, the only reasonable course of action that will avert catastrophe is to take the initiative in creating order by persuasively suggesting rules and procedures which will permit an organized exit from the situation before the fire rages out of control.

Some Suggestions for International Policy

But how does one create order out of potential chaos? How does one take the initiative in such an attempt? What rules and procedures should be developed? How can one be confident that the rules will be followed? These are difficult questions, but I venture to sketch an answer in the following paragraphs. It is self-evident that to facilitate the development of order and justice in international relations we must weaken the conditions which promote disorder and injustice and strengthen the conditions which promote the opposite state of affairs.

Weakening the Conditions Leading to Disorder

The major conditions leading to disorder in the present international scene are:

1. The revolution in military technology and the arms race: To overcome the dangers inherent in this situation we need to: (a) develop a counterrevolution in disarmament technology; (b) negotiate agreements and take steps unilaterally which will decrease military instability by preventing the diffusion of nuclear weapons, by reducing the fear of surprise attacks, and by reducing the likelihood of devastating incidents through accident, misunderstanding, or insanity; and (c) move toward disarmament theory and technology which permits a reliable disarmament. It seems to me unlikely that substantial disarmament will be feasible before a marked change has occurred in the international atmosphere. Consider only the unrealism of disarmament negotiations without the participation of Communist China.

2. <u>The widening gap in standards of living between the rich</u> <u>countries of Europe and North America and the poor countries of</u> <u>Asia, Africa, and Latin America,</u> coupled with the increasing aware-ness of this difference and a rising "revolution of expectations." It is obvious that the rich countries must spend much more organized, research-tutored effort in the attempt to assist the people in the "underdeveloped" countries to acquire the educational, economic, and political skills and resources to become independent, thriving nations. I stress "independent" to emphasize the importance of not involving these underdeveloped nations in the cold war, the import-ance of allowing them to develop in ways which do not pressure them to be committed to one "bloc" or the other.

3. <u>The existence of two organized crusading ideologies, one</u> <u>centered in the United States and the other in the Soviet Union,</u> which <u>emphasize their antagonistic interests while neglecting their mutu-</u> <u>ally cooperative interests.</u> I think it is the special duty of the social scientists in each "bloc" to expose the mythologies of each system, to accurately describe and analyze the complexities of each society, and to point out the similarities as well as the differences. Our an-alysis can not be content with such ideologically determined categor-ies as "free enterprise system," "Communism," "Democratic," "totalitarian." This is not to deny that there are real and important differences between the United States and the Soviet Union, but we should attempt to understand these differences by objective analysis and description rather than by using political slogans as labels for very complex social systems. An objective analysis would see each society in an appropriate historical perspective, in terms of the con-ditions which have given rise to and which maintain its particular in-stitutions. In addition, such an analysis would point to the future by understanding the implications of the revolutionary changes in edu-cation, communications, industrial technology, and standards of liv-ing occurring in each society (12). Moreover, such an analysis would avoid the mythological tendencies which lead to the identification of oneself with the "angels" and the others with the "devils." It is in-teresting to note that in the mythology of each nation, the other na-tion is essentially characterized as a social system in which "the many are involuntarily exploited by the few," "the mass of the peo-ple are not really sympathetic to the regime," "the government is dominated by groups who will attempt to impose their views upon the rest of the world, by force if necessary" (11).

Strengthening the Elements of Order

International order presupposes rules which effectively regu-late the interaction among nations. Until there is a world government with sufficient power to coerce compliance with international rules, it is evident that powerful governments will comply with rules, whether they are formalized in treaties or not, only as long as they perceive that compliance is more beneficial than detrimental to their enlightened over-all self-interests. Any system of rules which is supported primarily through voluntary compliance is likely to be initiated and maintained only if sufficient communication among the potential participants in the system of rules is also maintained so that: (a) they can recognize that they hold certain values in common; (b) they can articulate rules which fairly represent the shared values without systematically disadvantaging a given participant; (c) they can be reasonably certain that compliance is mutual; and (d) they can agree on procedures to resolve the misunderstandings and disputes about compliance which will inevitably occur. The ability of a system of rules to weather disputes and short-run disadvantages to a given participant is a function of the strength of the internal commitment to the system of rules and of the strength of the cooperative bonds that exist among the participants.

I shall employ this rather condensed presentation of "the conditions of normative order" to make some proposals for our international policy.

1. We must be unremitting in our attempt to communicate with members of the Communist bloc in such a way that the mutual recognition of our sharing many values in common (e. g., peace, technological advance, prosperity, science, health, education, cultural progress) is fostered. We should neither initiate nor reciprocate barriers to communication. Clearly our policy of noncommunication with Communist China makes no sense if we ever expect it to participate in arms control or disarmament agreements.

2. To develop a system of rules, our course of conduct in international affairs should exemplify supranationalistic or universalistic values; it should constantly indicate our willingness to live up to the values that we expect others to adhere to. We must give up the doctrine of "special privilege" and the "double standard" in judging our own conduct and that of the Communist nations. In my view, only a double standard would suggest that Communist China is aggressive toward us, but that we have not been so toward it; that the use of military force to maintain the status quo is peace-preserving while the use of force to change it is aggressive; that Communist bases near the United States are menacing while United States bases adjacent to the Soviet Union are peaceful; etc.

3. To cut through the atmosphere of basic mistrust which exists, the United States should engage in a sustained policy of attempt-

ing to establish cooperative bonds with the Communist bloc. I emphasize "sustained" to indicate that the policy should not be withdrawn in the face of initial rebuffs, which may be expected. Our policy should be to avoid the reciprocation of hostility and always to leave open the possibility of mutual cooperation despite prior rebuff. This means that we should have a positive interest in helping people in the Communist nations toward a higher standard of living, and our trade policies should reflect this. It means that we should have an active interest in reducing their fears that they may be the victims of military aggression. It means, basically, that we should attempt to relate to them as though they are human. Relating to them as though they were devils, or some inhuman horde, will only help to confirm our nightmares.

The thesis of this paper has been that an orientation to the other's welfare, as well as to one's own, is a basic prerequisite to a peace sustained by mutual confidence rather than by mutual terror. "As well as to one's own (welfare)" is underlined here to emphasize that loss of self-identity is a poor foundation for cooperation in international as well as in interpersonal relations. Thriving societies that are coping successfully with their own internal problems have less ground for the fears and less need for the hostilities that interfere with the international cooperation necessary to construct a civilized world for the genus man.

REFERENCES

1. Wright, Q., Evan, W.M., and Deutsch, M. (eds.), Preventing World War III: Some Proposals, New York, Simon and Schuster.

2. Deutsch, M., "A theory of cooperation and competition," Human Relations, 1949, 2, 129-152.

3. Deutsch, M.,"Trust and suspicion," Journal of Conflict Resolution, 1958, 2, 265-279.

4. Deutsch, M.,"The effect of motivational orientation upon trust and suspicion," Human Relations, 1960, 13, 123-139.

5. Deutsch, M.,"Trust, trustworthiness, and the F scale, " Journal of Abnormal and Social Psychology, 1960, 61, 138-140.

6. Deutsch, M., and Krauss, R.M., "The effect of threat upon interpersonal bargaining," Journal of Abnormal and Social Psychology, 1960, 61, 181-189.

7. Deutsch, M., "The face of bargaining," paper presented at the Nineteenth Annual Meetings of The Operations Research Society of America, Chicago, May 25, 1961.

8a. Kahn, H., "The arms race and some of its hazards," Daedalus, 1960a, 89, 744-781.

8b. Kahn, H., The nature and feasibility of war and deterrence. Rand Corporation Report P-1888-RC, January 20, 1960b.

9.   Rand Corporation Study, Report on a study of non-military defenses. July 1, 1958. Hearings before the Subcommittee on National Policy Machinery of the Committee on Governmental Operations, United States Senate, Eighty-sixth Congress, Second Session, February 23, 24, and 25, 1960. Part 120. U. S. Government Printing Office, 1960.

10. Maccoby, E.E., Newcomb, T., and Hartley, E. (eds.), Readings in Social Psychology, New York, Henry Holt and Co., 1958.

11. Bronfenbrenner, U., "The mirror-image in Soviet-American relations," Journal of Social Issues, 1961, 17, 45-56.

12. Rostow, W.W., The Stage of Economic Growth, New York, Cambridge University Press, 1960.

Part II

SPECIAL FIELDS:
THE TOLL OF COLD WAR, THE PRICE OF PEACE

*Learning, experimenting, observing, try not to stay on the
surface of facts. Do not become the archivists of facts. Try
to penetrate to the secret of their occurrence, persistently
search for the laws which govern them.*

Ivan Pavlov

Each in its own way, the separate fields within the behavioral
sciences seek to clarify the meaning, the causes, and the consequences
of the international conflict. They are not independent one of the other,
but usually each specialist, like the three blind men and the elephant,
will examine a different aspect of the same phenomenon. A psychologist considers the psychological obstacles to conflict resolution,
while the economist examines the economic deterrents.

Unlike the astronomer, the physicist, and the chemist who study
the "glamorous unknown," the behavioral scientist observes the pro-
saic activities of daily life which hardly call for the cogitations of a
trained mind. Only when he analyzes man's behavior in depth, searching for explanatory principles, can he hope to venture into the unknown and to discover laws comparable to those in the physical sciences. Take the papers on psychology and psychiatry as an example.
On the face of it, the years of Cold War have had no effect on people,
for does not life go on as before? Psychiatrist Judd Marmor points
to numerous conditions of man today that are effects of the conflicts
of our time, and also obstacles to peace. One of these is dehumanization, a condition the psychiatrists Viola W. Bernard and Perry Ottenberg and psychologist Fritz Redl analyze in great and enlightening
detail. The psychologists Nathan Kogan and Michael A. Wallach, considering a subject important at a time when a few men have considerable control over the buttons of doom, demonstrate through their own
research that there are principles that explain who will take risks (as,
for example, in foreign policy) and who will be conservative. The internal and external factors that motivate risk-taking are delineated.

The public health implications of the international tensions are discussed by two persons. Psychiatrist Francis Cloutier, Director-General of the World Federation for Mental Health, warns against some typical errors in applying the behavioral sciences to the world scene. Among these errors is the tendency to apply theories about individual psychology to nations as a whole. He indicates the ways in which the sciences can have an impact, pointing up several roles discussed previously by Talcott Parsons. Economist Kenneth Boulding considers war the major public health problem of the day because this "revolution of the mega-death... threatens to become the major source of human mortality...." It must and can come under man's control. To that end he proposes the study of the ecology of conflict; that is, the relationship between the opposing factions in reference to their economic and geographic environment. Dr. Boulding analyzes conflict and its management.

A society whose economy has long been keyed to the production of armament and other war matériel must prepare for conversion if it is seriously interested in peace. Economists Emile Benoit and Seymour Melman, in separate papers, discuss the problem, the possibilities, and the outlook. They conclude on a note of optimism, for reconversion is possible without economic disaster.

Quite appropriately, the representative of the field of anthropology opens his paper by reporting on some of his experiences in a contemporary "primitive" culture, the Lower Kutenai Indians. Humans are able to exploit the regularities of nature without understanding them, Ray L. Birdwhistell explains. To understand is, of course, the scientists' task, a difficult one for those behavioral scientists who, cursed by "scientism"—the need to imitate the physical sciences—rip man out of the context of his social life and attempt to study him "under conditions appropriate for a complex hydrocarbon."

Psychological Obstacles to the Peaceful Resolution of the Cold War

_____ JUDD MARMOR

The problems which divide the great camps of the East and the West in the current Cold War are complex and formidable; and they involve many realistic political, economic, and ideological differences. The psychiatrically-aware person cannot fail to recognize, however, that intimately intertwined with these realistic elements are important psychological parameters of fear and mistrust between the leaders of the opposing sides and between their respective populations. These parameters not only contribute significantly to the difficulties involved, but also tend to stimulate impulses toward violence at crucial periods. It is the purpose of this brief communication to examine some of the underlying psychological factors that act as obstacles in the search for nonviolent solutions to existing international differences.

One of the most persistent of the psychological barriers is the widespread assumption that war is an intrinsic manifestation of human nature. This assumption grows out of the theory that war is an inevitable social expression of a fundamental instinct for destructive aggression in man, akin to that which is presumed to be present in predatory animals. The validity of this theory is open to serious question. Actually, as Fairfield Osborne has pointed out: "Warfare as practiced by man has no parallel in nature.... Within the more highly developed animal populations of the earth there is not now nor has there ever been similar destruction within a species itself. In fact, one has to go to the lowliest forms of animals, such as certain kinds of ants, to find anything comparable to human warfare. " (1)

Modern behavioral scientists in increasing numbers are coming to·the conclusion that man's violence is <u>not</u> spontaneously instinctive, but rather a <u>reactive response</u> either to a sense of frustration or to perceived threats involving some aspects of his psychological or physical security. This view does not deny that the <u>capacity</u> for violence is innate in man, but asserts that whether or not this capacity is <u>expressed</u> usually depends on environmental factors.

However, even if destructive aggression <u>were</u> an innate human instinct, it still would not follow logically that war is inevitable. It is meaningless to talk of war as though it were the sum total of countless individual human aggressions. War, particularly contemporary war, is a complicated social institution, the resultant of the intermeshing of many factors, social, economic, political, and psychological. It involves large and intricate social organizations. It requires armies, weapons, technology, recruitment, and propaganda. Like any other social institution, it is capable of evolution, change, and—eradication. Other widespread social institutions of man's past, like slavery, dueling, ritual human sacrifice, and cannibalism, which in their times and milieus seemed equally rooted in human nature and destiny, have been almost totally eliminated in the course of history. It is a fact, moreover, that various societies have existed without recourse to war for many generations.

Although it seems incontrovertible, therefore, that war is not an inevitable expression of man's nature, there are, nevertheless, certain aspects of human individual and group psychology that strongly predispose man to violence and thus do represent serious obstacles to the elimination of war as a societal institution.

Perhaps the most fundamental of these, although not necessarily the most important, is <u>fear.</u> Abundant clinical experience has shown that panic is a highly potent trigger for hostile behavior. Extreme fear of an adversary is as likely to provoke a violent act as is hatred of him. Yet fear is a basic biological reaction without which an individual might fail to take the proper actions needed for his protection and survival in the face of danger. Unfortunately, however, there is only a thin line between the amount of fear necessary to stimulate corrective behavior and the amount that leads to maladaptive responses. Psychologists have long been aware of what has been called the <u>primitivizing effect of fear</u> (2). The reactions of humans, like those of animals, tend to become more archaic and less rational under conditions of extreme fear or panic. The capacity for adaptive discrimination is lost, and habitual responses that are no longer appropriate are fallen back upon. When fire breaks out in a theater, for example, most people will rush for the main exits even though they are jammed, and will ignore the more passable but less customary exits. In the same way, when fears of an adversary are fanned to great heights by communication media, an unbearable tension is created in many people—tension that seeks relief at nearly any cost. Under such stress, almost any course may seem better than none at all. Hence the cry, so often heard, for "action" and "getting it over with," even though such action might be self-defeating or self-destructive. The certainties of war at such times may appear more endurable than the ambiguities of peace.

Fear also shortens time perspective. A fearful person becomes preoccupied with warding off the imminent danger, often to the neglect of the ultimate consequences of his behavior. Similarly, nations may counter what they perceive as an immediate threat by the adversary with action involving long-term consequences that may be much more serious than the initial hazard.

Other common psychological responses to danger that lend themselves to making violence feasible are the mechanisms of de-nial and isolation. Denial involves the failure to perceive or recog-nize certain aspects of reality in order to avoid becoming aware of something which might be unduly painful or threatening. It is the psychological equivalent of "burying one's head in the sand." In isolation these aspects of reality are perceived, but the painful or disturbing emotions associated with them are blocked out of conscious-ness. We recognize that mechanisms such as these make it possible for many people to cope with anxieties that might otherwise be incapa-citating for them. Nevertheless, it seems incontrovertible that a failure to react with at least some alarm to the possibility of nuclear annihilation must be considered maladaptive.

Denial and isolation are abetted by a number of factors. For one, most human beings cling to an illusion of personal immortality and invulnerability. The possibility of war is made tolerable by the thought, "It can't really happen to me; somehow or other I'll manage to survive." Another contributing element is the deep sense of per-sonal helplessness that most people feel regarding their ability to influence the crucial decisions of war and peace.

Still another element is the inability of people to conceptualize the magnitude of a danger with which they have had no prior experi-ence, and which therefore has no reality for them. This is particu-larly true of nuclear war, the consequences of which are beyond or-dinary imagination. Moreover, the inadequacy of language in char-acterizing such new phenomena is an additional barrier to the accur-ate perception of such dangers. New words like "megaton" lack emotional impact, since they have no reference to actual experience. The use of old terms, on the other hand, may engender a false sense of security because they fail to convey the impact of the new realities involved. Terms such as "civilian defense" and "national security" are examples of words that arouse reassuring images even though their traditional meanings have been drastically altered by the de-velopment of modern weapons.

In this area of language and conceptualization, we must take note also of some of the stereotypes concerning war that are deeply imbedded in our language and traditions and that foster attitudes con-ducive to group violence. The history books of every nation justify its wars as brave, righteous, and honorable. This glorification is charged with overtones of patriotism and love of country. Virtues such as heroism and courage are regarded as being "manly" and are traditionally associated with waging war, and the great popular heroes of history have mostly been soldiers. Conversely, the avoidance of war or the pursuit of peace are generally regarded as "effeminate," passive, cowardly, weak, dishonorable, or even subversive. The brutal realities of war are glamorized and obscured in countless tales of heroism and glory, and the warnings of an occasional Gerneral Sherman that "War is hell [and] its glory is all moonshine" go unheeded.

Another element which enters into the complex mosaic of denial is the de-individualization and dehumanization (3) of man in modern mass society. By these terms I refer to a complex phenomenon, which appears to be a consequence of increasing industrialization and urbanization, in which individual human beings and individual human values become lost in the mass. Under the pressures of group conformity and the standardized diet of the mass communication media, people tend to lose or never to acquire a sense of uniqueness and individuality. Persons with whom one has no direct relationship tend to become "anonymous" and dehumanized, numbers rather than individuals. This brings with it a sense of noninvolvement with and indifference to the actual or potential distress of other human beings and thus has a bearing on the capacity of people to tolerate psychologically the implications of mass destruction in a total war. The "organization man" becomes an item or tool which serves the mass machine—a means to an end, rather than an end in himself. In the technology of modern war theory, patterns of thinking that reflect this phenomenon are often observable. Concepts such as "first-strike," "overkill," "counterforce deterrence," etc., represent a move-countermove, game-theory type of thinking that treats the millions of potential human victims as mere statistics or pawns in a global chess game, and psychologically screens out the awesome consequences of the contemplated actions upon individual people, a full appreciation of which would make such actions emotionally intolerable.

But perhaps the most serious of the psychological obstacles to rational and nonviolent resolution of conflicts between nations are the mutual distortions of perception that take place under such circumstances. These distortions are often subsumed under the general concept of ethnocentric perception. This refers to the tendency of members of a group to perceive and evaluate events from the standpoint of their own group's interest and bias. The virtues of one's own side are magnified and its faults are not seen, while the evils of the adversary are exaggerated and his virtues ignored. Thus the identical behavior which is perceived as "standing firm" when exhibited by a member of one's own group is interpreted as "being pigheaded and obstinate" when manifested by a member of the opposing group.

This often leads to stereotyped conceptions, both of one's self and of the adversary, with the development of a self-righteous view of the in-group and a "bogeyman" view of the opponent. The motives of one's own group are always assumed to be morally honorable, fair, and decent; those of the opposing group are always suspect.

Ethnocentric perception also favors the development of polarized attitudes, in which everything is regarded as black or white, never as gray. All truth and morality are regarded as being on one's own side, all deceit and evil on the other. Neutrality is viewed with suspicion and hostility. Differences with the adversary tend to be exaggerated and similarities to be minimized.

Ethnocentric perception is not necessarily a matter of faulty access to information or to faulty intelligence. Although its extreme manifestations are more apt to be observed among people with little educational background, it occurs in greater or lesser degree among almost all people, in high stations as well as low ones, and even among those who have access to the widest sources of information. The reason for this lies in the homeostatic need of all human beings to organize their perceptions to fit into their pre-existent conscious and unconscious expectations, needs, and wishes, and to reject, minimize, or "fail to see" things that would upset their basic views about the nature of reality. This is an effort to keep the environment as constant and as meaningful as possible, and to avoid whatever might make it appear disturbing or unclear. This "intolerance of ambiguity" or "need for certainty" increases whenever individuals feel threatened, and tends to lessen with feelings of emotional security.

Another basic aspect of human psychology which is involved in ethnocentric distortions is the tendency to modify one's perceptions and reactions in response to group pressures. The effect of mob hysteria on individual behavior is a well-known phenomenon, but the ways in which more subtle group pressures affect people are often not as well recognized. This phenomenon was strikingly illustrated by an ingenious experiment performed some years ago by Asch, in which a subject is placed in a group of six to eight others, all of whom are asked to make certain perceptual or evaluative judgments. What the subject does not know is that the experiment is rigged, that the others all have been instructed to give false responses on a predetermined schedule. At first the subject finds himself in agreement with the others, but then finds his responses differing from all the others more and more often. He is initially puzzled, but then becomes more and more upset, begins to doubt his own judgment, and finally, in about one-third of the cases, actually begins to "see" things the way the others presumably do! There is little doubt that this kind of unconsciously influenced perception takes place widely in all countries, particularly when a conflict with an outside group increases the nationalistic pressures toward conformity.

All of these distortions inevitably lead to a <u>biased perception of what is fair and reasonable,</u> and thus not only render meaningful negotiations between adversaries difficult and sometimes impossible, but also fan the winds of fear and hate in their respective populations. The <u>mutual distrust</u> that inevitably develops under such circumstances becomes itself one of the most serious of the obstacles to nonviolent resolution of the conflicts between nations. The expectation that no agreement can be reached because "the other side doesn't really want peace" and "can't be trusted" inevitably leads to the anticipated failure and thus becomes a "self-fulfilling prophecy"— an expectation that by its very nature inexorably provokes the anticipated consequences.

Finally, no discussion of the psychological obstacles to nonviolence in international conflict can ignore the <u>significant interactions that exist between heads of governments and their peoples.</u> Many of the perceptual distortions of an adversary's actions and purposes are often deliberately created and manipulated by political leaders through the withholding of significant information or the dissemination of false information for the purpose of achieving certain strategic objectives in the power struggle with the adversary. Also, things may be said by them that are intended only for domestic consumption and domestic power politics but lend themselves to misinterpretation by the adversary. Once this has been done, however, the tensions, fears, and hostilities created in the minds of their populations become potent forces that control the subsequent freedom of the leaders to act. Thus a constant dynamic interplay exists between national leaders and their followers that often makes them both captives of a vicious cycle of increasing tensions. This is particularly true in open societies like our own, but the significance of such interactions should not be minimized, even in closed societies. Consequently, even when leaders may wish to make realistic compromises with the adversary, they may be unable to do so because of nationalistic pressures, the dictates of political expediency, the influence of power blocs within their own country, and the fears and suspicions that have already been aroused among their own peoples.

In this brief presentation I have not attempted to do more than merely touch on the more outstanding psychological obstacles to the nonviolent solutions of international conflicts. Although the basic causes of war cannot be said to be rooted in psychological sources alone, wars are waged by people, and the elimination of those factors that predispose men to violence is of major importance, therefore, in the search for a warless world.

Such a world does not mean a world without conflict. Conflict

between individuals, groups, and nations will always be part of the
human scene as long as there are diversities of human interests and
values. In this age of nuclear weaponry, however, it has become imperative to find ways of engaging in these inevitable conflicts without
resort to organized and institutionalized violence; to find, in William
James's apt phrase, the "moral equivalents of war." There is little
doubt that most people on our planet yearn consciously for a world
at peace, but man's unconscious irrationality may yet destroy him
despite his conscious wishes. One of the chief goals of behavioral
science is the increasing of man's self-understanding so as to bring
his unconscious attitudes and impulses under conscious control.
Never was such a goal more urgent than in today's world, lest the
awesome weapons that man in his ingenuity has constructed become
the Frankenstein's monster that will encompass his destruction.

REFERENCES

1. Osborn, F., Our Plundered Planet, Little Brown & Co., Boston,
   1948.
2. Osgood, C. E., An Alternative to War or Surrender, Urbana, Ill.,
   University of Illinois Press, 1962.
3. Bernard, V., Ottenberg, P. and Redl, F., "Dehumanization: A
   Composite Psychological Defense in Relation to Modern
   War," this volume, pp. 63-82.

Dehumanization: A Composite Psychological Defense in Relation to Modern War

VIOLA W. BERNARD
PERRY OTTENBERG
FRITZ REDL

We conceive of dehumanization as a particular type of psychic defense mechanism and consider its increasing prevalence to be a social consequence of the nuclear age. By this growth it contributes, we believe, to heightening the risks of nuclear extermination.*

Dehumanization as a defense against painful or overwhelming emotions entails a decrease in a person's sense of his own individuality and in his perception of the humanness of other people. The misperceiving of others ranges from viewing them en bloc as "subhuman" or "bad human" (a long-familiar component of group prejudice) to viewing them as "nonhuman," as though they were inanimate items or "dispensable supplies." As such, their maltreatment or even their destruction may be carried out or acquiesced in with relative freedom from the restraints of conscience or feelings of brotherhood.

In our view, dehumanization is not a wholly new mental mechanism, but rather a composite psychological defense which draws selectively on other well-known defenses, including unconscious denial, repression, depersonalization, isolation of affect, and compartmentalization (the elimination of meaning by disconnecting related mental elements and walling them off from each other). Recourse to dehumanization as a defense against stresses of inner conflict and external threat is especially favored by impersonal aspects of modern social organization, along with such special technological features of nuclear weapons as their unprecedented destructive power and the distance between push button and victim.

We recognize that many adaptive, as well as maladaptive,[1]

---

*The authors have revised this paper since it was presented in March 1963.

[1]Adaptive and maladaptive refer to a person's modes of coping with internal and external stress. The distinction hinges on the extent to which such coping is successful with respect to the optimal over-all balance of the individual's realistic interests and goals.

uses of self-protective dehumanization are requisite in multiple areas of contemporary life. As a maladaptive defense in relation to war, however, the freedom from fear which it achieves by apathy or blindness to implications of the threat of nuclear warfare itself increases the actuality of that threat: the masking of its true urgency inactivates motive power for an all-out effort to devise creative alternatives for resolving international conflict. Dehumanization also facilitates the tolerating of mass destruction through by-passing those psychic inhibitions against the taking of human life that have become part of civilized man. Such inhibitions cannot be called into play when those who are to be destroyed have been divested of their humanness. The magnitudes of annihilation that may be perpetrated with indifference would seem to transcend those carried out in hatred and anger. This was demonstrated by the impersonal, mechanized efficiency of extermination at the Nazi death camps.

The complex psychological phenomenon which we call dehumanization includes two distinct but interrelated series of processes: self-directed dehumanization relates to self-image, and denotes the diminution of an individual's sense of his own humanness; object-directed dehumanization refers to his perceiving others as lacking in those attributes that are considered to be most human. Despite the differences between these two in their origins and intrapsychic relationships within over-all personality development and psychodynamic functioning, both forms of dehumanization, compounded from parts of other defenses, become usable by the individual for emotional self-protection. These two forms of dehumanization are mutually reinforcing: reduction in the fullness of one's feelings for other human beings, whatever the reason for this, impoverishes one's sense of self; any lessening of the humanness of one's self-image limits one's capacity for relating to others.

It seems to us that the extensive increase of dehumanization today is causally linked to aspects of institutional changes in contemporary society and to the transformed nature of modern war. The mushrooming importance in today's world of technology, automation, urbanization, specialization, various forms of bureaucracy, mass media, and the increased influences of nationalistic, totalitarian, and other ideologies have all been widely discussed by many scholars. The net long-term implications of these processes, whether constructive or destructive, are beyond the scope of this paper, and we do not regard ourselves qualified to evaluate them.

We are concerned here, however, with certain of their more immediate effects on people. It would seem that, for a vast portion of the world's population, elements of these broad social changes contribute to feelings of anonymity, impersonality, separation from the decision-making processes, and a fragmented sense of one's in-

tegrated social roles, and also to pressure on the individual to con-
strict his affective range to some machine-like task at hand. Similarly,
the average citizen feels powerless indeed with respect to control
over fateful decisions about nuclear attack or its aftermath.

The consequent sense of personal unimportance and relative
helplessness, socially and politically, on the part of so many people
specifically inclines them to adopt dehumanization as a preferred defense against many kinds of painful, unacceptable, and unbearable
feelings referable to their experiences, inclinations, and behavior.
Self-directed dehumanization empties the individual of human emotions and passions. It is paradoxical that one of its major dynamic
purposes is protection against feeling the anxieties, frustrations and
conflicts associated with the "cog-in-a-big-machine" self-image into
which people feel themselves pushed by socially induced pressures.
Thus, it tends to fulfill the very threat that it seeks to prevent.

These pervasive reactions predispose one even more to regard other people or groups as less than human, or even nonhuman.
We distinguish among several different types and gradations of object-directed dehumanization. Thus, the failure to recognize in others
their full complement of human qualities may be either partial or
relatively complete. Partial dehumanization includes the misperceiving of members of "out-groups," en masse, as subhuman, bad human,
or superhuman; as such, it is related to the psychodynamics of group
prejudice. It protects the individual from the guilt and shame he
would otherwise feel from primitive or antisocial attitudes, impulses,
and actions that he directs — or allows others to direct — toward those
he manages to perceive in these categories: if they are sub-humans
they have not yet reached full human status on the evolutionary lad-
der and, therefore, do not merit being treated as human; if they are
bad humans, their maltreatment is justified, since their defects in
human qualities are their own fault. The latter is especially true if
they are seen as having superhuman qualities as well, for it is one
of the curious paradoxes of prejudice that both superhuman and de-
based characteristics are ascribed simultaneously to certain groups
in order to justify discrimination or aggression against them. The
foreigner, for instance, is seen at once as "wicked, untrustworthy,
dirty," and "uncanny, powerful, and cunning." Similarly, according
to the canons of race prejudice, contradictory qualities of exceptional prowess and extraordinary defect — ascribed to Orientals, Negroes, Jews, or any other group — together make them a menace toward whom customary restraints on behavior do not obtain. The main
conscious emotional concomitants of partial dehumanization, as with
prejudice, are hostility and fear.

In its more complete form, however, object-directed dehumanization entails a perception of other people as non humans—as statis-

tics, commodities, or interchangeable pieces in a vast "numbers game." Its predominant emotional tone is that of indifference, in contrast to the (sometimes strong) feelings of partial dehumanization, together with a sense of <u>non-involvement in the actual or foreseeable vicissitudes</u> of others. Such apathy has crucial psychosocial implications. Among these — perhaps the most important today — is its bearing on how people tolerate the risks of mass destruction by nuclear war.

Although this communication is primarily concerned with the negative and maladaptive aspects of dehumanization, we recognize that it also serves important adaptive purposes in many life situations. In this respect, it resembles other mental mechanisms of defense. Some of the ingredients of dehumanization are required for the effective mastery of many tasks in contemporary society. Thus, in crises such as natural disasters, accidents, or epidemics in which people are injured, sick, or killed, psychic mechanisms are called into play which divest the victims of their human identities, so that feelings of pity, terror, or revulsion can be overcome. Without such selective and transient dehumanization, these emotional reactions would interfere with the efficient and responsible performance of what has to be done, whether it be first aid, surgery, rescue operation, or burial.

Certain occupations in particular require such selectively dehumanized behavior.[2] Examples of these include law enforcement (police, judges, lawyers, prison officials); medicine (physicians, nurses, and ancillary personnel); and, of course, national defense (military leaders, strategists, fighting personnel). Indeed, some degree of adaptive dehumanization seems to be a basic requirement for effective participation in any institutional process. Almost every professional activity has some specific aspect that requires the capacity for appropriate detachment from full emotional responsiveness and the curtailment, at least temporarily, of those everyday human emotional exchanges that are not central to the task at hand, or which might, if present, impede it. The official at the window who stamps the passport may be by nature a warm and friendly man, but in the context of his job. The emigrant's hopes or fears lie outside his emotional vision.

Margaret Bourke-White, the noted photographer, was at Buchenwald at the end of World War II as a correspondent. Her account of herself at that time aptly describes the adaptive use of dehumanization, both self-directed and object-directed: "People often ask me how it is possible to photograph such atrocities... I have to work with

---

[2]These occupations, therefore, carry the extra risk of their requisite dehumanization becoming maladaptive if it is carried to an extreme or used inappropriately.

a veil over my mind. In photographing the murder camps, the protective veil was so tightly drawn that I hardly knew what I had taken until I saw prints of my own photographs. I believe many correspondents worked in the same self-imposed stupor. One has to or it is impossible to stand it. " (1)

The only occasions to date on which nuclear bombs have been used in warfare took place when the "baby bombs" were dropped on the civilian populations of Hiroshima and Nagasaki. Lifton (2) has reported on reactions among the Hiroshima survivors, as well as his own, as investigator. His observations are particularly valuable to us since, as a research psychiatrist, he was especially qualified both to elicit and to evaluate psychodynamic data. According to the survivors whom he interviewed, at first one experienced utter horror at the sudden, strange scene of mass deaths, devastation, dreadful burns, and skin stripped from bodies. They could find no words to convey fully these initial feelings. But then each described how, before long, the horror would almost disappear. One would see terrible sights of human beings in extreme agony and yet feel nothing. The load of feeling from empathic responsiveness had become too much to endure; all one could do was to try to survive.

Lifton reports that during the first few such accounts he felt profoundly shocked, shaken, and emotionally spent. These effects gradually lessened, however, so that he became able to experience the interviews as scientific work rather than as repeated occasions of vicarious agony. For both the survivors and the investigator, the "task" provided a focus of concentration and of circumscribed activity as a means of quelling disturbing emotions.

In these instances, the immediate adaptive value of dehumanization as a defense is obvious. It remains open to question, however, whether a further, somewhat related, finding of Lifton's will in the long run prove to be adaptive or maladaptive. He learned that many people in Japan and elsewhere cannot bear to look at pictures of Hiroshima, and even avoid the museum in which they are displayed. There is avoidance and denial of the whole issue which not infrequently leads to hostility toward the A-bomb victims themselves, or toward anyone who expresses concern for these or future victims. May not this kind of defense reaction deflect the determination to seek ways of preventing nuclear war?

We believe that the complex mechanism of dehumanization urgently needs to be recognized and studied because its use as a defense has been stepped up so tremendously in recent times, and because of the grave risks it entails as the price for short-term relief. This paper represents only a preliminary delineation, with main attention to its bearing on the nuclear threat. [3]

Many people, by mobilizing this form of ego defense, manage to avoid or to lessen the emotional significance for themselves of today's kind of war. Only a very widespread and deeply rooted defense could ward off the full import of the new reality with which we live: that warfare has been transformed by modern weaponry into something mankind has never experienced before, and that in all-out nuclear war there can be no "victory" for anyone.

The extraordinary complacency with which people manage to shield themselves against fully realizing the threat of nuclear annihilation cannot be adequately explained, we think, by denial and the other well-studied psychological defense mechanisms. This is what has led us to trace out dehumanization as a composite defense, which draws upon a cluster of familiar defenses, magnifying that fraction of each which is most specifically involved with the humanness of one's self-image and the perception of others. It operates against such painful feelings as fear, inadequacy, compassion, revulsion, guilt and shame. As with other mental mechanisms of defense, its self-protective distortions of realistic perceptions occur, for the most part, outside of awareness.

The extent to which dehumanization takes place consciously or unconsciously, although of considerable interest to us, is not relevant enough to this discussion to warrant elaboration. This also holds true for questions about why dehumanization as such has not hitherto received more attention and study in clinical psychiatry. [4] At least one possible reason might be mentioned, however. Most defense mechanisms were not studied originally in relation to such issues as war and peace, national destiny or group survival. Instead, they came under scrutiny, during the course of psychotherapy, as part of the idiosyncratic pathology of individual patients. This could have obscured the recognition of their roles in widespread collective reactions.

In order to avoid confusion we should also mention that the term "dehumanization" as we are using it, refers to a concept that is different from and not connected in meaning with the words "humane" and "humanitarian." "Inhumane" cruelty causes suffering; maladaptive dehumanization, as we point out, may also lead to suffering. Yet even these seemingly similar results are reached by very different

---

[3]Because of this primary emphasis, we shall refrain from exploring many important facets of dehumanization which seem less directly relevant to the threat of nuclear warfare. Yet, it permeates so many aspects of modern life that, for clarity in describing it, our discussion must ramify, to some extent, beyond its war-connected context. Still, we have purposely neglected areas of great interest to us, especially with regard to psychopathology, psychotherapy, and community psychiatry, which we think warrant fuller discussion elsewhere.

[4]No doubt, when the phenomenon is part of a mental disorder, it has been dealt with therapeutically, to some degree, under the names of other defense mechanisms.

routes; to equate them would be a mistake. A surgeon, for example, is treating his patient humanely when, by his dehumanization, he blots out feelings of either sympathy or hostility that might otherwise interfere with his surgical skill during an operation.

No one, of course, could possibly retain his mental health and carry on the business of life if he remained constantly aware of, and empathically sensitive to, all the misery and injustice that there is in the world. But this very essentiality of dehumanization, as with other defenses, makes for its greatest danger: that the constructive self-protection it achieves will cross the ever-shifting boundaries of adaptiveness and become destructive, to others as well as to the self. In combination with other social factors already mentioned, the perfection of modern techniques for automated killing on a global scale engenders a marked increase in the incidence of dehumanization. Correspondingly, there is intensified risk that this collective reaction will break through the fragile and elusive dividing line that separates healthy ego-supportive dehumanization from the maladaptive callousness and apathy that prevent people from taking those realistic actions which are within their powers to protect human rights and human lives.

A "vicious cycle" relationship would thus seem to obtain between dehumanization as a subjective phenomenon and its objective consequences. Conscience and empathy, as sources of guilt and compassion, pertain to human beings; they can be evaded if the human element in the victims of aggression is first sufficiently obscured. The aggressor is thereby freed from conscience-linked restraints, with injurious objective effects on other individuals, groups, or nations. The victims in turn respond, subjectively, by resorting even more to self-protective dehumanization, as did the Hiroshima survivors whom Lifton interviewed.

One might argue, and with some cogency, that similar conversion of enemies into pins on a military map has been part of war psychology throughout history, so are we not therefore belaboring the obvious? The answer lies in the fundamental changes, both quantitative and qualitative, that nuclear weapons have made in the meaning of war. In fact, the very term "war," with its pre-atomic connotations, has become something of an outmoded misnomer for the nuclear threat which now confronts us. "Modern war" — before Hiroshima — reflected, as a social institution, many of the social and technological developments which we have already noted as conducive to increased dehumanization. But with the possibility of instantaneously wiping out the world's population — or a very large section of it — the extent of dehumanization as well as its significance for human survival have both been abruptly and tremendously accelerated.

In part, this seems to be due to the overtaxing of our capacity really to comprehend the sudden changes in amplitudes that have become so salient. In addition to the changed factors of distance, time, and magnitude in modern technology, there is the push-button nature of today's weaponry and the indirectness of releasing a rocket barrage upon sites halfway around the world, all of which lie far outside our range of previous experience. When we look out of an airplane window, the earth below becomes a toy, the hills and valleys reduced to abstractions in our mental canvas; but we do not conceive of ourselves as a minute part of some moving speck in the sky — which is how we appear to people on the ground. Yet it is precisely such reciprocal awareness that is required if we are to maintain a balanced view of our actual size and vulnerability. Otherwise, perceptual confusion introduces a mechanistic and impersonal quality into our reactions.

The thinking and feeling of most people have been unable as yet to come to grips with the sheer expansion of numbers and the frightening shrinkage of space which present means of transportation and communication entail. The news of an animal run over by a car, a child stuck in a well, or the preventable death of one individual evokes an outpouring of sympathetic response and upsets the emotional equanimity of many; yet reports of six million Jews killed in Nazi death camps, or of a hundred thousand Japanese killed in Hiroshima and Nagaski, may cause but moderate uneasiness. Arthur Koestler has put it poignantly, "Statistics don't bleed; it is the detail which counts. We are unable to embrace the total process with our awareness; we can only focus on little lumps of reality." (3)

It is this unique combination of psychosocial and situational factors that seems particularly to favor the adoption of the composite defense we have called "dehumanization" — and this in turn acts to generate more and more of the same. The new aspects of time, space magnitude, speed, automation, distance, and irreversibility are not yet "hooked up" in the psychology of man's relationships to his fellow man or to the world he inhabits. Most people feel poorly equipped, conceptually, to restructure their accustomed picture of the world, all of a sudden, in order to make it fit dimensions so alien to their lifelong learning. Anxiety aroused by this threat to one's orientation adds to the inner stress that seeks relief through the defense.

We are confronted with a lag in our perceptual and intellectual development so that the enormity of the new reality, with its potential for both destructive and constructive human consequences, becomes blurred in our thinking and feeling. The less elastic our capacity to comprehend meaningfully new significances, the more we cling to dehumanization, unable to challenge its fallacies through knowledge and reason. Correspondingly, the greater our reliance on dehumanization as a mechanism for coping with life, the less readily can the new facts of our existence be integrated into our full psychic functioning, since so many of its vital components, such as empathy, have been shunted aside, stifled, or obscured.

Together, in the writers opinion, these differently caused but mutually reinforcing cognitive and emotional deficiencies seriously intensify the nuclear risk; latent psychological barriers against the destruction of millions of people remain unmobilized, and hence ineffective, for those who feel detached from the flesh and blood implications of nuclear war. No other mechanism seems to fit so well the requirements of this unprecedented internal and external stress. Dehumanization, with its impairment of our personal involvement, allows us to "play chess with the planets."

Whether it be adaptive or maladaptive, dehumanization brings with it, as we have noted, a temporary feeling of relief, an illusion of problems solved, or at least postponed or evaded. Whatever the ultimate effects of this psychic maneuver on our destiny, however, it would seem to be a wise precaution to try to assess some of its dangerous possibilities.

Several overlapping aspects of maladaptive dehumanization may be outlined briefly and in oversimplified form, as follows:

1. Increased emotional distance from other human beings. Under the impact of this defense, one stops identifying with others or seeing them as essentially similar to oneself in basic human qualities. Relationships to others become stereotyped, rigid, and above all, unexpressive of mutuality. People in "out-groups" are apt to be reacted to en bloc; feelings of concern for them have become anesthetized.

George Orwell illustrates this aspect of dehumanization in writing of his experience as a patient (4). His account also serves as an example of the very significant hazard, already mentioned, whereby professionally adaptive uses of this defense (as in medical education and patient care) are in danger of passing that transition point beyond which they become maladaptive and so defeat their original purpose.

"Later in the day the tall, solemn, black-bearded doctor made his rounds, with an intern and a troop of students following at his heels, but there were about sixty of us in the ward and it was evident that he had other wards to attend to as well. There were many beds past which he walked day after day, sometimes followed by imploring cries. On the other hand, if you had some disease with which the students wanted to familiarize themselves you got plenty of attention of a kind. I myself, with an exceptionally fine specimen of a bronchial rattle, sometimes had as many as a dozen students queuing up to listen to my chest. It was a very queer feeling — queer, I mean, because of their intense interest in learning their job, together with a seeming lack of any perception that the patients were human beings. It is strange to relate, but sometimes as some young student stepped forward to take his turn at manipulating you, he would be actually tremulous with excitement, like a boy who has at last got his hands on some expensive piece of machinery. And then ear after ear... pressed against your back, relays of fingers solemnly but clumsily tapping, and not from any one of them did you get a word of conversation or a look direct in your face. As a non-paying patient, in the uniform nightshirt, you were primarily a specimen, a thing I did not resent but could never quite get used to. "

2. Diminished sense of personal responsibility for the consequences of one's actions. Ordinarily, for most people, the advocacy of or participation in the wholesale slaughter and maiming of their fellow human beings is checked by opposing feelings of guilt, shame, or horror. Immunity from these feelings may be gained, however, by a self-automatizing detachment from a sense of personal responsibility for the outcome of such actions, thereby making them easier to carry out. (A dramatic version of the excuse, "I was only carrying out orders, " was offered by Eichmann at his trial.)

One "safe" way of dealing with such painful feelings is to focus only on one's fragmented job and ignore its many ramifications. By blocking out the ultimately destructive purpose of a military bombing action, for instance, one's component task therein may become a source of ego-acceptable gratification, as from any successful fulfillment of duty, mastery of a hard problem, or achievement of a dangerous feat. The B-29 airplane that dropped the atomic bomb on Hiroshima was named Enola Gay, after the mother of one of its crew members. This could represent the psychological defense of displacing human qualities from the population to be bombed to the machine.

One of the crew members is reported to have exclaimed: "If people knew what we were doing we could have sold tickets for $100,000!" and another is said to have commented, "Colonel, that was worth the 25¢ ride on the 'Cyclone' at Coney Island. " (5) Such reactions, which may on the surface appear to be shockingly cynical, not only illustrate how cynicism may be used to conceal strong emotions (as seems quite likely in this instance); they also suggest how one may try to use cynicism to bolster one's dehumanization when that defense is not itself strong enough, even with its displacement of responsibility and its focusing on one's fragmented job, to overcome the intensity of one's inner "humanized" emotional protest against carrying out an act of such vast destructiveness.

3. Increasing involvement with procedural problems to the detriment of human needs. There is an overconcern with details of procedure, with impersonal deindividualized regulations, and with the formal structure of a practice, all of which result in shrinking

the ability or willingness to personalize one's actions in the interests of individual human needs or special differences. This is, of course, the particular danger implicit in the trend toward bureaucracy that accompanies organizational units when they grow larger and larger. The task at hand is then apt to take precedence over the human cost: the individual is seen more as a means to an end than as an end in himself. Society, the Corporation, the Five-Year Plan — these become overriding goals in themselves, and the dehumanized man is turned into a cost item, tool, or energy-factor serving the mass-machine.

Even "scientific" studies of human behavior and development, as well as professional practices based on them, sometimes become dehumanized to a maladaptive extent (6). Such words as "communicate," "adjust," "identify," "relate," "feel," and even "love" can lose their personal meaningfulness when they are used as mere technical devices instead of being applied to specific human beings in specific life situations. [5] In response to the new hugeness of global problems, patterns of speech have emerged that additionally reflect dehumanized thinking. Segmented-fragmented concepts, such as "fallout problem," "shelter problem," "civil defense," "deterrence," "first strike," "pre-emptive attack," "overkill," and some aspects of game theory, represent a "move-countermove" type of thinking which tends to treat the potential human victim as a statistic, and to screen out the total catastrophic effect of the contemplated actions upon human lives. The content of strategy takes on an importance that is without any relation to its inevitable results, the defense of dehumanization having operated to block out recognition of those awesome consequences that, if they could be seen, would make the strategy unacceptable. The defense, when successful, narcotizes deeper feelings so that nuclear war, as "inevitable," may be more dispassionately contemplated and its tactical permutations assayed. In the course of this, however, almost automatic counter-actions of anxiety are frequently expressed through such remarks as : "People have always lived on the brink of disaster," "You can't change human nature; there will have to be wars," and "We all have to die some day."

---

[5]Within our own discipline this is all too likely to occur when thousands of sick individuals are converted into "cases" in some of our understaffed and oversized mental hospitals. Bureaucratic hospital structure favors impersonal experience. In an enlightening study (6), Merton J. Kahne points up how this accentuation of automatic and formalized milieu propensities thwarts the specific therapeutic need of psychiatric patients for opportunities to improve their sense of involvement with people.

On another occasion we hope to enlarge on how and why maladaptive uses of dehumanization on the part of professionals, officials, and the general public hamper our collective effort as a community to instill more sensitivity to individual need into patterns of congregate care, not only in mental hospitals but also in general hospitals, children's institutions, welfare and correctional facilities, etc.

4. <u>Inability to oppose dominant group attitudes or pressures</u>.
As the individual comes to feel more and more alienated and lonely
in mass society, he finds it more and more difficult to place himself
in opposition to the huge pressures of the "Organization." Fears of
losing occupational security or of attacks on one's integrity, loyalty,
or family are more than most people can bear. Self-directed dehumanization is resorted to as a defense against such fears and conflicts:
by joining the party, organization, or club, and thus feeling himself
to be an inconspicuous particle in some large structure, he may find
relief from the difficult decisions, uncertainties, and pressures of
nonconformity. He may also thereby ward off those feelings of guilt
that would arise out of participating in, or failing to protest against,
the injustices and cruelties perpetrated by those in power. Thus,
during the Nazi regime, many usually kindhearted Germans appear
to have silenced their consciences by emphasizing their own insignificance and identifying with the dehumanized values of the dictator-
ship. This stance permitted the detached, even dutiful, disregard of
their fellow citizens, which in turn gave even freer rein to the systematic official conducting of genocide.

5. <u>Feelings of personal helplessness and estrangement</u>. The
realization of one's relatively impotent position in a large organization engenders anxiety[6] which dehumanization helps to cover over.
The internalized perception of the self as small, helpless, and insignificant, coupled with an externalized view of "Society" as huge,
powerful, and unopposable, is expressed in such frequently heard
comments as: "The government has secret information that we don't
have"; or, "They know what's right, who am I to question what they
are doing?"; or "What's the use? No one will listen to me..."
The belief that the government or the military is either infallible or impregnable provides a tempting refuge because of its renun-
ciation of one's own critical faculties in the name of those of the powerful and all-knowing leader. Such self-directed dehumanization has
a strong appeal to the isolated and alienated citizen as a protective
cloak to hide from himself his feelings of weakness, ignorance and
estrangement. This is particularly relevant to the psychological at-
traction of certain dangerous social movements. The more inwardly
frightened, lonely, helpless, and humiliated people become, the
greater the susceptibility of many of them to the seductive, prejudiced
promises of demagoguery: the award of spurious superiority and
privilege achieved by devaluing the full humanness of some other
group — racial, religious, ethnic, or political. Furthermore, as an
added advantage of the dehumanization "package," self-enhancing

---

[6]This has been particularly well described in novels by Kafka and Camus.

acts of discrimination and persecution against such victim groups can be carried out without tormenting or deterrent feelings of guilt, since these are absorbed by the "rightness" of the demagogic leader.

In recent decades and in many countries, including our own, we have seen what human toll can be taken by this psychosocial configuration. It has entered into Hitlerism, Stalinism, U. S. A. "lynch-mobism." If it is extended to the international arena, against a "dehumanized" enemy instead of an oppressed national minority, atomic weapons will now empower it to inflict immeasurably more human destruction and suffering.

The indifference resulting from that form of dehumanization which causes one to view others as inanimate objects enables one, without conscious malice or selfishness, to write off their misery, injustices, and death as something that "just couldn't be helped." As nonhumans, they are not identified with as beings essentially similar to oneself; "their" annihilation by nuclear warfare is thus not "our" concern, despite the reality that distinctions between "they" and "we" have been rendered all the more meaningless by the mutually suicidal nature of total war.

Although this type of dehumanization is relatively complete, in the sense of perceiving others as not at all human, it may occur in an individual with selective incompleteness under certain special conditions only, while his capacity for other emotional ties is preserved. This may prove socially constructive or destructive, depending on the purposes to which it is put. Thus, we have already noted how "pulling a veil" over her mind helped Bourke-White adaptively in her socially positive job of reporting atrocities. But it was compartmentalized dehumanization that also helped many to commit those very atrocities; they were able to exterminate Jews with assembly-line efficiency as the Nazi "final solution" while still retaining access to their genuine feelings of warmth for family members, friends and associates.

These contradictory emotional qualities, often appearing side by side in the same person, are also evidenced — in the opposite direction — by outstanding deeds of heroic rescue by those who, under different circumstances, might well exhibit dehumanized behavior. Almost daily, the newspapers carry stories of exceptional altruism; individuals or whole communities devote their entire energies to the rescue of a single child, an animal, or perhaps (in wartime), a wounded enemy soldier. What accounts for the difference between this kind of response to the plight of others, and that of dehumanized callousness? How are the adaptive humanized processes released?

One research approach might consist of the detailed description and comparative analysis of sample situations of both kinds of these collective reactions, which have such opposite social effects. A case history of community apathy which could be compared in such a study with instances of group altruism already on record, was recently provided by A. M. Rosenthal, an editor of The New York Times (7). At first glance, perhaps, his account of dehumanization, involving but one individual and in peacetime, may not seem germane to our discussion about nuclear war. But the macrocosm is reflected in the microcosm. We agree with Mr. Rosenthal that the implications of this episode are linked with certain psychological factors that have helped pave the way for such broad social calamities as Fascism abroad and racial crises in this country, both in the North and South. It does not seem too farfetched, therefore, to relate them to the nuclear threat as well.

For more than half an hour, one night in March, 1964, thirty-eight respectable, law-abiding citizens in a quiet middle-class neighborhood in New York City watched a killer stalk and stab a young woman in three separate attacks, close to her home. She was no stranger to these onlookers, her neighbors, who knew her as "Kitty." According to Rosenthal, "Twice the sound of their voices and the sudden glow of their bedroom lights interrupted him and frightened him off. Each time he returned, sought her out and stabbed her again. Not one person telephoned the police during the assault; one witness called after the woman was dead." Later, when these thirty-eight neighbors were asked about their baffling failure to phone for help, even though they were safe in their own homes, "the underlying attitude or explanation seemed to be fear of involvement — any kind of involvement." Their fatal apathy gains in significance precisely because, by ordinary standards, these were decent, moral people — husbands and wives attached to each other and good to their children. This is one of the forms of dehumanization that we have described, in which a reaction of massive indifference — not hostility — leads to grievous cruelty, yet all the while, in another compartment of the self, the same individual's capacity for active caring continues, at least for those within his immediate orbit.

Rosenthal describes his own reaction to this episode as a "peculiar paradoxical feeling that there is in the tale of Catherine Genovese a revelation about the human condition so appalling to contemplate that only good can come from forcing oneself to confront the truth...the terrible reality that only under certain situations, and only in response to certain reflexes or certain beliefs, will a man step out of his shell toward his brother. In the back of my mind... was the feeling that there was, that there must be some connection between [this story and] the story of the witnesses silent in the face of greater crimes — the degradation of a race, children hungering.... It happens from time to time in New York that the life of the city is frozen by an instant of shock. In that instant the people of the city are seized by the paralyzing realization that they are one, that each man is in some way a mirror of every other man.... In that instant of shock, the mirror showed quite clearly what was wrong, that the face of mankind was spotted with the disease of apathy — all mankind. But this was too frightening a thought to live with, and soon the beholders began to set boundaries for the illness, to search frantically for causes that were external and to look for the carrier. "

As we strive to distinguish more clearly among the complex determinants of adaptive-maladaptive, humanized-dehumanized polarities of behavior, we recognize that stubborn impulses toward individuation are intertwined with the dehumanizing trends on which we have focused. Both humanization and dehumanization are heightened by interpenetrating social and psychological effects of current technological and institutional changes. The progress of the past hundred years has markedly furthered humanization: it has relieved much of human drudgery and strain, and helped to bring about increased leisure and a richer life for a larger part of the world's population. Despite the blurring of personal distinctiveness by excessive bureaucracy, there are now exceptional opportunities, made possible by the same technology that fosters uniformity, for the individual to make rapid contact with, and meaningful contribution to, an almost limitless number of the earth's inhabitants. The same budgets, communication networks, transportation delivery systems, and human organizations that can be used to destroy can also be turned toward the creative fulfillment of great world purposes.

Our situation today favors contradictory attitudes toward how much any individual matters in the scheme of things, both subjectively and from the standpoint of social reality. At one extreme a few individuals in key positions feel — and are generally felt to have — a hugely expanded potential for social impact. Among the vast majority there is, by contrast, an intensified sense of voiceless insignificance in the shaping of events. Objectively, too, there is now among individuals a far greater disparity in their actual power to influence crucial outcomes. More than ever before, the fate of the world depends on the judgment of a handful of heads of state and their advisers, who must make rapid decisions about actions for which there are no precedents. Ideas and events, for better or worse, can have immediate global impact. [7] A push-button can set a holocaust in motion; a transatlantic phone call can prevent one.

In spite of humanizing ingredients in modern life, and the fact that men of good will everywhere are striving ceaselessly toward goals of peace, freedom and human dignity, we nevertheless place

---

[7]The news of President Kennedy's assassination circled the earth with unparalleled speed, and evoked a profound worldwide emotional response.

primary emphasis, in this paper, on dehumanization because we feel that the dangers inherent in this phenomenon are particularly pervasive, insidious, and relevant to the risk of nuclear war.

From a broad biological perspective, war may be viewed as a form of aggression between members of the same species, homosapiens. The distinguished naturalist, Lorenz, has recently pointed out a difference, of great relevance to the relationship between dehumanization and nuclear warfare, in the intraspecies behavior of animals who live in two kinds of groups (8). In the one, the members live together as a crowd of strangers: there are no expressions of mutual aggression, but neither is there any evidence of mutual ties, of relationships of affection, between individuals in the group. On the other hand, some of the fiercest beasts of prey — animals whose bodily weapons are capable of killing their own kind — live in groups in which intense relationships, both aggressive and affectionate, exist. Among such animals, says Lorenz, the greater the intraspecies aggression, the stronger the positive mutual attachments as well. These latter develop, through evolution, out of those occasions, such as breeding, when cooperation among these aggressive animals becomes essential to their survival as a species.

Furthermore — and this is of the utmost importance for survival — the greater the capacity for mutual relationships, the stronger and more reliable are the innate inhibitions which prevent them from using the species-specific weapons of predatory aggression, fangs, claws or whatever, to maim or kill a member of their own species, no matter how strong the hostile urge of one against another. For example, when two wolves fight, according to Lorenz, the potential victor's fangs are powerfully inhibited at what would be the moment of kill, in response to the other's ritualized signal of immobile exposure to his opponent of his vulnerable jugular.

Man's weapons, by contrast, are not part of his body. They are thus not controllable by reflexes fused into his nervous system; control must depend, instead, on psychological inhibitions (which may also function through social controls of his own devising). These psychic barriers to intraspecies aggression — which can lead to our becoming extinct — are rooted in our affiliative tendencies for cooperation and personal attachment. But these are the very tendencies that, as this paper has stressed, dehumanization can so seriously undermine.

Lorenz speaks of a natural balance within a species — essential to its preservation — between the capacity for killing and inhibition. In that sense, perhaps, man jeopardizes his survival by disturbing, with his invention of nuclear bombs, such a balance as has been maintained throughout his long history of periodic "old-style" wars. Such a dire imbalance would be increased by any shift on the part of the "human animal" toward a society essentially devoid of mutual relationships. For this would vitiate the very tendencies toward emotional involvement and cooperation which are the source of our most reliable inhibitions against "overkilling." Therefore, in terms of the parallels suggested by Lorenz, in order to protect ourselves against the doom of extinction as a species, we must encourage and devise every possible means of safeguarding the "family of man" from becoming an uncaring crowd. Not merely the limiting or halting, but the reversing of maladaptive dehumanization emerges as a key to survival.

What can be done to counteract these dangers? Assuredly, there is no single or ready answer. The development of psychic antidotes of rehumanization must involve a multiplicity of variables, levels of discourse and sectors of human activity, commensurate in complexity with the factors that make for dehumanization. Our attempt in this paper to identify this mental mechanism, and to alert others to its significance, its frequency and its inter-relatedness to nuclear risk, represents in itself a preliminary phase of remedial endeavor. For the very process of recognizing a psychosocial problem such as this, by marshalling, reordering and interpreting diverse sets of facts to find new significances in them, is a form of social action, and one that is especially appropriate to behavioral scientists. Beyond this initial posing of the problem, however, any chance of effectively grappling with it will require the converging efforts of those in many different professions and walks of life.

Rehumanization as a mode of neutralizing the dangerous effects that we have stressed should not be misconstrued as aiming at the reestablishment of pre-nuclear age psychology — which would be impossible in any case. We cannot set history back nostalgically to "the good old days" prior to automation and the other changes in contemporary society (nor were the conditions of those earlier days really so "good" for the self-realization of a large portion of the population.) On the contrary, the process of rehumanization means to us a way of assimilating and re-integrating, emotionally and intellectually, the profound new meanings that have been brought into our lives by our own advances, so that a much fuller conviction than ever before of our own humanity and interdependence with all mankind becomes intrinsic to our basic frame of reference.

The imperative for speeding up such a universal process of psychological change is rooted in the new and specific necessity to insure survival in the face of the awesome irreversibility of nuclear annihilation. The most essential approaches toward achieving this goal, however, lead us into such general and only seemingly unrelated issues as the degree of political freedom and social justice; our patterns of child care and child-rearing; and our philosophy of education, as

well as the quality of its implementation. For the process of dehumanization, which eventuates in indifference to the suffering implicit in
nuclear warfare, has its beginnings in earlier periods and other areas
of the individual's life. It is through these areas that influences conducive to rehumanization must be channeled.

We need to learn more, and to make more effective use of what
is already known about how to strengthen people's capacity to tolerate
irreducible uncertainty, fear, and frustration without having to take
refuge in illusions that cripple their potential for realistic behavior.
And we urgently need to find ways of galvanizing our powers of imagination (including ways of weakening the hold of the emotionally-
based mechanisms that imprison it).

Imagination and foresight are among the highest functions of
the human brain, from the evolutionary standpoint, and also among
the most valuable. They enable us to select and extrapolate from
previously accumulated experience and knowledge, in order to create
guidelines for coping with situations never before experienced, whose
nature is so far unknown.

Other kinds of learning ordinarily serve us well in the complicated process of establishing behavior patterns for meeting new life
situations. We are able to learn by trial and error, for example,
from our firsthand experiences and from successively testing the
value of alternative approaches as similar situations arise. Also,
we learn much by vicariously living through the reported experiences of others.

Through imagination, however, a completely new situation can
be projected in the mind in its sensate and vivid entirety, so that the
lessons it contains for us can be learned without the necessity of going through it in real life. This form of "future-directed" learning,
which creative imagination makes possible, is therefore uniquely ad-
vantageous in dealing with the problematic issues of thermonuclear
war; it permits us to arrive at more rational decisions for preventing it without having to pay the gruesome price of undergoing its
actuality.

The fact is that the "once-and-for-all" character of full-scale
nuclear war renders the methods of "learning through experience" —
our own or others' — not only indefensible (in terms of the human
cost) but also utterly unfeasible. The empirical privilege of "profit-
ing" from an experience of that nature would have been denied to most
if not all of humanity by the finality of the experience itself.

Accordingly, it would seem that whatever can quicken and extend our capacity for imagination, in both the empathic and conceptual
spheres, is a vital form of "civil defense". It requires, to begin with,
all the pedagogic ingenuity that we can muster to overcome the lag in
our intellectual development that keeps us from fully comprehending

82

the new dimensions of our existence. Yet, our endeavors to develop new modes of thinking can be cancelled out by the constricting and impeding effects of dehumanization. The terrible potential of this subtle mechanism to facilitate the depopulating of the earth lies in its circumventing human restraints against fratricide. We are faced, therefore, with the inescapable necessity of devising ways to increase opportunities for meaningful personal relationships and maximum social participation throughout the entire fabric of our society.

REFERENCES

1. Bourke-White, M., Portrait of Myself, New York, Simon and Schuster, 1963.
2. Lifton, R., "Psychological effects of the atomic bomb in Hiroshima; the theme of death," Daedalus, Journal of the Amer. Acad. of Arts and Sciences, 462–497, Summer, 1963.
3. Koestler, A. "On disbelieving atrocities," in The Yogi and the Commissar, New York, Macmillan, 1945.
4. Orwell, G. "How the poor die," in Shooting an Elephant, New York, Harcourt, Brace, 1945.
5. Yank, the Army Weekly, New York, Duell, Sloane and Pearce, 1947, p. 282.
6. Kahne, M. J., "Bureaucratic Structure and Impersonal Experience in Mental Hospitals," Psychiatry, 22, 4, 363–375, 1959.
7. Rosenthal, A. M., Thirty-Eight Witnesses, New York, McGraw-Hill, 1964.
8. Lorenz, K., Das Sogenannte Böse — Zur Naturgeschichte der Aggression, Vienna, Dr. G. Borotha-Schoeler Verlag, 1963.

Risks and Deterrents: Individual Determinants and Group Effects

NATHAN KOGAN
MICHAEL A. WALLACH

For several years we have been engaged in research on the psychological factors predisposing individuals toward the taking of greater or lesser risks in decision situations, and on some of the consequences of such risk-taking. * We propose to pass the texture of some of our findings in review, pointing out, as we proceed, some of their possible implications for the kinds of risks and deterrents involved in decision-making concerning questions of human survival.

Effects of Personality

The first point of note is the relatively high degree of consistency found among various behaviors which possess implications for risk or conservatism. There is, in other words, empirical warrant for assuming the existence of a broad and unified dimension of risk and conservatism along whose extent certain kinds of individuals array themselves. Consider the various dispositions which, under certain conditions, form a consistent pattern.

First, there is the degree of risk or caution which the respondent will urge upon a central person who is described as faced with a choice between two courses of action, one more risky but more rewarding if successful, the other more secure but less rewarding (7, 14, 15, 17). In each of a range of dilemmas of this kind, covering diverse areas of content, the respondent is to advise the protagonist by deciding what probability of success for the risky alternative would suffice to warrant its choice. Some situations concern risk of

*The research reported in the present paper was partially supported by grant M–2269 from the National Institute of Mental Health, United States Public Health Service, by grant G–17818 from the Division of Social Sciences, National Science Foundation, and by an Auxiliary Research Award from the Social Science Research Council.

financial loss; others, risk of death; still others, risk of loss of prestige.

So, too, the same type of caution or risk-taking will be evinced, under some conditions, in the degree of risk individuals are willing to tolerate in gambling situations when they bet on the outcomes of dice throws for money, and in skill contexts when they likewise are making money wagers but are betting on their own achievements rather than on chance phenomena (8). Some of the strategy indices that have been used for defining risk in such situations include the tendency, over a series of choices between pairs of offered bets, to maximize possible winnings, to minimize possible losses, to prefer long shots with their attendant chances for greater gains, and to prefer the more moderate risks of a fifty-fifty probability of success or failure.

The risk-taking syndrome that we have been describing also turns out to be relevant to performance in an information-seeking context. In one of our experimental procedures, for example, clues are provided one at a time, the respondent being required to guess the identity of the object suggested by the clues (8). The risk element enters as the subject balances the monetary prize associated with a correct decision against the progressively increasing monetary costs attached to each clue. The prize is forfeited for an incorrect decision, hence the subject must attempt to decide just when it would be safe to venture a final decision. Individuals differ, depending on their risk-taking propensities, in the degree of unequivocality which they require incoming information to possess before they are willing to make a decision on the basis of it.

Of the various decision-making procedures employed in our work, it is quite likely that the information-seeking paradigm is most descriptive of military strategy in the nuclear age. Consider the decision arrangements that the major powers have presumably set up for evaluating information about the imminence of a potential enemy attack. One can anticipate a staff of experts communicating with each other about the import of information provided by a computer system. This information may well be equivocal in its initial phases. Yet a decision most likely will have to be reached quickly, lest one's nuclear deterrent be rendered ineffective by the enemy's blow. In short, we have here a task of information-seeking and evaluation in which the prizes and costs assume values of enormous magnitude.

In sum, we appear to have uncovered what amounts to a risk-taking syndrome encompassing decision-making in hypothetical and monetary payoff contexts. One may legitimately inquire at this juncture about the statistical evidence for the syndrome. We must confess that the magnitudes of relationships among the various decision-making tasks employed, while meeting acceptable levels of statistical significance, were, nevertheless, fairly low.

We could have stopped at this point, satisfied with the fact of low but statistically significant relationships among a variety of risk-taking indices. This distressed us, however, and accordingly, we began wondering whether the various risk-taking dispositions described earlier might cluster together as a syndrome or constellation more clearly for some individuals than for others. In other words, it seemed reasonable to us that certain other factors—call them moderator variables—determine whether or not the kinds of relationships that we have been considering will occur, and also determine their strength. The critical problem, of course, is one of locating and specifying these moderator variables. The task before us is one of delineating one or more subsamples of persons who are likely to view large segments of their environment through risky or conservative spectacles, so to speak. At the same time, we should like to isolate analytically those persons who do not approach all or most decision-making tasks in either a consistently risky or a conservative manner.

On theoretical grounds, two particular personality dimensions seemed promising for being cast in a moderating role. One of these is overt anxiety experienced under stressful conditions—what some investigators have called test anxiety (9, 1); the other is defensiveness (12)—a concept that is closely related to White's (18) construct of "defensive inhibition," and to the psychoanalytic defense mechanisms of repression and denial.

We expected that individuals reporting symptoms of anxiety when asked about their performance in stressful situations would be highly sensitized to the success and failure aspects of the decision-making tasks confronting them. This sensitization might well lead to a heightened consistency within the decision-making domain. Notice that we make no claims that test anxious persons are more conservative or more risky than their less anxious colleagues. Rather, we are suggesting that the test-anxious person, be he fundamentally risky or conservative in orientation, might well manifest that orientation consistently in responding to a variety of decision-making situations. Those persons who react to stressful situations with less anxiety, on the other hand, might well be more alert to the particular situational characteristics of the decision-making tasks posed for them. Being much less concerned about failure-avoidance, they might be expected to devote their attention to the specific stimulus characteristics of the diverse decision-making situations in which they participate.

We turn now to defensiveness. Of particular relevance here is the image-maintenance aspect of defensiveness. Considerations of risk and conservatism might well be an integral part of the self-image of the highly defensive person. For such persons, then, particular attention may be given to maintaining a conception of oneself as either a bold and daring or a careful and judicious decision-maker. If there is any basis for this expectation, we should find that the defensive individual exhibits a consistent orientation toward risk-taking or conservatism across a wide variety of decision-making tasks. In contrast, the person low in defensiveness, for whom considerations of risk and conservatism may be less paramount, might be expected to respond differentially in terms of the unique situational requirements of the various decision-making tasks employed.

Thus far, we have been considering test anxiety and defensiveness separately. This is somewhat artificial, of course, for these two dimensions may well exert an interactive influence upon risk-taking processes. We find, in fact, that test anxiety and defensiveness are statistically independent of each other in the samples studied: that is, a person high on one dimension may or may not be high on the other. This has permitted us to divide our samples into four subgroups of approximately equal size—the low test anxious and low defensives, the low test anxious and high defensives, the high test anxious and low defensives, and the high test anxious and high defensives. Within each of these subsamples, we have examined the interrelationships among our various risk-taking indices. Separate analyses were carried out for males and females. The research is reported in detail in Kogan and Wallach (8).

We should point out that sex constitutes an important and interesting moderator variable in its own right. The pattern of relationships among our risk-taking measures does not assume identical form in men and women. This is hardly surprising, of course, for risk-taking can be expected to have distinctive connotations for each sex. We do not imply, however, that the differences between the sexes in the present study assume drastic proportions. Rather, we find a pattern of similarity and difference that serves to reinforce the major outcomes of the study. Where differences between the sexes do occur, they make reasonable sense in terms of general expectations regarding sex differences in risk-taking. For the purpose of the present discussion, we shall ignore the matter of sex differences, since it is quite evident that critical decision-making respecting national policy is largely a masculine affair. Those of our readers who are women may feel that this constitutes a rank injustice on the grounds that women seem to value peace more highly than do men, and hence would make more intelligent decisions affecting it. There may be some basis for this view, but we are sorry to say that our data do not reinforce it. First, our female sample (which, by the way, closely matches our male sample in intelligence, educational level, and socioeconomic status) is more predisposed than our male subjects to respond to a wide array of decision-making in terms of a consistently risky or conservative orientation. Males, by con-

trast, seem to make somewhat sharper differentiations among decision situations in terms of specific characteristics, with the consequence that they exhibit less consistency in risk-taking behavior
throughout bet strategy and information-seeking contexts, for example. In short, our results suggest that a woman's decision-making
performance is more strongly determined by what she brings to it in
the way of internal dispositions than that of a man, whose risk-taking
behavior is more strongly influenced by what the external situation
has to offer. These results hardly constitute a mandate for changing
the sex composition of our national decision-making bodies.

Lest anyone take offense, it is only fair to point out that we
have been talking about the general pattern for the male and female
samples as a whole. When one turns away from entire samples to
the personality subgroups delineated above, the evidence points to
intra-sex variation as great as, if not greater than, cross-sex variation. We should like to turn now to a more detailed consideration
of the effects of our personality moderators—test anxiety and defensiveness—upon the generality of risk-taking behavior in males.
Consider first the relationship between decision-making in a hypothetical and payoff context. Are individuals consistent in the risk and
conservatism they display under the conditions in which nothing is at
stake and those in which substantial monetary gains and losses are
involved? It might be noted in the latter connection that our subjects'
winnings ranged from zero to approximately twenty dollars for an
experiment of about three hours' duration.

When the choice dilemmas procedure is related to strategy
preferences in a payoff context, consistencies do emerge; those deterred by failure in a hypothetical decision task tend to adopt a strategy that will minimize their losses, while those for whom failure is
less of a deterrent in resolving a hypothetical dilemma tend to select
a strategy that will maximize their gains. Of considerably greater
interest is the marked variation in the strength of these relationships
across the four personality subgroups delineated earlier in the paper.
The relationships in question achieve their greatest magnitude in the
subgroup high in both test anxiety and defensiveness. It appears that
the strong defensive structures, in the present instance, have a risk-
regulatory function. For the highly test anxious and defensive male,
any choice situation very likely arouses anxiety, for the possibility
of a faulty decision is ever present. The anxiety aroused in the present sample, however, occurs against a background of strong defenses,
one of whose functions is to preserve a highly desirable self-image.
Indecision or lack of decisiveness is hardly consistent with such an
image. Hence, the decision situation, regardless of its manifest
character, trips off a consistent prepotent risky or conservative response.

Let us turn now to the men who are low in both test anxiety and defensiveness. These individuals can be characterized as the least disturbed members of our sample. They do not report anxiety symptoms under the pressure of academic stress situations and, at the same time, their defensive structures are sufficiently flexible to permit the admission into consciousness of certain moderately undesirable personal attributes. How do these men handle our decision tasks? Basically, they show a moderate degree of generality. Thus, they respond in a consistently risky or conservative way to a choice dilemmas and a chance strategies task. The association, however, is markedly attenuated when the choice dilemmas task is related to skill strategies. Chance and skill strategies differ, of course, in terms of the personal control one can exercise over decision outcomes. Hence, the choice dilemmas and chance strategies situations have in common a lack of control over outcomes, while choice dilemmas and skill strategies have little in common beyond the fact that considerations of risks and deterrents are involved. Thus, our least disturbed males behave consistently when the decision-making contexts are formally or stylistically similar; they do not behave in a consistently risky or conservative direction when the situational contexts are highly dissimilar. In short, these individuals appear to be highly sensitized to the particular task requirements of the various decision-making situations with which they are confronted.

We turn next to relationships among decision-making indices derived from different payoff contexts. Consider, in particular, the association between the strategy indices and the information-seeking procedures. In the male sample as a whole there is a negligible relationship between these distinctive decision-making domains. Yet when the various personality subgroups are examined, we note that our highly test-anxious and defensive subjects follow a unique course. For them, risk-taking consistencies emerge—the men who are willing to gamble on their motor skill for high stakes also tend to demand fewer clues before committing themselves to a decision in an information-seeking context. Correspondingly, for these subjects, conservatism in strategy preference in a motor-skill is associated with the demand for more information in a clues task.

These results are quite consistent with those previously reported. They serve to emphasize the important role played by test anxiety and defensiveness jointly in bringing about consistencies in risk-taking behavior within diverse decision-making contexts.

Also of interest is the behavior of the personality groups in response to the success or failure of the strategy that they have been pursuing. Consider the following findings regarding skill bets. Only in the case of the low test anxious-low defensive males is the degree of satisfaction with bet outcomes proportional to level of winnings.

In contrast, for high test anxious-high defensive males, just the opposite is found; the less they have won, the more satisfaction they express. Since failure is more likely when a person is following a risky strategy, this means that the motivationally disturbed subgroup expresses all the greater satisfaction with a risky strategy when it is found to fail. The minimally disturbed subgroup, on the other hand, expresses reduced satisfaction with a risky strategy if it fails. The behavior of the former subgroup is indeed paradoxical, while the behavior of the latter subgroup seems appropriately responsive to the information provided by the environment.

To sum up the present phase of our research endeavor, we are forced to conclude that the study of risk-taking behavior cannot be complete without detailed consideration of the moderating influence of particular personality variables. Thus, the evidence strongly suggests that highly test anxious and defensive males, figuratively speaking, view most decision-making situations through risky or conservative lenses. For such subjects, the resolution of choice situations appears to be predetermined on the basis of the motivational processes that are engaged whenever a decision must be made. When either test anxiety or defensiveness is present separately, the consistencies that appear are more selective, but apparently again dependent upon distinctive motivational forces rather than on particular situational properties. Finally, the low test anxious and low defensive males seem best able to differentiate decision-making situations in terms of their structural features. It is in this sub-group that the response to a choice situation appears least determined by internal motivational forces and most influenced by distinctive environmental forces.

What implications can we draw from these findings for the kinds of risks and deterrents with which the present volume is immediately concerned? What has become strikingly clear in the nuclear age is the inability to assign a positive value judgment to either end of the risk-conservatism dimension. Either alternative may be equally disastrous, depending upon the circumstances that prevail at the time. One can, however, begin to attach value judgments to consistently risky or conservative behavior that relegates situational inducements and constraints to a secondary role. It is such blind consistency of risky or conservative behavior which seems to us to pose a prime threat. It is here that issues of risk and conservatism become quite relevant to matters of rationality and irrationality. Osgood (11) in his inaugural address at the 1961 International Congress of Applied Psychology spoke eloquently of the dangers of irrationality in the present international arena. To quote him, "In a situation where the consequences of wrong decisions are so awesome, where a single bit of irrationality can set a whole chain of traumatic events in motion, I do not think that we can be satisfied with the assurance that 'most people behave rationally most of the time'" (p. 120). Osgood then goes on to inquire into the conditions that foster nonrationality in decision-making. To quote him once more, "increases in tension, beyond some optimal level, serve to magnify the ratio of non-rational to rational alternatives. Under stress men are more likely to act irrationally, to strike out blindly, or even to freeze into stupid immobility. In other words, both flexibility and rationality 'ride on the back' of tension-level" (p. 121).

We are in complete agreement with the views expressed by Osgood, but it is quite evident that he has not extended his argument quite far enough. While stress and tension can increase the nonrationality of decision-making for men in general, our findings strongly suggest that particular kinds of individuals are especially susceptible to such nonrationality. Further, it appears that various forms of nonrationality can be delineated and indeed, the presence of relatively high levels of rationality in decision-making may characterize but a minority of men.

We should like to think that the political and military leaders of the United States and the Soviet Union are members of this rational minority. Writing in a recent issue of Daedalus, Brodie (3), a member of the RAND Corporation, is quite discouraging in this regard. He thinks it a mistake to assume that any political leader will not act irrationally, especially on issues that involve the threat of violence. Brodie insists that, "It is in fact reasonable to assert the exact contrary: that they are bound to act at times irrationally, even in important matters, simply because all men do so. Neurotics tend to do so more than others, but there is not the slightest evidence that the Soviet Union has a lower incidence of neurosis than other countries or that neurotics are less likely there to climb into high political positions" (p. 744). Lest we become self-righteous in this respect, he points out that, "In periods of intense crisis, we are probably as capable as the Russians of acting out what may seem to be the imperatives of the moment. Our conceptions of what we are compelled to do will be molded like theirs, by a range of rational, semi-rational, and non-rational judgments or impressions, all coming out of human beings charged with emotion, including emotions of which the possessors are not even conscious" (p. 745).

These sentiments are echoed by Deutsch (4), who points out that "nervousness, the need to respond quickly because of the fear that one will lose either the desire or ability to respond, enhances the likelihood that a response will be triggered off by an insufficient stimulus and thus, makes for instability. " p. 62). Note the use of the phrase "insufficient stimulus" and consider its relevance to our earlier discussion of the personality determinants of decision-making processes.

Finally, note should be made of Kahn's (6) rank-ordering of the ways in which a nuclear war might arise. Though acknowledging that accidents are improbable, he nevertheless assigns accidental war the top ranking. Included within the rubric of accidents are the kinds of human irrationality that we have been discussing. The dangers of war by accident have also been stressed by Deutsch (4) and Frank (5). The former author expresses concern about the "possibility that the decision to use the bomb would be made by an irresponsible local unit— by a 'mischievous' missile squad, a 'grandiose' bomber crew, a 'paranoid' submarine crew—which could carry out its own decision" (p. 62). Frank notes that the multiplication of nuclear weapons and the reduced warning time for retaliation necessarily implies a progressive filtering of responsibility down the chain of command. Hence, individual psychology becomes highly relevant. We are very much in agreement with this conclusion. Further, the issues that Deutsch and Frank have raised also bear upon decision-making in a small group context. We shall consider the matter of such group effects below.

There is, then, in the published literature, considerable emphasis on the irrational aspects of decision-making and their possible impact on international conflict. Nowhere have we found any specific attempts to assess empirically the form of irrationality that is relevant to the type of decision-making that bears on matters of human survival. We should like to think that our work represents a start in this direction—a very small start, to be sure. At those times when we manage to suppress our modesty, we are burdened by a nagging curiosity about how those persons controlling our destiny would distribute themselves within the personality subgroups outlined earlier in the paper.

Effects of Group Interaction

Our discussion thus far has concentrated on the individual person's level of risk or conservatism. We now turn to research that we have conducted on the question of what happens when several individuals enter into a discussion and reach a consensus concerning how risky or how conservative a course of action to adopt (16, 17, 2). Obviously, the outcome will in part be dependent on the proclivities toward risk-taking or caution brought by each individual to the discussion context. But the outcome also appears to be importantly determined by processes that originate in the discussion situation itself.

On the face of it, the most likely expectation seemed to be that group discussion and consensus would lead either to an averaging effect or to increased conservatism when compared to the average risk-taking revealed in the previous individual decisions. An averaging effect would have been predicted from research on group judgment, in which it has been found that the group's attempts to induce compromise are exerted most intensively toward those members whose prior individual judgments are furthest removed in either direction from the average. A group-induced move toward greater conservatism, on the other hand, would have been expected on the basis of the frequent anecdotal observation that decision-making in a committee or team context generates a reticence to "stick one's neck out" by extreme recommendations which might make one seem rash and foolhardy in the eyes of others.

Contrary to both of these expectations, however, it turns out that the effect of asking a group of individuals to reach a consensus about the level of risk to accept in decision-making results in a stronger move toward greater risk-taking than is found in the average of the risk levels adopted by the same individuals in private decisions made before the group discussion. The decision situations in which this result was first obtained consisted of the advice-giving dilemmas described at the beginning of this report, in which the respondent was to recommend the degree of caution or risk that the protagonist in each of a variety of diverse situations should adopt. Not only did the requirement of a group discussion and consensus cause a shift toward recommending more risky courses of action than would be calculated from the average of the individual recommendations made before the group meeting, but this group-induced move toward increased risk-taking was found to maintain itself over subsequent time. When the individuals were asked to arrive at private recommendations as long as six weeks after the group meeting, under instructions that even urged them to deviate from the earlier group decision, their personal decisions still reflected the risk-inducing effect that had been exerted by the group discussion process (16). The results just reported were obtained with liberal arts college students of both sexes. A group-induced shift toward greater risk-taking, using the same decision task, also has been obtained with male graduate students of business administration by Stoner (13), and with middle-aged male business executives by Marquis (10).

These findings suggested the possibility that there occurred in this group setting a diffusion or spreading of responsibility—a decrease in the perceived negative consequences of failure as a result of knowing that the decision was arrived at in consultation with others rather than alone. With a reduced feeling of personal responsibility, license for greater risk-taking would thereby be provided. This interpretation necessarily remained tentative in view of certain limitations present in our first experiment. Inference to the diffusion of responsibility explanation was rather indirect, and the decision situations used had involved only hypothetical risks and payoffs rather than actual ones.

Our next experiment (17) hence was designed with the objective of remedying these limitations. Rather than making recommendations to protagonists who were in hypothetical situations, we devised tasks in which the decisions involved direct consequences in monetary payoffs and ego gratifications for the respondents. Their decision dilemma concerned, in each of a number of intellectual ability areas, how high a level of difficulty to set for themselves—how hard a test question to try to answer. The monetary rewards for correctly answering harder problems were commensurately greater than those for correctly answering the easier ones. Besides greater monetary gain from correctly answering questions at higher difficulty levels, there also was, of course, greater ego gratification from having proven oneself to be more capable at intellectual tasks. In the university subculture, intellectual competence constitutes an important enough area of concern to make the situation just described a highly important one for the respondent.

With this situation, we found, for males, that requiring group discussion and consensus concerning choice of difficulty levels eventuated in stronger risk-taking—selection of higher difficulty levels—than had occurred under individual decision conditions. This second study not only generalized the relevance of our earlier results from decision situations in which risks and payoffs were hypothetical to ones where they were actual and direct, but the findings of various experimental manipulations also provided support of a more direct kind for the view that the cause of the obtained group-induced shifts toward greater risk-taking consists of sharing or diffusing the responsibility for failure.

Our third experiment (2), in turn, extended the generality of our previous findings to a type of group decision-making in which negative consequences are emphasized. In order to accomplish this end, we selected physical pain and discomfort, coupled with monetary loss, as the potential outcomes of risk-taking. Once again, group consensus achieved through discussion was displaced in the risky direction relative to the average of the group members' prior individual decisions. Subsequent private decisions also exhibited this shift toward greater risk-taking. These results once again were explained in terms of a process of responsibility diffusion.

We will admit that the decisions reached in our experiments affected only the group members participating in the study; the decisions had no impact on the larger population from which the subjects were drawn. Nevertheless, it would be most surprising if the group-induced shifts toward risk-taking that we have observed did not have implications for some aspects of decision-making regarding political and military policy matters. Consider a group of experts reaching a decision on how to handle a troublesome problem of foreign policy. Or, consider a group of specialists evaluating information about the possible imminence of an enemy nuclear attack and reaching a decision about whether or not to unleash their own nuclear weapons against the enemy. Finally, consider a Strategic Air Command bomber crew, or a Polaris submarine crew, whose communication contact with home breaks down in the middle of a period of critical tension, making necessary a decision about how to proceed under these ambiguous circumstances.

As we stated earlier, risk-taking as such is not necessarily bad. The prevailing situation may demand it. The problem that arises is again one of overgenerality—the biasing of all or most group decisions in a risky direction as a consequence of dynamic forces at work in group interaction. These group effects are analogous in many respects to the overgeneralized risk-taking manifested by a single person with a particular pattern of motivational dynamics.

To sum up, we have explored various conditions that enhance and deter risk-taking behavior in individuals and groups. Further, we have tried to show how the issue of risk and conservatism in decision-making has considerable relevance for the problem of rationality and irrationality. The latter concepts have been invoked by a number of experts concerned with matters of international conflict and defense policy. These references to irrationality have been quite diffuse and, accordingly, we have tried to spell out the forms that rationality and irrationality might assume in decision-making contexts. It is quite clear that the risk or conservatism of a decision is a combined function of the personality of the decision-maker, the nature of the decision task, and the presence or absence of other people in the decision situation. We have tried in this paper to describe some of the ways in which these factors act to influence decision-making, and to point out some of the implications these findings may have for decision-making concerning national policy in times of military and political crisis.

REFERENCES

1. Alpert, R. and Haber, R. N., "Anxiety in academic achievement situations," J. Abnorm. Soc. Psychol., 1960, 61, 207-215.
2. Bem, D. J., Wallach, M. A. and Kogan, N., "Group decision-making under risk of aversive consequences," J. Pers. Soc. Psychol., 1965, in press.

3. Brodie, B., "Defense policy and the possibility of total war," Daedalus, 1962, 91, 733-748.

4. Deutsch, M., "Some considerations relevant to national policy," J. Soc. Issues, 1961, 17, 3, 57-68.

5. Frank, J. D., "Breaking the thought barrier: Psychological challenges of the nuclear age," Psychiatry, 1960, 23, 245-266.

6. Kahn, H., "The arms race and some of its hazards," Daedalus, 1960, 89, 744-780.

7. Kogan, N. and Wallach, M. A., "The effect of anxiety on relations between subjective age and caution in an older sample," in P. H. Hoch & J. Zubin (eds.), Psychopathology of aging, New York, Grune & Stratton, 1961, pp. 123-135.

8. Kogan, N. and Wallach, M. A., Risk taking: A study in cognition and personality, New York, Holt, Rinehart & Winston, 1964.

9. Mandler, G. and Sarason, S. B., "A study of anxiety and learning," J. Abnorm. Soc. Psychol., 1952, 47, 166-173.

10. Marquis, D. G., "Individual responsibility and group decisions involving risk," Indus. Mgmt. Rev., 1962, 3, 1, 8-23.

11. Osgood, C. E., "Toward international behavior appropriate to a nuclear age," in G. S. Nielsen (ed.), Psychology and International Affairs, Copenhagen, Munksgaard, 1962, pp. 109-132.

12. Rogers, C. R., "A theory of therapy, personality, and interpersonal relationships, as developed in the client-centered framework," in S. Koch (ed.), Psychology: a study of a science, Study I, Vol. III, formulations of the person and the social context, New York, McGraw-Hill, 1959, pp. 184-256.

13. Stoner, J. A. F., "A comparison of individual and group decisions involving risk." Unpublished master's thesis, Massachusetts Institute of Technology, School of Industrial Management, 1961.

14. Wallach, M. A. and Kogan, N., "Sex differences and judgment processes," J. Pers., 1959, 27, 555-564.

15. Wallach, M. A. and Kogan, N., "Aspects of judgment and decision making: Interrelationships and changes with age," Behav. Sci., 1961, 6, 23-36.

16. Wallach, M. A., Kogan, N. and Bem, D. J., "Group influence on individual risk taking," J. Abnorm. Soc. Psychol., 1962, 65, 75-86.

17. Wallach, M. A., Kogan, N. and Bem, D. J., "Diffusion of responsibility and level of risk taking in groups," J. Abnorm. Soc. Psychol., 1964, 68, 263-274.

18. White, R. W., The abnormal personality, New York, Ronald, 1956.

International Tensions and Mental Health

_____ FRANCOIS CLOUTIER

Whenever I am asked to speak on the possible contribution of the behavioral sciences to the difficult field of international tensions, I am always reminded of a story. It is an international story, and it could happen anywhere. A motorist, driving in a lonely part of the country, finds that he has lost his way. He sees a farmer walking on the road and stops his car.

"I want to go to such a place, " he says. "Could you tell me how to get there?"

"Well, " answers the farmer, "it is not too easy. Let me see. Yes. You drive on for another mile, then the road divides in two. You turn left till you see an old church. . . . " The man hesitates: "No, I guess it won't work that way. You turn right instead. You drive on for half a mile to a dirt road on the left. . . . " He stops, shakes his head, and adds: "I guess it doesn't work that way either. Tell me, Sir, do you really want to go there? Because if you do, you might have to change your plans. I do not think that it can be done from here. You will have to start from somewhere else!"

Now, why does that story come to me? The unconscious reason might be that the subject of international tensions makes me uneasy and that my defense mechanism is to laugh. The conscious reason is that I have serious doubts about some of our contentions as specialists in human behavior with respect to world tensions. I wonder if sometimes we are not assuming a function that does not rightly belong to us, if we are not thinking that we can offer more than we actually can, if, in a word, we are not overselling psychology. I wonder if our genuine desire to help in the most tragic dilemma of human history does not distract us from measuring our limitations at a practical level. It is a problem of methodology. If we want to get there, that is to peace and to survival, we might have to leave from somewhere else—that is from what we really can achieve and not from what we would like to do—from a reality situation, not from hope.

The one question to ask ourselves is simple enough. Has psychology anything to offer to alleviate international tensions? If so, what? I shall endeavor to answer this question, both in a negative and in a positive way. In a negative way, I will attempt to point out the errors made, in my opinion, when one applies psychological knowledge to political issues. In a positive way, I will try to define the areas where I think behavioral sciences might have the greatest impact.

Errors Commonly Made

The first mistake to avoid is to apply too rigidly notions deriving from individual psychology to nations as a whole. It is doubtful if any real analogy can be drawn between a person and a group in terms of behavior patterns and in terms of psychological understanding. To describe a country as paranoid, for instance, is rather farfetched. I fail to see the validation. For the same reason, the truth, if any, in the statement that international tensions proceed from individual tensions escapes me. I cannot help feeling also that another claim referring to war as the result of aggressive trends in individuals is a dangerous oversimplification. When one adds the belief that adequate child-rearing practice will prevent aggression and therefore will prevent war, I feel even more sceptical.

I do not venture to say that there is no truth in all this. I am concerned with the validity of the approach more than with the actual content. As a matter of fact, psychologists today tend to be more careful in their analyses of the causes of war than they were some fifteen years ago, However, my impression is that many of the half-truths of the postwar period are still finding their way into contemporary thinking. This period was characterized by an optimism which has clouded the real issues. No theory, no explanation should be suggested unless substantiated.

Another error, related to the preceding one, is to consider international tensions pathological. This is certainly what is implied when one speaks, as is often the case, of the psychopathology of international tensions. How tensions between countries can be pathological in any real sense, I cannot understand. They can be anything like good, bad, deteriorated, improving, but can they be symptoms? Where is the norm? Does it mean that the ideal relationship between countries is one entirely devoid of tensions? History, coupled with the slimmest psychological insight, teaches us that tension is a normal phenomenon. The problem, then, is not to look at tensions as morbid reactions to avoid, but to find the ways to handle them.

It brings us to another pitfall: the tendency toward systematically reducing political problems to psychological terms. We should remember that there are such things as political issues, that all conflicts are not based on misunderstanding, but can be the result of real clashes between divergent interests. We should not forget that, whether we like it or not, political problems in the forseeable future will be settled by politicians and not by psychologists or by psychiatrists. We ought also to keep in mind when we analyze a situation that we are not always in a position to know all the facts and to take all the factors into account.

Some time ago I heard somebody identified with activities for peace since the First World War say that disarmament was a psychological problem. Let me use this statement as an example of the type of generalization to avoid. Personally, I do not see how disarmament could be so described unless the term "psychological" is used all too loosely. Surely disarmament is a political problem. The same applies to the wider issue of the prevention of war, in which disarmament is an extremely important step. This kind of problem is being, and will continue to be, tackled by traditional diplomacy. Hopefully, some degree of agreement will be reached through compromise in the course of negotiations and discussions. This is how historical events, the world being what it is, usually present themselves.

There is no doubt that the whole situation is charged with emotion. Obviously, there is a lot of distrust, fear and misunderstanding. One might think that a different approach based on psychological insight would have a great influence in settling the issues. Granting this, I do not think that it makes the problem of disarmament or of prevention of war a psychological problem. Basically, it remains a conflict of interests extraordinarily complex, characterized by tremendous technical difficulties, deeply rooted in the history and in the culture of both sides.

Of course, there are psychological implications. I am not suggesting that psychology cannot be useful in clarifying the conflict and even in influencing its actual resolution. I am convinced that it can. We might not be invited to do it, but there is no reason why we should not make our views heard. It is our duty to bring into international politics any contribution arising from a deeper knowledge of human nature. These contributions are as important as those made by the physical sciences, for instance. My only point, and the rationale behind my reservations, is that our position will be stronger if we know our limits, if we define our golas, and if we do not present ourselves as crusaders.

Areas of Impact

Behavioral scientists, and the term includes anybody trained in the field of human conduct and of human relations, can contribute to the problem of international tensions in two main areas, the area of action and the area of research.

In terms of action, enough is known nowadays about the theory of personality and about group interactions to enable us to be immediately helpful. As a matter of fact, psychologists, social scientists, anthropologists, and, to a much lesser extent, psychiatrists, are already engaged in activities which have an indirect influence on international tensions. This is true particularly of people connected with the United Nations, its Specialized Agencies, and other international organizations, governmental or nongovernmental. If we wish, and if we feel that we need to have, a deeper influence, something else is required.

What is required is a program. What can we propose? How can we do it? It seems rather obvious that the decision-makers, those who have the final responsibility of a policy, or those at another level, who are engaged in its preparation and implementation, would benefit greatly by having psychological training or psychological insight. It is not excluded that people with such capacities might accede to political or top administrative posts. It can certainly not be the rule.

What we want, then, is to give some kind of psychological understanding to those in high office or to those who might influence the leaders to a certain extent. It means getting to the advisers to governments, diplomats, experts, exchange personnel, administrators, high officials, etc. There are already good examples of programs meant for certain groups like the teaching sessions for diplomats run by the Carnegie Endowment for International Peace, and the seminars organized by the American Friends Services Committee. More initiatives of that kind are needed, but they should be planned along psychological lines. Many examples could also be given of fruitful meetings, grouping statesmen and people who have a say in the affairs of their country and of the world. These meetings are usually limited to political and economic aspects. They would gain much by a sociopsychological approach.

Another thing to do in terms of an action program is to impress on the authorities in each country the urgent necessity for introducing social psychology as a subject in the training of civil servants and diplomats. Is it not as important as technical subjects? If history or strategy is taught, why not also the art of understanding human nature? Let us not forget, however, that the teaching of psychology and psychopathology is not easy, and cannot really be done through didactic courses only. Insight comes as a process of learning through living and experiencing. New methods might have to be devised.

We should also play an important role in the selection of these people. It is a well-known fact that the failure as well as the success of negotiations can depend on the personalities of the participants.

Technical training does not really make up for a deficient personality. A certain degree of rigidity, for instance, too great a personal involvement or emotional difficulties, does interfere with efficiency and does create distortions. It has been suggested that our leaders should be psychoanalyzed and that politicians should go through psychological tests before being allowed to run for office. This is certainly not a realistic suggestion! To be sure, I doubt that, if the leaders were psychoanalyzed, it would change things. They might decide to give up their jobs! What we can do, however, is to introduce sound selection techniques, based on the latest psychological discoveries, in government administration and in the international field.

A new function for the behavioral scientists would be to gain recognition as experts in their own right and to be invited to act as advisers to government at the level of policy planning. In the same capacity, they could attend certain conferences and participate in the negotiations. Technical experts in almost all disciplines are doing precisely that. When a problem requiring specialized knowledge arises, for instance, in the field of agriculture, an expert agronomist is asked for consultation. The leaders of this world and the decision-makers find themselves surrounded by experts of all kinds. Strangely enough, they seldom call in experts in human relations and human personality, which the psychologist and the psychiatrist really are. When one thinks that the majority of problems have psychological implications, this seems quite illogical. When one thinks that the conferences fail not always through lack of agreement on basic issues, but on account of emotional forces influencing the communication process, one wonders. It might even be a good idea to think of training psychiatrists especially for this function through special courses in economics and in political science.

Now, there is the whole field of education and mental health. Any group or any individual who promotes the principles of positive mental health has a definite influence on the betterment of human relationships and, ultimately, on international peace. There are in this world of ours numerous national and international organizations dedicated to this task. Improvement in child-rearing practices might not prevent war, but it might in time produce more mature individuals whose aggressive trends could be canalized toward creative instead of destructive activities. Programs related to eradication of prejudices cannot but benefit the community as a whole. These are only two examples. What we have to avoid is preaching. The mental health movement needs service-oriented approaches and realistic programs.

Besides the area of action, there is the area of research. I am thinking especially of the type of research aimed at acquiring new knowledge which somehow could be used in a practical way. Such research is not hopeless as is sometimes suggested. I believe that it can be planned on a relatively short-term basis and yield quick results. It is a problem of organization and of finance. Why should it be so difficult to find money for the activities that ought to matter most in terms of the survival of the human race? I can think of enough reasons to fill a book. The fact remains, however, that it is a desperately needed task. In spite of all difficulties, a surprising amount of good work has already been done. International organizations of the United Nations family or of the nongovernmental sector, universities, private institutes and groups have been involved in surveys and actual research. A repertory of what has been achieved in this field, a bibliography of all the publications, might seem impressive. Unfortunately, these efforts are quite limited. We have just been scraping the surface of the possibilities.

In my wildest dreams, I think that what is really required is some sort of international institute dedicated to peace research. Such an institute could coordinate what is being done in different countries and plan high-level programs on a world-wide basis. There are a few organizations which might claim to fulfill this function, or some part of it. As far as I know, none so far has a truly interdisciplinary approach. Emphasis is usually laid on the political or the socioeconomic aspects. The orientation should be more psychological, based on the principles promoted by the mental health movement from its very beginning.

There is a need for sociopsychological investigations on specific subjects like the nature of conflict and intergroup tensions. We have to study and to analyze further the psychology of nationalism; we have to understand better what constitutes leadership and to identify the ideal conditions conducive to it. We ought to know more about stereotypes and symbols, which sterilize our thinking more often than not, and which are at the bottom of much of the misunderstanding between people. An adequate program should also include studies on child-rearing, on personality development, on the validation of certain concepts of psychopathology, etc. Most of the problems of this century have mental health implications and call for research from the point of view of the behavioral scientists. We have to give more attention to such issues as population increase, town-planning, delinquency, technical assistance.

One promising field of research relates to the process of communication between human beings, specifically with respect to international tensions. Investigations in this area should be given high priority in view of the world situation. If disputes are not to be settled by the use of force, meaning by war, our only hope is that they will be settled through successful negotiations. In this period of history, negotiations are made in the course of conferences, although we should not underestimate the importance of traditional diplomacy in bringing about negotiation and tension-reduction. As a matter of fact, the United Nations has been thought of as a forum in which representatives of different countries could meet in order to discuss their difficulties or their common problems. Again, this emphasizes the role of the conference setting.

Anybody who has been involved in international conferences has experienced their limitations and their shortcomings. There are the problems of translation from one language to another, of the different cultural backgrounds of the participants, the clashes of personalities, the part played by chairmanship, etc. It is not always easy to evaluate the success or failure of a given meeting. Sometimes compromises are reached that, instead of resolving the conflict as they ought to do, create further misunderstanding. All this to say that we know little about what is happening during a conference, though this seems to be, for the time being, the only technique at our disposal. What research might bring, we do not know, of course. Conferences might not be the only device through which negotiations could be achieved, and they have not always been. The problem of communication has barely been studied. We have already invented the language, who could say that we cannot invent something else!

In spite of the doubts expressed here, I hope that I have conveyed my conviction that the behavioral scientists could and ought to play an important part in the problems of international tensions. I have tried to show how this could be done at the level of action and at the level of research. I would like to repeat that our efficiency might very well depend on our attitudes in assuming this new role, and that we should never lose sight of our limitations.

In a cartoon recently published in the United States, two groups of children are represented, ready to fight with each other. We are given to understand that there is a moment of hesitation. The caption reads: "What are we fighting, a war or a peace?" Let us hope that for us also there will be a moment of hesitation and that we will be given enough time to realize whether it is for war or for peace that we are being blown up.

War as a Public Health Problem: Conflict Management as a Key to Survival

The philosophy of public health envisages man as a species in an ecological framework. This ecological framework consists not only of other species but also of man's own institutions and artifacts. His houses, sewers, weapons, corporations, nations, and churches must be regarded as species in the grand ecosystem, just as wheat, rabbits, and field mice are. We must think of this whole system as exhibiting a dynamic course through time, the future of which is a function in some degree of its existing state at the present moment. We are certainly not in anything like an ecological equilibrium, and it is hard to predict at the present time what such an equilibrium would be. The expansion of the human population has gone hand in hand with the expansion of the population of various kinds of social species, such as machines, or even biological species of man-produced plants and animals. It has also gone along with a certain dimution in other species, especially those associated with forests and wildlife.

Man's present population explosion has been compared rather gruesomely to that of a colonizing species such as, for instance, the fireweed which takes over after a forest fire. Any major shift in the ecological environment is likely to produce an enormous expansion of a few populations, but the colonizers often lose out in the long run and may even disappear from the earth altogether is not as remote these days as it used to be, and it is certainly possible that the subspecies known as civilized man might disappear, together with the world of artifacts and organizations which surround him, and man might find himself reduced to a more primitive level of culture than he now enjoys. This may happen even without nuclear war, simply by a combination of the exhaustion of natural resources coupled with unrestricted population growth. We still do not have a permanent high-level technology, although this does seem to be almost within sight. If we do not achieve this, our present achievements are merely a flash in the pan of geological time, soon to be followed by the long, sad twilight of the

103

exhausted earth, where a small fraction of the present population scrabbles for a living on a planet devoid of ores or fossil fuels. This prospect may seem too far in the future to worry about, though it could certainly come about within a few hundred years if we are not careful.

For the immediate generation, however, the principal danger to man lies in his inability to manage conflict, especially international conflict. War, therefore, must be regarded as the major public health problem of the day. It has always been an important cause of death, though somewhat far down the list compared to most common diseases. Today we have had what has been called the "revolution of the mega-death," and war threatens to become the major source of human mortality, not only in the generation on which it actually falls but for many generations to come, through genetic mutation. It is surprising that the public health movement has been so little cognizant of this and so slow to recognize peace research as one of its major research components. In the absence of this concern, public health looks uncomfortably as if it is fattening us up for the eventual slaughter. We conquer tuberculosis and polio only to provide more people for the eventual roasting.

The ecological point of view, to which the public health movement is deeply committed, can make an important contribution to the study of war and peace itself, and to the conquest of war. The view still lingers that war is an act of God, essentially uncontrollable by man. We used to think the same about disease, and even a generation ago we thought the same about economic depressions. In the early 1930's we talked about the "economic blizzard" as if an economic depression were much the same as a depression on the weather map. Most of us now no longer accept this view, and regard the control of depressions as a legitimate function of government — and a function, moreover, of which it is perfectly capable. It has taken us longer to come to the view that war likewise is not merely a matter of the international climate, but is something which can be mastered and controlled by man. In the last resort, the epidemiology of war is not tremendously different from the epidemiology of malaria. Just as malaria is the product of a biological system that includes man and the Anopheles mosquito, so war is the product of a social system that includes independent national armed forces and certain tendencies toward infectious mental diseases without adequate institutions for checking them. War, in other words, is a product of some social systems and not of others. The systems which imply it should be identifiable, and the minimum institutions for the maintenance of stable peace should be capable of specification. Then the problem becomes one of the dynamics of social systems, by which we may be enabled to move from the present system, which does not have stable peace, to some future system which possesses this happy property.

We do not have to study the whole social system in order to find those parts of it which are peculiarly relevant to the problem of war and peace. We can identify war and peace very readily as properties of conflict systems, and, among conflict systems, only of those which involve large-scale organizations specialized for violence. Of the latter, international systems comprise by far the larger part, though the occasional existence of civil war, insurrections, or riots, and so on, within the body politic necessitates a certain broadening of the concept of war beyond that of the international system as such. The logical relations are illustrated in Figure 1, which shows that all war systems are conflict systems, some war systems are international systems, and some international systems are conflict systems.

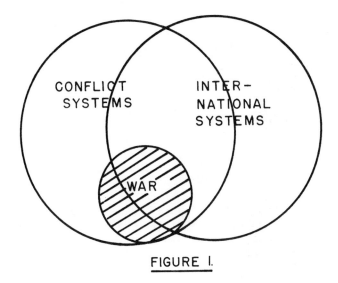

FIGURE I.

The study of the ecology of war and peace, therefore, begins with the study of the ecology of conflict itself. Conflict is carried on typically by a reaction process in which, for example, A makes a move which changes B's perception of the state of the world and his optimum position in it, so that then B moves. This changes A's perception in turn, and he moves again, which leads to further moves by B, and so on. A conflict move is then defined as one in which one party becomes better off and another party becomes worse off. This process is illustrated in Figure 2. Here we plot A's welfare vertically and B's welfare horizontally. A move from, say, P_1 to P_2 is a conflict move because it diminishes A's welfare and increases B's welfare. We will neglect the difficult problems involved in the perception of welfare and assume for the moment that some objective measure is possible. In a field such as this, a move in either a southeasterly or a northwesterly direction is a conflict move; a move in a northeasterly direction may be defined as a "benign" move, for this increases the welfare of both parties; similarly, a move in a southwesterly direction may be defined as a "malign" move in which both parties are worse off. An important proposition here is that a succession of conflict moves, that is, a conflict process, may be either benign or malign depending on the exact parameters of the process itself. Thus, again in Figure 2, suppose we start

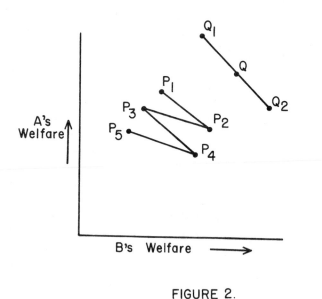

FIGURE 2.

at P_1. B makes a move to P_2, where he is better off but A is worse off, whereupon A responds by moving to P_3, where he is better off but B is worse off. B responds to P_4, A to P_5, and so on. The succession of conflict moves here results in a malign process in which both parties are getting worse off in the process as a whole. Although each time a party makes a move he gets better off, this improvement is more than cancelled by the next move of the other party. Suppose, however, that we move from P_5 to P_4 to P_3 to P_2 to P_1: we would have a succession of conflict moves in a generally benign direction. On the whole, economic competition tends to be benign in its over-all effect, though not universally so, whereas international competition, especially arms races, almost always tends to be malign. Interpersonal or interorganizational conflict can easily be of either character. We all know families or organizations shaken to pieces by malign conflict processes, and we also know those whom conflict has seemed to strengthen.

Neither malign nor benign processes can go on forever. A malign process, if it goes on long enough, will reach some kind of a boundary at which the process will break down. An arms race leads to a war, marital quarrels lead to divorce, industrial conflict leads to a strike. One party may be eliminated, or some drastic reorganization may take place. The existence of a boundary of this kind at which the system breaks down is highly characteristic of conflict systems. benign moves, too, are not likely to go on forever; a system of this kind is likely to exhibit some upper boundary which is imposed by the sheer scarcities of the system, such as Q_1 to Q_2 in Figure 2. When the conflict process reaches this upper boundary, further benign moves are no longer possible, and the only possible moves are conflict moves. From the point Q, for instance, we can only go either toward Q_1, in which case A is better off and B is worse off, or toward Q_2, where B is better off and A is worse off. Even these scarcities, however, are not absolute. What economic development means, in fact, is pushing out this boundary of scarcity in a generally benign direction. The more resources that are devoted to diminishing scarcity, the better chance there is of maintaining in the system benign moves which make everybody better off.

Conflict management is essentially a developmental or learning process. It has two aspects: first, the prevention of malign conflict processes, and second, the diminution of scarcity by economic, political, and social development. Both these cases have a centralized and a decentralized aspect. In avoiding malign conflict processes an important element is the development of skills in the management of conflict by the parties themselves. We see this, for instance, in the development of the child, at least in a middle-class environment, when the fist-fights of first grade are gradually replaced by the more subtle conflicts of adult life. We see this also in the "gentling" process of social learning, through which we have attained personal disarmament, the abolition of dueling, and the almost complete disappearance of personal combat in very large sections of society. Supplementary but also essential to this process has been the development of a centralized process of conflict management, such as law, arbitration, conciliation, and so on. This might be called third-party control. Ideally, it should involve two things: the first is a reserve power, as it were, on the part of the third party which can be thrown toward one or the other of the contending parties in order to prevent malign conflict processes. The second aspect is the impact of the third party on the learning processes of the parties in conflict, by means of which certain attitudes and values are legitimatized and accepted by the conflicting parties as norms of behavior. Unless the fear of the law passes over into respect for law, the power of the legal institution, or of government itself, is very limited. Unless, therefore, the payoffs, both positive and negative, actual and potential, which third-party control introduces contributes to the learning process of the other parties, third-party control is likely to be ineffective. It is hard for anyone who has grown up in a society like that of the United States, where the law is largely respected and indeed almost taken for granted, to realize how precarious this consent may be and how impotent the law is in a society where it does not command respect.

The development of decentralized control depends on the growth of three factors in the images, value systems, and behavior patterns of the parties concerned. The first of these is accuracy in the perception of the nature and intentions of the other party by each of the parties to conflict. There is a good deal of empirical work which shows that individuals can manage conflicts even when there are wide incompatibilities and possibly conflicts of interest between the parties, if each has a realistic appraisal of the character of the other. When the image that each party has of the other diverges sharply from the image which the party has of itself, each party is behaving, as it were, in an unreal world, and it is not surprising that the management of conflict becomes difficult. We see this in the most extreme form in the schizophrenic or the paranoid, whom every act of the other party is interpreted as hostility, and benign moves become impossible.

The second characteristic is perhaps an aspect of the first, but it is so important that it deserves special mention. This is the character of long-sightedness on the part of the parties. Malign processes frequently arise because the party making the conflict move does not anticipate the reaction of the other. Thus, in Figure 2 again, if B is shortshighted, he may make a move from, say, P_1 to P_2. If A's reaction to this is to move to P_3, B is worse off than he was before. If B is longsighted, therefore, he will not make the move to P_2, but will make some less extreme move which will provoke either no response, or a less violent one, by A. The "prisoners' dilemma" in game theory is a good example of a situation in which a succession of shortsighted moves is invariably malign, but in which, if each of the parties is longsighted, a benign move can be made. The difficulty here is that benign moves frequently require both parties to be longsighted, and if one of the parties is shortsighted this may force the other one to be shortsighted too. This is one of the major reasons why decentralized control alone is not usually adequate, and why centralized or third-party control usually has to be brought in to protect society against what might be called "unilateral shortsightedness." This is done by changing the payoff in such a way that shortsightedness does not profit the shortsighted even in the first instance.

The third source of success in decentralized conflict management is empathy, or the identification of each party with the interests of the other. Parties who are friendly toward each other are likely to

make benign moves, for moves which benefit both parties simultaneously will be strenuously sought after and conflict moves will be made
reluctantly and with as little loss to the other party as possible. By
contrast, when the parties are hostile, so that each rejoices in the
misery of the other, the probability of a malign succession of moves
is much enhanced.

It is one of the great weaknesses of game theory as a guide to
the interpretation of social systems that it fails to take into account
this factor of empathy or identification. This is the basis of much that
is fallacious in what has been called "strategic thinking," which takes
the existing hostilities of the international system for granted and does
not inquire how to change them. Without a strong element of what I
have called the "integrative system," however, no social system could
possibly survive, and it is surprising that this element in the social
system has been so little studied and, indeed, has been treated almost
with contempt by those who fancy themselves sophisticated.

Both hostility and friendliness are essentially learned attitudes,
and one of the most important contributions which the behavioral sciences could make to this infant science of conflict management would
be to investigate the origin of these states of mind. What is it, for instance, in the experience of individuals which makes some people generally benevolent and eager to identify with others, while some people
are malevolent in disposition and seem to need a positive hatred in
order to organize their own personalities? There is a great deal of
evidence which suggests that early childhood experience is a crucial
factor in determining these predispositions, but we are still a long way
from really identifying their causes, and there seems to be surprisingly little work specifically directed toward this problem. The study of
integrative systems, therefore, would seem to me the most exciting
and also the most important frontier of all behavioral science, both at
the theoretical and at the empirical level.

The study of centralized conflict management, or third-party
intervention in the form of law, police, judiciaries, arbitration or
conciliation, and the like, has an enormous literature. Yet much of
the effect of this discussion is lost by the failure to realize that third-
party intervention is not a system in itself, but is merely one aspect
of a much larger system of the dynamics of social conflict. There is,
of course, a quite legitimate study of the formal aspects of third-party
intervention in the study of law, constitutions, and so on. This covers
a large part of the traditional ground of political science. Unless third-
party intervention, however, is seen as part of a larger process of
social learning by which the elements that lead to decentralized control are also enhanced, we will certainly fail to understand why given
institutions are successful in some environments and not in others.
The fallacy of much legal and political thinking is that it tends to identi-

fy the institutions of third-party control as self-contained systems, whereas in fact the significance and the success of these institutions rests to a considerable degree on the extent to which they supplement and enhance a system of decentralized control. Unless the political and legal institutions of a society create a learning process in which individuals learn to handle their own conflicts, they can easily become ineffective or possibly move toward breakdown. If democratic government, for instance, does not result in a process of social learning which accumulates over a period of time, it is almost bound to fail. The success of political and legal institutions, therefore, often depends on the existence of other, complementary institutions, through which these political and legal processes themselves are fed into the overall learning process of the society. These integrative institutions — the family, the church, and the school—provide the soil in which the dry seeds of legality can either come to life or remain barren.

Just because we claim that it is possible to learn to manage conflict, we do not mean that conflict is illusory. The world is full of perfectly real conflicts of interest and, in the great dynamics of the social system, some parties "win" and become relatively better off, and other parties "lose" and become relatively worse off. In a society with a stationary, low-level technology, conflict can be very real and very severe indeed. A high-level, expanding technology, on the other hand, is in a very real sense a substitute for conflict, because it constantly yields situations in which everybody can be better off and most moves are benign. This is why technology represents such an enormous political change. In a society with a stationary technology, almost the only way to become better off is to make somebody else worse off. In a society with an advancing technology, we can become better off without making anybody worse off, and indeed we can all get better off together.

In all societies it is important to avoid malign processes, for these are always pathological and it is to the interest of all parties to avoid them. Insofar as these processes rest on illusions and on failures of social perception, the elimination of these illusions would be an important contribution to the elimination of malign processes. It is possible that some benign processes also rest upon illusion, but this is much less likely. But in a technically developing society, malign processes become all the more intolerable simply because benign processes are so much more possible. In this fact, perhaps, lies one of the major hopes for the future of mankind.

The Economic Impacts of Disarmament

_____ EMILE BENOIT

(N. B. This paper was prepared essentially in 1962, and has
not been updated. Some estimates and some statements are no longer
realistic or applicable.)

I should like first to record my conviction that up to now economic considerations have been of negligible significance in our failure to achieve disarmament. We do not go on pouring funds (and real
resources) into armaments because we need the work that armaments
provide, or are unable to imagine alternative types of economic activity. We do it because we depend for our physical security on national
armaments. To be sure, the evolution in military technology has made
this an extraordinarily hazardous way of trying to achieve security —
so hazardous, indeed, that it is imperative that we find a better way.
Nevertheless, the rational purpose of national defense is physical
security.

The major reason for disarmament is not the economic cost of
armaments, but their danger — their inability to safeguard our security effectively. Even on the purely economic plane, the cost of producing armaments is insignificant in relation to what we would lose if
we had to fight a major war, or if we had to surrender to a hostile
power out of fear of a war.

While vested interests have struggled over the distribution of
the defense dollar and have tried to get more for their own communities or their own weapons systems, and have sometimes caused the
defense dollar to be allocated at less than achievable efficiency, I
see no convincing evidence that vested interests in defense have been
generally triumphant over the economy bloc. Democratic nations have
tended to put too few resources into armaments rather than too many.
Before World War II, Britain, France and the United States were un-
willing to put as large a fraction of their national output into defense
as the Fascist Alliance, and since 1953, the Western powers have
put a far smaller proportion of their resources into defense than the
U. S. S. R. This is particularly apparent if one recognizes the relative

111

underpricing of Russian defense goods and services and the qualitative superiority of the resources they absorb. It also seems likely that some of the most ominous and disturbing aspects of our present armaments reflect not the desire to spend more money, but the desire to save it. "A bigger bang for a buck" — the rationale for the massive retaliation doctrine and the endless proliferation of nuclear weapons — reflected not the expensiveness but the cheapness of nuclear armed ICBMs. For efficient mass killing of human beings at a low unit-cost, such weapons are absolutely unsurpassed. The justification for the massive deterrence doctrine was developed by an administration that was basically hostile to government spending, worried more about budget deficits than about falling behind the Russians in defense, space, growth rates, or anything else, and which passed from the scene in a jeremiad against the military-industrial complex.

So far, then, the real obstacle to disarmament is not economic. The real obstacle is a political one. National governments have as yet shown little evidence of understanding what would actually be required in order to have a type of disarmament one could trust, or willingness to accept the profound changes in the system of international relations which would be required. Even the conceptual problem of disarmament, i. e., the nature of the political institutions which could make disarmament dependable and still no danger to national independence and individual liberties, has not yet been solved by anybody. It is scandalous that our political scientists have until now given it so little attention. I myself believe that a solution does exist, but along hitherto unsuspected lines that would require fundamental innovations in political thinking as well as political practice.

This, however, is not my present topic; my topic is, rather, the economic effect of disarmament if it should actually occur. This is a subject about which I have been directing a research program for several years, and the interim report of this research has been published (1).

The economic effects of disarmament can be analyzed only if one first starts with a well-defined concept of what disarmament is. One version of disarmament as it is often conceived is what I call "bilateral disarmament." In this concept, each side reduces its arms to a low or negligible level, but still counts on itself to protect its liberties. This seems impracticable and dangerous to me, since it promises to be even less stable than what we have now. Such a solution would inevitably give rise to fears, and possibly to the reality, of secret violations of the agreement. Moreover, it would make it seem less dangerous to begin a war, but war could quickly escalate to the highest level of violence. The arms race would then assume the form of a race to prepare methods for the quickest possible nuclear rearmament — a race in which an open society would suffer a considerable handicap.

I therefore think there is little use in considering anything other than what I call "multilateral disarmament," which is essentially characterized not by the elimination of arms, but by the shifting of decisive weapons to a supranational authority charged with keeping the peace. It would do so by enforcing agreements voluntarily made among the nations to abstain from major armaments and from direct and indirect aggression defined in advance, but identified if necessary by a supranational judiciary. Such a proposal raises many obvious and serious problems. I believe they are soluble. If they are not, then disarmament may prove unattainable. Let us, for the purpose of discussion, assume they are soluble. What then would be the economic problems raised and the solutions to them?

Disarmament Impact

Political Military Model   Table 1 shows the politico-military steps included in our disarmament model. They are broadly consistent with the official "United States Program for General and Complete Disarmament in a Peaceful World" presented at Geneva in 1962. However, they diverge on some points and are far more specific than the government's proposals on others, and, in any case, should be regarded as provisional and hypothetical. Space is lacking for a detailed discussion of the politico-military assumptions on which the model is based, but summarily stated, the main assumptions are as follows:

1. It would not be feasible, politically or administratively, to negotiate and ratify a sound disarmament agreement before 1965, nor fully to implement it in fewer than a dozen years after that. This judgment is not based on economic considerations, but solely on what it takes to install a properly inspected and enforced disarmament system. These estimates were made in 1960 and 1961. The model would need to be pushed several years into the future to provide enough lead time if it were done today.

2. The United States would bear one-third of the costs of the inspection, police, and strategic deterrent functions of an international disarmament organization. This would cost the United States about 7 billion dollars a year.

3. Cutoffs in weapons production would precede cutbacks in stocks of weapons, and would begin in the first stage.

4. Soft, unstable weapons systems (such as bombers or liquid fuel rockets in unhardened bases) would have production cutoffs before the more stable systems (such as Minuteman in reinforced bases, and Polaris).

5. Manpower cutbacks would begin immediately, and about a third would be cut back in the early stages.

6. The United States armed forces would ultimately be reduced to a size below that of 1939 in relation to population, but would retain a small and essentially defensive capability. Even this, with equipment, would cost 10 billion dollars a year.

7. Inspection would remain on a bilateral basis in the first stage, and be shifted to the I. D. O. (International Disarmament Organization) in the second stage.

It is assumed that destructive capacity by 1965 will be so large that the risks in production cutoffs will be slight and not seriously destabilizing.

Expenditure Model   The expenditure model of disarmament shown in Table 2 was first prepared by the R. E. A. D. (Research Program on Economic Adjustments to Disarmament) and later modified in details through discussion within the Consultant Panel on Economic Impacts of Disarmament in the United States Arms Control and Disarmament Agency — although, of course, it has no official status. It is not intended to be a literal forecast, but simply a means of illustrating the kinds of economic problems to which disarmament would give rise.

As indicated in Table 2, disarmament on the scale and at the tempo assumed in our model would involve a decline in United States defense expenditure of about 46 billion dollars (in 1960 dollars), of which about 17 billion dollars would occur in the first three years. If allowance is made for the offsets provided by the estimated United States contribution to the International Disarmament Organization and the planned expansion in civilian and atomic energy programs, then the net decline would not be more than 32 billion dollars in all, and not more than 5 billion dollars a year, even during the first three-year period, when the maximum impact would be felt.

Employment Model   Table 3 shows the essential changes in employment which would occur in the implementation of a disarmament program based on the R. E. A. D. model. The estimates are based upon an input-output matrix prepared by Leontief and Hoffenberg and correspond to the expenditure model shown in Table 2 (2).

The employment model projects a total of defense-dependent employment of about 7. 3 million persons by 1965 — 3 million in industry, 3 million in the armed forces, and nearly 1. 2 million civilian employees in defense agencies. The total projected decline during disarmament is about 6. 25 million.

These declines are by no means equivalent to a prediction of

Table 1
DISARMAMENT MODEL. POLITICO-MILITARY MEASURES
(Model of general and complete disarmament as developed by READ — the Research Program on Economic Adjustments for Disarmament)

	STAGE I: 1965-68	STAGE II: 1968-71	STAGE IIIA: 1971-74	STAGE IIIB: 1974-77
U.S. DEFENSE FORCES REDUCED	From 3.0 to 2.5 million	From 2.5 to 2.0 million	From 2.0 to 1.0 million	From 1.0 to 0.5 million
CUTOFFS IN NATIONAL PRODUCTION OF	"Soft" strategic delivery systems, e.g., bombers, liquid fuel rockets in unhardened bases, etc., tactical nuclear weapons	"Hard" strategic delivery systems: nuclear fuel	Conventional weapons, except spare parts and replacements	Unconventional weapons, e.g., chemical, biological, radiological warfare matériel, etc.; "dangerous" R&D — development of new weapon concepts, etc.
CUTBACKS IN NATIONAL INVENTORIES		50 per cent cut in "soft" strategic delivery vehicles and systems; one-half destroyed, one-half stockpiled for destruction in Stage IIIA.	75 per cent cut in conventional weapons, of which one-third destroyed, one-third stockpiled for destruction in Stage IIIB, one-third transferred to IPF; remaining "soft" strategic delivery systems destroyed; all tactical nuclear weapons destroyed.	All "hard" strategic delivery vehicles and systems except "reassurance reserve,"a e.g., 10 low yield Minuteman or Polaris missiles and delivery systems.
BASES	Denuclearization of "soft" foreign bases	Denuclearization of "hard" foreign bases	Transfer to IDO police force (IPF) of foreign bases	Transfer to IDO deterrent force (IDF) of "hard" domestic bases; except "reassurance reserve,"a transfer to IPF of 50 per cent of nonnuclear domestic bases
INSPECTION MEASURES	Test ban inspection; inspection of missile launching pads; surprise attack inspection — all with bilateral or UN inspection	Transfer of national inspection functions (except secret intelligence) to IDO inspection force (IIF)		IDO research and development group (IRD) maintains inventory and inspection of national research and development
ARMS UTILIZATION AGREEMENTS ON	Nuclear test ban: restrictions on deployment of submarines, carriers, and forward flights of air wings; orbiting weapons	Missile testing: regional or zonal agreements	National withdrawal from tension boundaries	
INTERNATIONAL CONVENTIONS ACCEPTED ON	International Disarmament Organization (IDO); IDO inspection force (IIF)	IDO police force (IPF)	IDO deterrent force (IDF) IDO research and development group (IRD)	
INTERNATIONAL DISARMAMENT ORGANIZATION (IDO) OPERATIONS	IDO administration begins	IDO judiciary; IDO inspection force (IIF) begin	IDO police force (IPF) builds up to 0.5 million men, receives 25 per cent of national stocks of conventional weapons; stationing of IPF along tension boundaries	IPF raised to 1 million; IDO deterrent force (IDF) begins — rises to 0.5 million; receives all "hard" bases and delivery systems from national forces (except "reassurance reserve";a) IDO research and development group (IRD) given a monopoly of "dangerous" R&D

a The "reassurance reserve" would be intended to increase willingness to accept GCD by making it unlikely that any attack could be made on the present nuclear powers without heavy sacrifices, but would leave the primary deterrent responsibility to IDO and would not enable any nation to destroy any other nation or to deter the IDO.

Table 2
MODEL OF GENERAL AND COMPLETE DISARMAMENT

	U. S. Expenditures for Security and Associated Programs[1] (in billions of 1960 dollars)					
	1960	1965	Stage I 1965–68	Stage II 1968–71	Stage IIIA 1971–74	Stage IIIB 1974–77
U. S. Defense[2]						
Personnel	11.7	15.1	13.1	11.1	6.7	4.7
Operation and maintenance	10.2	12.6	8.9	6.0	3.9	2.1
Procurement (inc. research & development)	18.0	20.9	12.2	6.3	4.8	1.5
Aircraft	(6.9)	(6.0)	(2.0)	(0.5)	(0.5)	(0.5)
Missiles	(5.1)	(5.4)	(0.5)	(0.1)	(0.1)	(0.1)
Military space..............	(0.5)	(2.6)	(4.4)	(2.5)	(2.5)	(0.0)
Ships	(1.9)	(2.4)	(1.5)	(0.2)	(0.2)	(0.2)
Other......................	(3.6)	(4.5)	(3.8)	(3.0)	(1.5)	(0.7)
Construction	1.6	2.0	0.5	0.2	0.2	0.2
Military assistance program.....	1.6	2.4	2.0	1.5	0.0	0.0
Military AEC	2.1	1.4	0.5	0.2	0.0	0.0
Civil defense[3].................	(5)	1.7	1.7	1.7	1.7	1.7
U. S. Defense — Total	45.2[6]	56.1	38.9	27.0	17.3	10.2
U. S. contribution to international functions[4]						
Inspection	....	....	....	3.2	2.6	1.3
Police forces	....	....	....	....	1.8	2.7
Deterrent forces	....	....	....	....	....	2.6
Juridical & administrative functions.....................	....	....	....	0.5	0.5	0.5
U. S. contribution — Total	....	....	....	3.7	4.9	7.1
TOTAL U. S. EXPENDITURES ON SECURITY PROGRAMS.......	45.2	56.1	38.9	30.7	22.2	17.3
Associated programs						
NASA	0.4	2.7	4.5	5.9	7.4	8.9
Civilian AEC	0.5	1.4	2.0	2.0	2.0	2.0
Associated programs — Total	0.9	4.1	6.5	7.9	9.4	10.9
GRAND TOTAL	46.1	60.2	45.4	38.6	31.6	28.2

[1]These estimates were prepared in 1961. The grand total projected for 1965 is approximately correct, but there are considerable deviations in the individual items. Disarmament assumptions are intended to be broadly consistent with the U. S. program.

[2]Defense expenditure estimates made by R. E. A. D. based on Bureau of the Budget projections, published in _Special Study_ (Jan. 1961); George Steiner's unpublished manuscript, "Defense Activities in Southern California in the 1960's"; and confidential industry sources.

[3]These estimates were based on the assumption that in a period of disarmament the United States would be glad to adopt any measures of a defense character which would increase its physical security and not be incompatible with the disarmament agreement. They might be viewed as a desirable form of insurance against possible breakdowns in the disarmament program, especially during a period before all nations were participating. Nor would such a program reduce the deterrent power of the Peace Force; on the contrary, it alone could render the exercise of such power credible.

[4]The U. S. contribution to the international control organization and the Peace Force is assumed to cover one-third of total costs, but no charge is assumed for existing weapons or bases transferred to the international control organization or the Peace Force.

[5]Less than $50 million.

[6]Excluding revolving fund.

Table 3
PROJECTED PRIMARY IMPACT ON EMPLOYMENT OF REDUCTION
IN NATIONAL DEFENSE EXPENDITURES[1]

Industry	% Output used by military 1958	Defense employ-ment (000) 1965	Decrease in defense employment[2] (000)				
			Stage I 1965-68	Stage II 1968-71	Stage IIIA 1971-74	Stage IIIB 1974-77	Total Decrease
Chemicals	5	63	23	15	9	9	57
Fuel & power	7	86	29	20	13	11	73
Petroleum	(10)	(52)	(16)	(12)	(9)	(7)	(44)
Primary metals	13	198	81	51	22	27	182
Iron & steel	(10)	(90)	(35)	(23)	(11)	(12)	(82)
Fabricated metals	8	150	54	35	24	20	132
Nonelec. machinery	5	92	30	22	18	12	82
Elec. machinery	21	376	126	85	68	61	341
radio, commun.	(38)	(279)	(100)	(64)	(43)	(48)	(256)
Trans. equip. & ordnance	38	1302	505	376	146	173	1199
Aircraft & parts	(94)	(739)	(361)	(193)	(36)	(115)	(705)
Ships & boats	(61)	(239)	(87)	(123)	(5)	(3)	(218)
Ordnance	(100)	(291)	(45)	(52)	(97)	(52)	(245)
Instruments	20	67	30	17	4	11	63
Transportation	6	129	45	29	19	16	109
RR & trucking	(5)	(101)	(37)	(23)	(14)	(12)	(86)
Trade	1	159	60	36	24	16	137
Service, etc.	1	260	85	60	40	33	219
Business services	(4)	(105)	(36)	(25)	(16)	(13)	(91)
Prof. & serv. industries	(2)	(129)	(39)	(29)	(20)	(17)	(105)
Construction	2	82	37	7	0	0	45
Other industries[3]	2	228	85	53	31	26	195
Total Industry[4]	6	3193	1191	807	419	417	2835
Government[4]	85[5]	4171	827	770	1179	678	3454
Armed Forces	100	(3000)	(500)	(500)	(1000)	(500)	(2500)
Civilian	11	(1171)	(327)	(270)	(179)	(178)	(954)
Total Industry & Government[4]	5	7364	2018	1577	1598	1095	6289

[1]"Primary Impact" refers to direct and indirect effects as measured by input-output analysis but ignoring possible multiplier effects or final demand offsets.

[2]The assumed reductions in expenditures are in accord with the hypothetical model of general and complete disarmament as follows: Stage I, $17.2 billion; Stage II, $11.9 billion; Stage IIIA, $9.7 billion; Stage IIIB, $7.1 billion.

[3]Food and kindred products, apparel and textile mill products, leather products, paper and allied products, rubber and rubber products, lumber and wood products, nonmetallic minerals and products, and miscellaneous manufacturing industries.

[4]Totals not exactly equal to sum of parts because of rounding.

[5]Federal purchases of goods and services for national defense as percent of total Federal purchases of goods and services.

Source: Leontief-Hoffenberg 1958 matrix, adjusted to 1965. Table prepared by R. E. A. D. (Research Program on Economic Adjustments to Disarmament).

Table 4
IMPACT OF ALTERNATIVE FISCAL PROGRAMS IN AN ADJUSTMENT
TO A $32 BILLION DEFENSE CUT
(dollars in billions)

CHARACTER OF ADJUSTMENT		IMPACT		
		Changes In		
Type of Adjustment Policy	Specific Measures Involved	Gross National Product	Employment (millions)	Budget Surplus or Deficit (-)[a]
1. Laissez-Faire	No offsets	$-48.0[b] -37.0[c]	-5.3[b] -4.1[c]	$+19.8
2. Balanced Budget with Tax Cut	Tax Cut $31.9[d]	-12.3[b]	-2.9[b]	0.0
3. Balanced Budget with Partial Tax Cut & New Government Programs	Tax Cut $21.9[d] New Government Programs $10.0	-8.4[b]	-2.0[b]	0.0
4. Three-way Split	Tax Cut $11.0[d] New Government Programs $11.0 Debt Retirement $10.0[d]	-19.2[b] -14.8[c]	-2.6[b] -2.0[c]	+6.2
5. Production Stabilization Tax Cut	Tax Cut $43.0[d]	0.0	-2.0	-6.8
6. Employment Stabilization Tax Cut	Tax Cut $69.3[d]	+29.6	0.0	-23.3
7. Balanced Stabilization Offsets	Tax Cut $18.5[d] New Government Programs $18.5	+0.4	-0.8	-3.1

Note: Defense cut based on R.E.A.D. disarmament model — consisting of $21.6 billion in defense purchases from the private sector, and $10.4 billion cut in expenditures in defense personnel. Tax cuts assumed to be across-the-board on personal income tax.

[a] ex post based on minimum impact estimate.
[b] Minimum estimate. Maximum estimate is up to double this figure.
[c] Minimum estimate after correction for the monetary expansion resulting from use of the surplus to reduce the national debt.
[d] ex ante.

Source: Benoit, E. & Boulding, K. Disarmament & The Economy, Chaps. 6 and 8.

increases in unemployment; they would be a function not only of the rate of release of manpower from defense activities, but also of the rate of build-up of the demand for non-defense goods and services, as well as of the success achieved in redeploying equipment and manpower to satisfy the new demand. At this point, we do not know the magnitude, type and effectiveness of the adjustment program. However, the model does provide some indication of the relative severity of the redeployment problem within the various industries.

The over-all magnitude of the redeployment problem is estimated at about 8 per cent, this being the total size of the cutback in
estimated employment in defense industry, the armed forces, and
the defense agencies expressed as a percentage of the labor force.
However, offsets will be supplied by the expansion in the civilian
space and atomic energy programs, and from the United States' contribution to international inspection, police and deterrent functions.
If their labor requirements per dollar of expenditure were roughly
in line with those of the defense activities they replace, they should
offset about 30 per cent of the estimated cutbacks in defense employment. Net defense cuts after such offsets would then be only 5.5 per
cent of the labor force and only 1.75 per cent of the labor force in the
first three years.

One important qualification is necessary. If the postulated defense cutbacks were not offset by expansion of private or public nondefense expenditures, their multiplier effects could create a far more
severe impact than so far indicated in our model.

Regional Deployment   There is a considerable regional concentration of defense-dependent economic activity, and this fact will un-
questionably create a major set of readjustment problems in the event
of disarmament. Kansas, Washington, New Mexico, California, Con-
necticut, Arizona, and Utah have 20 to 30 per cent of their manufacturing employment in four major fields of defense procurement:
ordnance, electronics, aircraft and missiles, and shipbuilding and
repairing. Alaska, Hawaii, Washington, D.C., and Virginia have a
tenth to a quarter of their incomes provided by defense agency payrolls. Clearly, these areas are likely to face readjustment problems
of above the average difficulty.

Within these and other states there are counties which have an
even more highly concentrated dependence on military contracts, and
a thorough-going analysis of the problems would require a much more
detailed survey of the location of defense activities in particular areas,
together with indications of where the defense cuts would be most
likely to come and the alternative employment opportunities existing
and likely to develop in these particular places. Such estimates are
very difficult to make because of the widely ramified network of defense subcontracts which is largely unrecorded, making it extremely
difficult or impossible to trace out the full geographic distribution of
the economic activity generated by defense contracts.

Econometric Analysis of Policy Alternatives

The econometric model used for analysis of fiscal impacts is
an adaptation of the 32-equation model of the United States economy

developed by Professor Daniel B. Suits of the University of Michigan, from the old Klein-Goldberger model. Table 4 shows the impacts of various fiscal programs in an adjustment to the projected 32-billion-dollar defense cuts, using the multipliers developed by Professor Suits. It is important to bear in mind that these multipliers understate the investment effects and are much lower than those used in most other econometric models. The estimated declines in income and employment should therefore be viewed as conservative and minimal; it is possible that the adverse effects could be as much as twice as bad. On the other hand, the Suits model makes an allowance for the expansionary effects of using a budget surplus to reduce national debt, implicitly handling the surplus as if it were an increase in Treasury cash or deposits. I have made an adjustment for this based on some original research of Warren Smith (1, Chapter 8).

The first type of program — a laissez faire policy — which would provide no offsets to the defense cuts, would produce declines of at least 37 billion dollars in Gross National Product and 2 million in employment, even allowing for the stimulating effects of a substantial reduction in the national debt. These declines could be as much as twice these figures if the secondary or multiplier effects proved to be larger than assumed. Moreover, during the first few years, when 46 per cent of the net defense cuts in the model would occur, and when part of the impact of later scheduled cutbacks could be created by announcement effects, it is possible that in the absence of offsets, disarmament could provoke declines in Gross National Product of 15 to 20 billion dollars a year. This would clearly involve a real depression — though not, of course, on the 1929-34 scale. It is hard to believe that we would be so foolish as to let this happen.

A more likely danger is that we would seek at least a balanced budget. This could be achieved under Policies 2 and 3 by means of either full tax cuts, or partial tax cuts, supplemented by new government spending programs. This would lead to minimal contractions of 8 to 12 billion dollars in Gross National Product and 2 to 3 million in employment. Here again, these estimates could be doubled if the multiplier effects were worse than assumed. What is implied is a recession or a significant interruption in economic growth.

A fourth policy which would doubtlessly have much political appeal would probably produce even worse results. It involves a "three-way split" between tax cuts, new government programs, and the creation of a budget surplus for reduction of the national debt. The probable results would be a 15 to 30-billion-dollar decline in Gross National Product and a 2 to 4 million rise in unemployment. This implies a fairly serious recession — or a mild depression.

Policies 5 and 6 are designed to stabilize the economy solely by means of tax cuts, but prove to be rather impractical. The former would stabilize Gross National Product but would permit a decline of 2 to 4 million in employment. The latter would require tax cuts and deficits so large — of approximately 70 billion dollars and 23 billion dollars respectively — as to set it outside the boundaries of serious political discussion. Both would introduce severe structural inflationary strains into the economy by endeavoring to shift such an enormous volume of resources so quickly from the public to private sectors of the economy.

To my mind, program 7, a balanced stabilization offsets program, offers the best solution. It provides tax cuts about equal in size to new government expenditure programs, the total of the two being slightly (about one-seventh) in excess of the 32-billion-dollar defense cutback. Such a program prevents any significant decline either in production or in employment. It shares the benefits of the cutback equally between the taxpayer and the communities desiring expanded welfare programs. The budget deficit involved would not be large by the standards of recent experience and current planning.

Lessons of Past Defense Cuts

Optimists about our chances of making a good economic adjustment to some future disarmament are apt to point to our "painless" defense cuts after 1945 and 1953 as evidence. A closer look at these episodes may dispel some of the reassurance.

While the 1945-48 reconversion was accomplished with an unexpectedly low rate of unemployment, it did involve sharp declines in the total labor force, hours of work and industrial output. These reductions were a reaction to the relaxation of the unusual economic pressure of the war years. In a peacetime situation in the 1960's, such a decline in the supply of labor is neither to be expected nor welcomed.

The 1945-48 adjustment was also facilitated by a condition of hyperliquidity arising out of the 182 billion dollars of federal deficits (on income and product account) during the war years with 136 billion dollars of exceptional individual savings (beyond prewar trends), plus an extraordinarily easy postwar credit policy, with mortgages and consumer debt more than doubling between 1945 and 1948. The money supply rose from 41 per cent of G. N. P. in 1940 to 47 per cent in 1945, and fell back to 35 per cent in 1953, and to only 28 per cent in 1960. With far lower liquidity in the sixties, we are much more vulnerable to deflationary shocks if they occur.

Viewed soberly, the post-Korean experience is even less reassuring. In fact, we are still suffering today from our poor adjustments to the defense cuts made at that time. Defense expenditures dropped

12. 1 billion dollars (annual rates at current prices) between the second quarter of 1953 and the last quarter of 1954. Instead of increasing federal nondefense purchases as an offset, the government cut these back also — by one-third in three years. Total federal expenditures (on income and product account) from 1954 to 1957 inclusive, averaged 5. 2 billion dollars annually <u>below</u> the 1953 level. The tax cut of 1954 helped, but it was entirely insufficient to offset this cut in expenditures. There was a substantial rise in revenues, and a total federal budget surplus (on income and product account) of 11. 5 billion dollars over the years 1955, 1956 and 1957. The result of this failure to replace defense demand with adequate alternative demand — private or public — has been a severe slowdown in our growth.

Despite the record rate of real private investment in new plants and equipment in 1956 and 1957, there was a quick leveling off in industrial production. The index, both in 1956 and 1957, averaged slightly below the December 1955 level, and by the end of 1958 it was still lower. In effect, three years of industrial growth were wasted. The level of final demand that would have justified the volume of private investment from 1955 to 1957 was simply not allowed to materialize.

In real terms, discounting for price increases, defense cuts continued down to 1960, while revenues kept rising; and in 1960 there was another substantial budget surplus (on income and product account) of 3. 8 billion dollars, provoking our third recession in six years. Largely as a result of the deflationary fiscal policies followed, our rate of industrial growth in the period 1953-60 was only about half that achieved in the preceding seven years, and only a quarter of that concurrently attained by the countries of the European Economic Community. Average unemployment rose from 3 to 6 per cent of the civilian labor force and in the latter part of this period we were using only four-fifths of our industrial capacity or less, according to the McGraw-Hill estimates.

The Outlook for Successful Readjustment

How successful we are in the future in adjusting to major defense cutbacks depends essentially on whether we have learned enough from our recent mistakes not to repeat them. This, of course, requires that we learn to recognize that they <u>were</u> mistakes. The big obstacles are three: disbelief in the efficacy of tax cuts, hostility to government spending, and fear of government debt.

Disbelief in tax cuts has little scientific foundation but is hard to dissipate by argument. The percentage of disposable income that consumers spend has been remarkably stable: since 1950 it has not gone outside the range of 91 to 94 per cent in any single quarter; and windfall receipts, such as unanticipated Service insurance payments, have been spent at least that freely. Corporations have invested half to three-quarters of their cash flow in new plants and equipment and, on the average, have distributed about one-third of it in dividends. There is no sound reason whatever to fear that if government leaves more income in private hands, it will not be spent. Our ability to handle disarmament effectively may depend on whether the public is given a prior opportunity to learn how effective deficit-financed tax cuts can be in stimulating the economy and improving our rate of growth. Even a single violation of an irrational taboo, if unpunished, can readily lead to its discard.

Ideological hostility to federal spending is one of those unreasoning prejudices which can be reduced only very gradually. Because of it, people have vastly exaggerated ideas about the growth of such spending. In fact, nondefense spending on goods and services, discounting price increases, is now less than in 1939, and nondefense federal, state and local expenditure on goods and services constitute a smaller proportion of the economy. There are many valuable research, educational, public health, and welfare programs into which resources released from defense spending could go. High priority programs in these categories could readily absorb at least twice the resources likely to be released from the defense program in the event of disarmament (1, Chapter 12).

As for the fear of national debt as an economic burden, this is a shibboleth that can be dissipated only by elementary economic education. People will have to learn that just as they understand that they ought to borrow when necessary for their education or to increase their earning capacity, and just as businesses find it sensible to float bond issues to finance expansion when this enables them to raise the rate of profits on their equity capital, so too it makes sense for the government to assume a moderate amount of debt (in relation to the size of the economy) to increase the output of the economy and the profits of business. A government debt, rising gradually in proportion to the growth of the economy and which is owned by its own citizens, is a sign of health and vitality, not a menace, as it is too often portrayed. In fact, government debt is today much smaller in relation to the size of our economy than it was at the end of World War II.

I realize that even if demand is successfully maintained, there will be plenty of problems of a structural sort arising from the concentration of defense activity in particular areas, occupations and industries. These problems are the more obvious ones which people usually worry about, but they are far less important, in my opinion, than the ones I have been discussing in this paper. If we do not solve the problem of adequate demand, it makes very little difference what else we do or don't do: we will be in a bad way, and retraining or other structural adjustment measures will be seen as no more than ineffective palliatives, quite unable to solve our serious problem.

I am confident, however, that if we can solve the problem of adequate demand, we will not find the structural problems insoluble. In part, they will solve themselves, owing to the mobility of American labor and the ingenuity of American management when over-all markets are adequate.

The most serious structural problem is likely to arise from the highly specialized and unique characteristics of industrial defense activity and industrial defense firms, which would render very difficult any transition to routine commercial work. In part, this difficulty will require the creation of large new government-financed research and development programs which could be carried out by existing defense companies but which are devoted to pioneering attempts to improve man's mastery of nature for peaceful, welfare objectives. Programs of this sort would provide an ideal opportunity for the offsetting expansion of nondefense federal expenditure, which will also be required for a satisfactory fiscal policy adaptation to major cuts in defense spending.

REFERENCES

1. Benoit, E. and Boulding, K. (eds.), Disarmament and the Economy, New York, Harper and Row, 1963.
2. Leontief, W. and Hoffenberg, M. "Economic Effects of Disarmament," Scientific American, 204 (4):47-55, April 1961.

From Military to Civilian Economy
_____ SEYMOUR MELMAN

American society must have the competence to deal effectively
with the problems of converting industry from military to civilian
production if it is to deal effectively with present economic problems
and with future disarmament. For the last two years at least, Professor Emile Benoit[1], Gerard Piel[2], a few other colleagues and I
have been meeting on public platforms to discuss various aspects of
the economics of converting from military to civilian production. One
of the most striking features made apparent by these discussions is
how little has been done in private industry, by local communities,
and by the federal government to implement some of the plausible
notions of how to cope with these problems.

At the end of the last World War, more exactly beginning about
1944, every industrial firm of size had a vice president who was
characteristically called the Vice President in Charge of Postwar
Planning. The detailed blueprinting done at that time was an important part of the competence of American industry, even in the presence of large consumer markets, to bring about the shift from muni-
tions manufacture to the manufacture and successful marketing of
other goods. There are few post-arms-race-planning vice presidents
in American firms. Some important industrial contractors have made
initial individual efforts to study the possibility of alternative products
and alternative markets.

However, the very size of the military budget during the last
years is a major deterrent to such activity. The military budget has
passed the 50-billion-dollar mark; hence, for those in the fortunate
position of securing large contracts from these budgets, there is a
manifest deterrent against searching for avenues of activity other
than those required by the present and forecasted work. The Arms
Control and Disarmament Agency, which one might expect to take a

---

[1]Professor of International Business, Columbia University; _Europe at Sixes and
Sevens_, Columbia University Press, 1961; Editor: _Disarmament and the Economy_,
Harper and Row, 1963.
[2]Publisher of _Scientific American_.

125

lead in these matters, is a new agency, has a relatively modest budget, and is not equipped with the wide-ranging network of contacts in American industry necessary for stimulating at least the beginnings of a discussion on these topics. Indeed, only when the Commerce Department of the federal government, and private groups such as the Committee for Economic Development, the American Management Association, or the National Association of Manufacturers, are moved to discuss these matters on a serious, workaday, how-to basis will we have the crucial indications that this activity is being seriously undertaken in American society.

Much of the discussion of the economics of disarmament and the problems of industrial conversion has been conducted within the framework of the problems that might reasonably arise if agreement were reached on international disarmament. And owing to the varied political exigencies at any given moment, there has been a varying estimate of the plausibility of undertaking such activities. Recently, however, certain data concerning the military competence of the United States, and its implications for our military budgets, have served to put these basic questions in a fresher light.

Is it possible that problems of industrial conversion may be faced even before an international political agreement on disarmament is reached? In order to shed light on the significance of this question, I wish to present a few estimates on the military competence of the United States and then to discuss some implications with respect to our military budget for the coming fiscal year.

One way of gauging a nation's military competence is to estimate its ability to deliver nuclear warheads of enormous destructive power. In 1963 the armed forces of the United States possessed about 3,400 major nuclear delivery vehicles. By nuclear delivery vehicles, I mean aircraft and missiles primarily, and by major, I mean those of large carrying capability and intercontinental range. In that spectrum, the smallest delivery vehicle is the Polaris submarine and the smallest missile is the Polaris missile. Therefore, in the estimates I am about to summarize, we omit entirely intermediate- and short-range missiles, fighter aircraft, fighter bombers, and a host of other devices like cannon, mines, missiles of shorter tactical range (such as the Davy Crockett rocket launcher that can be carried by infantrymen). Thus, assuming 3,400 strategic weapons, we can estimate that we possess a combined delivery capability equivalent to 22 billion tons of TNT. The meaning of these figures may be made clear by a synthetic exercise in which we will utilize a value that I will call a "Hiroshima equivalent."

One hundred thousand people were killed at Hiroshima by the explosion of the equivalent of 20 thousand tons of TNT. Utilizing that value, we ask, What is the destructive competence of these 3,400 delivery vehicles which are competent to deliver 22 billion tons of TNT equivalent?

Now, on the earth there are about 2,000 cities of 100,000-or-over population. If every one of these cities in this speculation were marked off as a target, and further, if we allowed a 30 per cent failure in arrival of these delivery vehicles, then the surplus of delivery vehicles and of the destructive capability now at hand would be in the order of magnitude of an overkill capability (on a global scale) of 125 times. The destructive power, in other words, present in the major strategic vehicles in the U.S. Air Force and the U.S. Navy is sufficient to destroy all cities of 100,000-and-greater population on earth about 125 times, even making allowance for a 30 per cent technical failure for all causes. In the Sino-Soviet bloc there are 370 cities whose population is such that we can calculate again that, with 30 per cent attrition, the United States overkill capability is 500 times. In the Soviet Union alone are 140 cities of 100,000 population and over; the United States overkill capability with respect to these cities and their people is now in the order of magnitude of 1250 times. Finally, we should note that even if United States strategic forces lost 90 per cent of the missiles and 75 per cent of the big planes, the residual overkill on the U.S.S.R. would be 231 times. These estimates increase as weapons continue to be perfected.

It may also be noted that the stockpile of warheads capable of being carried by major strategic delivery vehicles is only a fractional part of the total stockpile of warheads available to the United States armed forces. That stockpile, whose exact magnitude is publicly unknown, may very well be of the order of magnitude of twice, or even greater than two times, the deliverable stockpile of warheads. The implications include offensive and defensive considerations. First, let us examine the implications for military operations on the offensive side: once destructive capability has reached "overkill" (an irrational notion, of course, implying an ability to destroy a human being more than once), then adding to that competence does not give military gain.

On the defensive side, the meaning of these data is that there now exists, in the hands of each of the major nuclear powers, such a variety and such a quantity of nuclear warheads and delivery vehicles that all known and all technically plausible modes of defense can be saturated by the variety and the quantity of offensive capabilities. There is no defensive system known to be of such reliability as to preclude saturation. Calculations of a similar sort have been estimated for the Soviets. Thus, the Soviets, with their strategic delivery vehicles, are estimated to have an overkill capability for the United States (again measured in units of cities of 100,000 population and over) on the order of a magnitude of 145 times.

As a result of this line of thought, attention has been turned to the military budget — a matter now being discussed[3] in the United States Congress. It is a military budget of a size unprecedented for the United States to maintain when not engaged in major hostilities. The proposed military budget totals 56.7 billion dollars. A major part of this budget is for additions to present forces, hence for an enlargement of this already very, very large destructive competence.

Accordingly, I have turned my attention to formulating a revised military budget based on the principle of maintaining the present armed forces in their present condition of strength, already enormous. And this, it should be understood, is a pre-disarmament, pre-international agreement, pre-agreed arms reduction budget. From this standpoint, the military personnel proposals of the budget are to be left intact, as are the complete operational- and maintenance-budgeted funds. For these are an essential part of the maintenance of the present forces in being.

However, the procurement item in the budget is here marked for a cut of between 6 and 10 billion dollars. The research, development, test, and evaluation portion of the budget is marked for a cut of 7 billion dollars, assigning only about a quarter of a billion for that purpose.

May I note that the value of a research and development budget is suggested by my previous argument concerning additions to offensive or defensive capability. Unless one finds a way to refute this argument, there is no essential justification for major extension of these military capabilities beyond present competence. The military construction item in the budget is marked for a cut; the civil defense item is marked for complete elimination, on the grounds that it is technically implausible, as well as a politically dangerous, exercise.

Military assistance is marked for elimination. The justification for this has been extensively discussed in a variety of books and periodicals, the conclusion having been drawn that military assistance abroad has not tended to support the cause of personal and political freedom in society.

The atomic energy program, originally budgeted at 2.9 billion dollars, is marked for a cut of 2 billion on the ground that further production of nuclear warheads is an unreasonable act. Hence, the large factories at Oak Ridge, Tennessee, Hanford, Washington, Paducah, Kentucky, and elsewhere should be shut down.

Similarly, the stockpiling of strategic materials and various minor emergencies-preparedness activities may reasonably be curtailed. The result of this reasoning suggests a budget cut on the order of magnitude of 18 to 22 billion dollars.

---

[3]This is a reterence to the United States military budget proposed for 1963-64.

Again, I wish to emphasize that this is a budget reduction based on a maintenance-of-present-military-forces. What are the implications of this budget reduction? First, in the area of procurement, that is, in the area of industrial production, clearly a 10-billion-dollar reduction of procurement budget from 16 billion to 6 billion dollars would involve major curtailment in new contracting activity to the aerospace, the missile, and the electronic industries. Since these industries tend to be concentrated in particular states and even in particular regions within these states, it is perfectly clear that this cut would in due course produce a major impact on employment and industrial activity. While we may regard this concentration as having a certain penalizing effect, we may look at it in another way by considering that certain of the adjustment problems would be more manageable because they would be more concentrated. They could therefore be dealt with in a reasonably integrated way. Thus, when the governor of the State of California takes note of these possibilities and, in the name of ordinary truth, takes the lead in offering the industry of his state a prospect of alternate activity, then the managements of these industries will be able to apply their talents to formulating programs for activities in directions other than armaments.

Major reduction on the research and development side of the military budget would have a great impact upon a wide array of vocations. Much of the research activity now being conducted in our industrial firms is government-supported, and the military side of that is the preponderant share. From industry's viewpoint, this would have the immediate effect of releasing large reserves of engineering and scientific talent for nonmilitary industrial research of all sorts that in many of our industries now are being sustained at a very modest level (so modestly, as a matter of fact, that the President's Office of Science and Technology was recently moved to inquire into these matters, and an Under Secretary of Commerce has been designated, with a budget for encouraging civilian technical research). That the problem should have been so formulated and that a budget should have been recommended within the Commerce Department for civilian technical research indicates that serious persons have become persuaded that civilian industrial research in the United States has become a substantially neglected activity.

The "maintenance-of-a-present-forces" military budget would bolster the civilian sector of the economy. But such a budget would itself create problems in other areas. For example, many of our universities and leading technical institutes are heavily engaged in activities financed by the Department of Defense. Parts of these activities are in the realm of basic science, the sort of work that is financed also by the National Science Foundation, the Public Health Service, and similar bodies. One might think that ordinary prudence here, too, suggests the importance of early considering steps for transferring the basic research funds now administered by the Department of Defense to federal agencies that have been established to deal with precisely this activity. Nevertheless, some readjustment will surely be required and, if not prepared for, painful results can be anticipated. I would also hope that universities and technical institutes equipped with a wide array of talents would have the wit to cope with their own problems in this field.

The Atomic Energy Commission, by reducing its manufacturing activity, would generate a variety of problems whose scope may be briefly suggested. If certain of these major manufacturing plants are closed down, then the requirements for major blocks of electric power are cut off. Since these blocks of electric power are largely produced from steam generating plants, then the product of these power plants and the fuel that enters into them are no longer needed. One might therefore expect some ramified effects in the coal fields in those states where there is already considerable unemployment in these very industries.

I have enumerated these problems, not to suggest that they are difficult or insuperable. On the contrary, in my judgment these problems are soluble. Indeed, the very emergence of these problems into prominence can be made into a major opportunity for our society — an opportunity to cope with a set of problems that has been neglected, and whose generation, independently, is a source of considerable concern to many people.

I would like to identify five problems that have come to be of pressing importance to our society, and whose solution will be vastly facilitated by the release of technical manpower and capital resources from military production. The first concerns the civilian economy of the United States. Important sectors of that economy have suffered grave deterioration and technological stagnation; the machinery-producing industries of the United States have in large part become less than competent to compete, not only in the world market but in the American market as well. The absence of adequate technological manpower in these industries, the absence of new capital investment, the absence of schemes required to stabilize the operation of these industries has allowed many of these industries — themselves the producers of basic machinery — to be equipped and to use production methods that are elsewhere recognized as obsolete. The result is that many of these crucial industries, such as shipbuilding, machine tools, heavy electric machinery, printing machinery, textile machinery, and the like are at a point at which they require and can utilize major infusions of technological manpower and new productive capital.

Our condition can be somewhat better understood, I think, if we see what has happened in these industries in the United States as compared, for example, to the situation in countries in the Common Market. In the Common Market countries, of all the goods and services (i. e., the Gross National Product), produced in a recent year, 1960, 10 per cent were used for the purchase of new machinery and equipment. In the United States, in that same period, our industries spent, all told, 5 per cent of our Gross National Product for new machinery and equipment. In the Common Market, again, the expenditure for all military purposes in this same year was 4 per cent of their Gross National Product, and in the United States it was 10 per cent. This inversion in those proportions of our productive wealth which are placed into new means of production as against instruments of a military sort has as its consequence the rapid growth rate and rapid expansion of economic opportunities for the countries of the Common Market, and the deflation of such opportunity in the last years in the United States. This is a major clue to why there is a substantial rate and quantity of unemployment in the United States, even with unprecedentedly large governmental peacetime spending. This anamoly results from the fact that government spending is predominately in an area in which the production of goods and the performance of services leads to no further production of goods and services.

Military products do not lead to other production. Neither are they used in any other economic exchange. Even the technologies that are developed for military purposes do not tend to flow or spill over into the civilian side of the economy. With notable exceptions, such as the use of radar for finding things, the massive infusion of capital and manpower into military technology has not been resulting in allied development, spillover development, or multiplier development in civilian technology. On the contrary, the result has been to detract from civilian technological development.

A second problem facing our country, a problem known mainly to a group of financial specialists, though it concerns all of us, is the flight of the dollar, or the flight of gold from the United States. What is involved here, very briefly, is this: The United States Treasury held 24 billion dollars of gold bullion twelve years ago. [4] It now holds 15 billion dollars. Against this 15 billion dollars, there are claims held abroad of 19 billion. Certain countries, in their state banks, hold important blocks of these chips, so to speak, against the United States Treasury. The Bank of France, for instance, recently held about 1. 1 billion dollars in claims against this stock of gold, a political economic factor of no small importance.

Why has there been this drain on gold in the United States? During the last decade, we have had a favorable balance of trade as a regular feature of our economic life, but we have also had an unfa-

---

[4] The figures used here are on the basis of 1963 statistics. —Editor

vorable balance of payments. How can this contrast? Why does a favorable balance of trade become an unfavorable balance of payments?
This has occurred because the favorable balance of trade has been
overwhelmed by the current spending abroad for military purposes,
which has been done in dollars each year. Thus, on the average, the
spending of about 3 billion dollars a year during the last half a dozen
years or so has caused a piling up of dollar claims abroad — hence
claims on the American gold reserve — dollar claims which are not
being used for the purchase of goods and services in the United States.
This process contains the possibility of jeoparidizing the international
value of the dollar and in this way jeoparidizing the international value
of American currency. That this problem exists is significant because it has already had ramified affects upon our government's policy. For example: one of the classic tools available to the federal
government for stimulating capital investment and therefore more
industrial and other activity is the device of lowering the interest rate,
which means making capital cheaper to buy. But the federal government cannot make capital cheaper today because lowering the interest
rate in the United States would be an incentive to many people to move
capital abroad, to other areas where a higher rate of return could be
expected. The inability of the federal government to make one of the
classically plausible moves to encourage domestic economic activity
is owing to the constraints placed on government policy by the problem of the gold reserve.

A third problem which we have developed in American society
is the remarkable and unprecedented concentration of production decision power within the hands of a single government agency. The Department of Defense alone wields decision power over the largest
industrial group in the United States. The Census of Manufacturers
is inadequate as a means to describe this concentration of decision
power in the hands of the Department of Defense, because the products that are required, and ordered, are located in many industries.
But they all have a common feature: a single customer, and that is
the federal government.

Now, about 10 per cent of all the goods and services we produce
have been ordered, directly or indirectly, by the Department of Defense. Since that activity is not evenly spread in the U.S., but is concentrated in particular states and regions, it is as if we had developed
baronies — entire areas of the country whose economic well-being is
controlled by managerial decisions made in the Department of Defense.
It is, indeed, entirely within the competence of the decision-makers
located there to generate conditions of employment or unemployment
in particular areas of the country, depending upon decisions made
about location of defense contracts.

There is the further fact that, as a result of this concentration

of economic power, there has arisen a new class of activity in which
members of the Congress compete with each other in delivering the
goods for the folks back home, by competing for orders from the Department of Defense for their areas. This has created a bureaucratic
statism of hitherto unknown dimensions and importance in American
society.

A fourth problem developed in this country is the sustained neglect of 30 to 40 million Americans who live in poverty. In March,
1961, the editors of Fortune described this occupation group not only
in words, but also in a special section of vivid photographic portraits.
Approximately one out of every six Americans is living in conditions
of deep, unmistakeable poverty: inadequate housing, poor food, poor
medical care, absence of ordinary amenities, such as proper running
water, plumbing, electricity, or the like. In order to lift this group
from a condition of poverty to one of sufficient affluence to become a
part of an American consumer market for soft and durable goods,
there is a clear need to make this group productive, that is, make it
possible for them to earn incomes. Then, and only then, will one-
sixth of the potential American consumer market become operative as
a consumer merket. Obviously this has the widest implications for
marketing managers of firms producing consumer goods.

Then there is a fifth problem. While we have been concentrating
on military development at home and abroad, we have allowed more
than half the world's population to remain in bleakest poverty, and
even in daily hunger. We have failed to use our unmatched technological resources for the acceleration of the economic development of
the rest of the world. The bitter price of this policy, and the concomitant emphasis on military assistance and military pacts with
these countries, is the very chain of development we have seen in
Cuba and the prospect of a chain of Cubas without end.

As long as the possibility of economic development is not offered, and offered under conditions which allow for an option of personal and political freedom to developing countries, it is clear why
the Soviet or the Chinese types of society appear as altogether reasonable models to be used by these countries. Economic development
carried out by the extraction of capital from impoverished people can
be done only by using severe police measures to discipline the population for this purpose. I am suggesting, literally, that none of us
placed in such a position would be able to operate otherwise. In order
to have the option of some personal and political freedom, or development to occur under conditions where there can be growth of industrialization and parallel growth of personal well-being. There are
feasible ways for making that possible. These require certain key
infusions of capital, a type of developmental "seed money" placed in
strategic places; they also require available capital in the form of

technological talent, machinery, and the like. There are feasible ways of accelerating these processes which we have hardly begun to tap.

Recently, Mr. Morris Forgash, president of the U. S. Freights Corp., formulated a plan for an international banking institution. His plan is to establish an International Bank for Accelerating Economic Development, whose primary task will be to undertake land reform in many areas of the world, on a conventional banking basis. The justification for this was that such loans, on an ordinary banking basis, are entirely plausible and prudent because land reform characteristically results in major increases in agricultural productivity and, therefore, a high plausibility of repayment of loans.

In 1945, during the occupation of Japan, land reform was carried out under the direction of General MacArthur, which resulted in a 20 per cent increase in Japanese agricultural productivity. The result was that in recent years Japan has become a net exporter of rice. There is no reason why, under appropriate conditions, similar results could not be attained in Asia, Africa, and Latin America, wherever a reasonable effort is made.

The United States Government has yet to give serious attention to the possibility of establishing such institutions. It is entirely possible to deal with the problem of generating human resources or capital in new ways in these underdeveloped countries. The absence of trained personnel is one of the major brakes on economic development in most of the world.

How do you overcome the illiteracy barrier? In _most_ countries this is attempted by teaching teachers, who in turn are expected to teach teachers to teach teachers. That kind of multiplication of human ability to communicate literacy and other basic knowledge takes a long time and is costly. There are ways of shortening this process. Certainly, for the communication of such basic knowledge as literacy, how to cook, how to care for one's self, how to care for a baby, how to improve the soil, how to make appropriate bricks for building a better house, television could be used. It is surely within the competence of the United States to prefabricate networks of television transmitters and receivers such that one hundred to two hundred persons could at one time watch the screen on a television set, at a cost of no more than $150 per unit, each unit having its own power generating source: a very inexpensive device for conducting mass teaching. There is no reason why it should not be possible by such means to break the literacy barrier in many underdeveloped countries within the span of a single year. There is no reason why such methods could not be used to produce a swift and extensive multiplying effect in accelerating the products of economic development.

The solutions of these five problems share a common requirement, and that is the necessity for transferring technological competence, manpower, and capital from the military-producing industries
in which they produce dead-end products, to industries and activities
in which the creative competence of our people can generate productive results on a wide scale. Each of these problems is the result of
the absence of productive resources in a particular sphere. Each of
them requires a shift of productive resources. And if my previous
line of reasoning has any merit at all, then we may well be at the
point where we are capable of moving resources of large size from
military to civilian industry and allied activities.

The conversion of resources on a large scale can not be carried
out automatically by push button, but requires thoughtful planning —
thoughtful planning in each firm, in each factory, in each laboratory,
in each university, in each technological institute. In large industrial
plants such planning could very well require a year's time and even
more. But that kind of lead time is not unreasonable and might even
be shortened, given a powerful incentive.

It is estimated that our society has requirements, in private
and public markets, for a great variety of products whose production
and use would vastly enhance our lives. These are in the areas of
our own housing, transportation, and education, and economic development in the rest of the world. The range of products needed for
these possible uses has been partly detailed in certain studies by the
Arms Control and Disarmament Agencies in reports to the Secretary
General of the United Nations. There is no great mystery here. The
range of activity actually covers all the areas of internal underdevelop-
ment in American society.

Are we equipped to undertake this development? To contemplate this conversion? To begin acting on it in a creative way? I believe that certain attitudes, widely spread in our society, may have
a very important role to play in this matter. Many Americans and I
say many because I am confident that the number is considerable
even though I do not know how many, hold with the following view:
that economic development in Asia, Africa, and Latin America is
necessarily and best carried out under dictatorial regimes.

The second view held by some substantial number of people is
that a hierarchical mode of society is a more efficient one, even in
already developed countries.

A third fear of many people is that even partial disarmament,
or cessation, or cutback in military activity, would result in an
economic depression in the United States. In short, this mode of
reasoning suggests that the United States cannot permit itself to be
involved in disarmament because that would be to leave us politically
naked.

On political and allied grounds, I do not accept any of these propositions. And I want to emphasize here only that the acceptance of these propositions involves a totally defeatist prognosis for American society — defeatist not only politically but, since the implied argument is the necessary commitment to military methods, this is a defeatism that implies the deepest kind of social pessimism. Since no one knows how to conduct and win a nuclear war, in any humanly meaningful sense of that term, and since a nuclear war means defeat for all of us, to hold the propositions that compel one to rely only on military methods and on the risk of nuclear war is tantamount to holding a view that presses governments to take this risk. Many of our countrymen hold the view that there is no alternative, today, other than to rely on the military as a basis for international power. The assumption is that only military methods can be efficiently used for resolving conflicts among nation-states, that political power is finally based on the wielding of military force, and that there is no other plausible basis for wielding political power.

These propositions, stated boldly in this way, immediately suggest an alternative proposition — that political power can be based on industrial and economic competence, that there is no reason why we should be compelled to organize ourselves so as to seek political power or political results only by military means.

I have suggested elsewhere, in a book called The Peace Race, that the United States today has the competence to mount a set of policies aimed toward scoring a win for personal and political freedom around the world if it will use its industrial ability to make possible the option of freedom in societies in Asia, Africa, and Latin America, and that such ability constitutes an industrial basis for political power.

In a forthcoming book on Our Depleted Society (Holt, Rinehart and Winston), New York, 1965, I have diagnosed the damage that has been done to America by sustained emphasis on overkill, and what must be done to move toward a productive society.

I submit to you that this power issue must be faced. We must ask ourselves, "Is it possible to organize an international community of nations on the basis of relationships in which conflict will exist, will be expected, but will be resolved by a resort to instruments of power other than military?" Those who hold that there is no alternative add that the United States would be helpless, vis-a-vis the Soviet Union or Chinese society, if these societies were confronted with other than military power, not only give a prognosis of political defeat for American society but for all human society. For we are now in the condition of multiplied military overkill, and the requirement for extricating ourselves from the implications of that condition and

from the use of this military competence is to discover and begin to
practice systems of international relationships in which constructive,
creative vigor replaces military force.

SELECTED REPORTS, 1961-63

Seminar on Problems of Conversion from Military to Civilian
Economy. Columbia University

**McDonnagh and Zimmerman, A Program for Civilian Diversification
of the Airframe Industry, 215 pp.
Dreiblatt, D., Estimated Direct Employment Effects of Selected
Programs of Public Works Projects—With Special Reference
to Disarmament, 98 pp.
Krause, R. P., Implications of Disarmament for the United States
Ship Building and Repairing Industry, 58 pp.
Guarino, T. A., Economic Capacity of the Soviet Union in a Disarma-
ment Environment, 77 pp.
Scheiber and Tchimenoglou, Brooklyn Naval Shipyard: A Program
for Conversion, 105 pp.
Bloch, A., U. S. Industrialization Assistance, 44 pp.
Gorgol, J., Economic Effects of Military Procurement in New
Jersey, 21 pp.
Shepard, S., Economic Aspects of Disarmament: Research and De-
velopment, 80 pp.
Spertus, E. D., An Investigation of the Relative Enterprise Costs
in the Common Market and the United States, 115 pp.
Araten, M., Housing Needs and Disarmament, 59 pp.
Sitlick, M., Market Analysis of Public Health in the United States,
97 pp.

Note: These reports are available in manuscript form at Columbia University.
Copies may be ordered at 10 cents per page plus $1 for handling. Prepaid check to
Columbia University. Order from Librarian, Engineering Library, Mudd Building,
Columbia University, New York, N.Y.. 10027.
**Available as part of the collection of papers on conversion problems: Vol I —
Impact of the Defense Program on National Manpower and Economic Growth;
Vol II — Conversion of Defense and Space Resources to Civilian Needs..Obtainable
from: Labor and Public Welfare Committee, U.S. Senate, Washington 25, D.C.

SELECTED BIBLIOGRAPHY

On Economics of Disarmament and Conversion to Civilian Economy

The United States position and proposals on general and complete disarmament:

> United States Arms Control and Disarmament Agency (US ACDA), Blueprint for the Peace Race, Superintendent Documents, US Government Printing Office, Washington, D. C., May, 1962, 30 cents.

A report by a distinguished panel of economists on the general economics of disarmament:

> US ACDA, Economic Impacts of Disarmament, Superintendent of Documents, US Government Printing Office, Washington, D. C., January, 1962, 15 cents.

For a more detailed economic analysis of the impact of disarmament, as well as the range of industrial opportunities to replace military programs:

> US ACDA, The Economic and Social Consequences of Disarmament (US reply to the inquiry of the Secretary General of the United Nations) Superintendent of Documents, US Government Printing Office, July, 1962, 35 cents.

Industrial and political implications of an American strategy in relation to the Soviet system, based upon US industrial power:

> Melman, Seymour, The Peace Race, New York, George Braziller, 1961, $3.95. In paperback, Ballantine Books, N. Y. 50 cents.

For a summary of a Senate study on industrial conversion feasibility:

> Humphrey, Sen. Hubert H., Economic Impact of Arms Control Agreements — Study by Senate Subcommittee on Disarmament. (Congressional Record, October 5, 1962.

Papers on industrial management problems in conversion to civilian industry:

> New York Regional Conference on Industrial Conversion and Development, June 12, 1962, Hofstra College, Hempstead, Long Island, N. Y. A conference initiated by Division of Business, Hofstra College, and Department of Industrial Management Engineering, Columbia University; report is 70 pages, and may be obtained for $1.00 from S. Melman, 320 S. W. Mudd, Columbia University, New York, N. Y. 10027.

Analyses of American security policy emphasizing economic aspect:

> A Strategy for American Security — An Alternative to the 1964 Military Budget: a report submitted by a group of inde-

pendent specialists; ed., Seymour Melman, April, 1963.
Copies available from Lee Service, Inc., 48 East 21st
Street, New York, N. Y. 10010. 50 cents.

A major collection of studies in economics of disarmament:

Benoit, Emile, and Boulding, Kenneth (eds.), Disarmament
and the Economy, New York, Harper and Row, 1963.

Benoit, Emile, "Adjustments to Arms Control, Journal of
Arms Control, 1:105-11, 1963.

Benoit, Emile, and Boulding, Kenneth, The Economic Consequences of Disarmament, Center for Research on Conflict
Resolution, 1961.

"The Economic Impact of Disarmament in the United States,"
in Seymour Melman's (ed), Disarmament: Its Politics and
Economics, American Academy of Arts and Sciences, 1962.

Boulding, Kenneth, "Economic Implications of Arms Control,"
in Donald Brennan's (ed) Arms Control, Disarmament,
and National Security, 1961.

Brand, Horst, "Disarmament and the Prospects of American
Capitalism," Dissent, Summer, 1962.

Feinstein, Otto, "Michigan Economic Myths: Defense Contracts,
Jobs, and Affluence," Monograph No. 1, Impact of Foreign
Policy on the Community, Wayne State Univ., 1963. Copies
by request to Monteith College, Wayne State Univ., Detroit 2, Michigan, attention Otto Feinstein.

Leontieff, Wassily W., and Hoffenberg, Marvin, "The Economic Effects of Disarmament", Scientific American
April, 1961.

Melman, Seymour, (ed.), Disarmament: Its Politics and Economics, American Academy of Arts and Sciences, Cambridge, Mass., 1962.

Melman, Seymour, "The Economics of Armament and Disarmament," Our Generation Against Nuclear War, Spring,
1962; also in New University Thought, Spring, 1962.

United Nations, Dept. of Economic and Social Affairs, Economic and Social Consequences of Disarmament, 1962.

Training for Basic Research in the Behavioral Sciences: A Necessary Direction in Human Survival

_____RAY L. BIRDWHISTELL

The story of Joseph, his dreams, their intrepretation, and Joseph's consequent promotion to high position have intrigued scholars from a multiple of disciplines. The inspirationist, the intuitionist, and the psychoanalyst have found Joseph's anticipation of the Egyptian disasters exemplary of their formulations.

I remember the night that I first thought about Joseph as an anthropologist. I was walking back to my cabin after a late evening session with Long John Alexander, my Kutenai informant. The Lower Kutenai Indians, living in the Selkirks that range west of the Rockies in British Columbia, depended for subsistence upon the fish traps set in spring along the Kootenay River. The fishing season began when the warming winds brought the quick thaw to the mountains and the snow water overflowed the river banks of the Kootenay and the Columbia. Fish traps, properly prepared and correctly set in the gullies along the river, provided the Kutenai with a harvest of fish as the receding waters from the subsiding flood returned to the original river bed.

That night Long John had told me how they chose the Fish Chief, the man responsible for organizing Kutenai fishing. If the choice of Chief was fortunate and the selected leader's timing correct, the Kutenai could lay by an enormous quantity of fish for the coming winter. A misjudgment, on the other hand, could leave the community dependent upon the autumn deer drive, led by a comparably chosen Deer Chief. Long John's description gave me real insight into the complex blend of mysticism and pragmatism centered around the Chief, his training, selection, and leadership. There is neither inherited leadership nor a simple election among the Kutenai. Conversely, a Kutenai does not knowingly seek to be selected as a leader. Leadership carries too much heavy responsibility and there is little reward other than prestige; absolute equality of division of the harvest and multiple leadership patterning prevents accumulation of power or goods through leadership position. Among the Kutenai there is no school for Chiefs.

According to Kutenai tradition, around the time of puberty a young man goes alone into the mountain. He fasts while awaiting the vision that will instruct him about his future life course, his responsibilities, and the talents with which the spirits of nature will equip him. Only he can know of his vision and its instructions; as he matures, his personality and performance will hint of these to his fellow tribesmen. The Kutenai know that from the novitiates will come their future Chiefs. As the young mature, they are watched carefully for clues indicating the directions of their emerging talents. Long John denied that they steered the special interests of these lads, but it is clear that a boy already alerted by vision would specially attend to certain teaching. (And no society could long exist blind to its replacement needs.)

As nature signaled the approach of spring, stories around the fire in the main lodge turned more and more to the mixed history and mythology of past fishing seasons. The man or the men whose performances or interests gave evidence that their power was related to fishing sat and stared into small sacred balsam smoke fires for visional instruction. In the smoke appeared figures which, when interpreted, would guide the building, the location, and the timing of trap placement. This was no simple matter. Unless properly placed, but a few fish would be caught, the main body of fish escaping into the river along new escape routes cut by the flooding river.

The Kutenai were not angry at their Chief when his miscalculations led to a poor harvest; they felt only that his Power was fading and that a new Chief should be chosen for the following season. No Kutenai is encumbered with chieftainship for life. In fact, the Kutenai were sure that such leadership was only for the young mature; as a man approached middle age his Power faded and he could enjoy life unburdened by special responsibilities. The spirits realized this and often, even before the Chief's harvests indicated declining Power, the figures in the smoke, either by their indistinctness or by direct instruction, signaled that it was time to choose a new Fishing Chief. Old Kutenai Chiefs did not "only fade away." Night after night they joined the other men in the storytelling sessions around the fire—memories resurrected and retold became part mythology and part natural history—the subject matter of the education of succeeding generations of leaders.

Even if we discount the nostalgia which sweetens an old man's memory, we must accept the fact that this was a relatively successful method for organizing the subsistence procedures of a hunting and gathering society. Protected from invading enemies by rough country around this fruitful area, Kutenai selection, training, and testing procedures were sufficient to keep several hundred Kutenai alive on some ten thousand square miles of game-filled land. It was a functional adaptation; that is, it was functional so long as the tight interdependence of the ecology of the Upper Columbia watershed was not thrown off rhythm by cataclysm.

There was nothing in Kutenai cosmology to give the Kutenai insight into the <u>principles</u> which governed the regularity, the cyclicity of the climatological factors which regulate the proportions of the spring flood and runoff. Natural variations in the population of fish and deer and in that of the predators, animal or bacteriological, who competed with man were probably seldom of consequence to the Kutenai, since they needed such a small proportion of the game to maintain themselves.

Kutenai religion instructed that everything in nature held something for man—that man had but to recognize his relationship to nature to receive its gifts. This optimistic philosophy was seldom contradicted by the experience of life in a benevolent land. Shortages were temporary, and while the Kutenai did tell stories of starvation times, such stories are better characterized as vehicles of moral instruction about sharing than as horror tales of starvation.

It is not difficult to see why eighteenth and early nineteenth century philosophers sentimentalized such an adaptation as this. The return to such an existence cannot fail to have allure for a thoughtful man beset by changes in his world which he cannot comprehend. <u>Natural</u> education with a <u>natural</u> emergence of leadership in a <u>natural</u> setting is seductive—if we limit the view of Kutenai history to a period extending from about 1700 until around the turn of this century.

The Kutenai, in their adaptation, demonstrate that attribute which distinguishes man from other animals. He has culture. That is, he is specially adapted to belong to a grouping able to accumulate experience, to abstract that experience, in or out of awareness, and to pass it on to succeeding generations, which are equally unaware of the processes which organize their existence. The Kutenai were fortunate in that their ecology was both fruitful and regular; it swings and vacillations were minimal and relatively inconsequential. This ability to exploit the regularities of nature without understanding them is human, not Kutenai. The wise old Bushman in the Kalahari Desert, the ancient Abo who can still find food when Australia has been burned by drought, use the same talent to live in far less hospitable lands. <u>But,</u> only if the cyclical swings of nature are within the range of human preparedness is this sufficient.

To return briefly to Joseph—it is easy to see how impressed the urban Egyptians must have been when this boy, raised around the herdsmen's campfires, drew together the minimal cues from his background and, fortified by their appearance in dreams, made his interpretation of the out-of-awareness knowledge which he shared with the Pharaoh. He abstracted the cycle of fertility and famine along the Nile and became the confidant of the king. Our delight in this story and its consequence (we remember that the Pharaoh, with his foreknowledge, hoarded food and, by judicious trading, gained control of all the wealth of Egypt,) obscures the earlier dream which had brought Joseph to the Pharaoh's attention. The reader will recall that Joseph's initial tour de force occurred when, as a shrewd observer of the Egyptian palace social organization, he interpreted the dreams of the imprisoned baker and butler. Correctly, he anticipated the hanging of the baker and the return to power of the butler. Shrewdly, he instructed the butler not to forget the incident and to bring it (and Joseph) to the Pharaoh's attention. We remember the Pharoh's dream and have only vague recall of the butler's and the baker's dreams. We have been able to understand the regularity of the Nile. Perhaps we have such a hazy recollection of the earlier dream because we cherish the fiction that the butler, the baker, and the Pharaoh had only individual histories— the butler's lucky (or blessed), the baker's unlucky (or cursed), and the Pharaoh's, like all leaders, wise, arbitrary, or foolish. Joseph as folk sociologist has remained hidden, adumbrated by his reputation as folk meteorologist and administrator.

The folk tales and the histories of many societies contain stories of the results of brilliant inductions from minimal cues. The names of the inductors are lost, their acts of insight having been assigned to anthropomorphic deities or even to zoomorphic progenitors. Until recently, the act of abstracting or generalizing from experience, an essentially human attribute, has been misunderstood. Man, as mystic, sought dignity in denial of the human characteristic. Crystal balls, tea leaves, or horoscopes manipulated by men inspired by the deity or in league with the devil are only slightly easier explanations of insight than some in vogue today. In effect, they do not differ qualitatively from more modern rationalizations which phrase insight in terms of particular but vaguely located neural and physiological superiorities. In a world which seeks gods and devils inside man's physiological or psychological frame, such rationalizations preclude the recognition of the unconscious and out-of-awareness social accumulate of information available to systematic observation and research. But little better equipped than preliterate man for understanding the mechanisms of ordered investigatory thought, we are continuously tempted to think of the innovative summarizer as a master of flash deduction. Without being aware of it, we retain old mysticisms when we explain his unusual organization of data as a result of a force called "genius." It is easy to forget that we are being poetic when we use terms like "gifted" and "talented" to describe unusual men of whom we approve. Our legitimate appreciation of special contributions becomes deleterious to the development of science when we allow such preformationistic judgments to rationalize poor recruiting, inept teaching, and the shortage of trained investigators.

As educators and as research administrators we have little need to reproach ourselves if, in the primary analysis, contributions to the comprehension of man rest upon talent rather than upon training, brilliance rather than upon application, upon serendipity rather than upon planning and systematic investigation. Educational and administrative responsibility is reduced if we can think of discovery as finally related to intellectual valence—if, after all, only every tenth or twentieth or hundredth student or professional will be productive. We cannot be blamed if productivity is, all other things ignored, dominated by probability.

Even the most ardent nativist must recognize the accelerating expansion of man's awareness of the decipherability of nature; there is no denying that a decade in the past century has produced more original thought than a millennium in the more distant past. Yet, as Boas (1) and Radin (2) pointed out so brilliantly, there is no qualitative biological, neurological, or even psychological difference between so-called primitive and modern man. The pre-literate native, so far as we can detect, lacks none of the physiological equipment of his counterpart in more technologically advanced societies. Early man did not, however, have the cultural equipment, the accumulated knowledge (or the methodology) to investigate nature purposively, without recourse to magical, extraordinary, transcendental, or supernatural explanations which inevitably limit observation and foreclose experimentation. Early man could observe nature, but he could not do it on purpose. He lacked explicit techniques which would make it possible for others to test his procedures and to apply their principles in other areas. His results could be tested pragmatically, but without procedures which could be abstracted and generalized, the universe to which they were applicable was special and limited. Furthermore, conclusions arrived at by hunch often become concretized in culture. Conventionalized into favored reifications, they preclude investigation and new comprehension. Most seriously, skills which are not conceptualized can not be taught, they can only be learned.

No realistic history of science can ignore the monumental advances in theory and methodology made by Western man during the past two or three centuries. Radical shifts in approach and methodology have preceded and followed every new perspective upon nature. Yet it would be easy to deceive ourselves by overconcentration upon the positive elements of what I feel to be less than a complete intellectual revolution. Methodologies can become as sacralized, as concretized, and as reified as any other idea. Secularity is easily overwhelmed by devotion, and methodology becomes ritual as it gains devotees. The borderline between magic and science is often vague. Merlin would not feel a stranger at many research conferences. As an anthropologist I have often been unable to distinguish at one conceptual level between many of the operations of a Siberian shaman in his ritual of divination and those of certain sociologists in their rituals of IBMification. There is a haunting similarity between the image of a West African exhorting his gods and of a young psychologist invoking chi square and plus or minus one sigma. It takes little stretch of theory to classify together the Arabic astrologer and the abstraction-juggling young anthropologist. Any time a method becomes the method, the forces of deceleration in science are set into action. When the object matter of a method is the behavior of man himself, such tendencies to sacralize are reinforced by man's need to hide the rationale of his behavior from himself.

It was popular twenty-five years ago to describe the distance between our knowledge about man and about the remainder of nature as a case of "cultural lag." No such easy tag can suffice to explain away our present anxieties over the growing need for knowledge about man. Sober men are increasingly driven to ask why we know so relatively little about man. The realities of life in a modern world demand reappraisal of both the state of this knowledge and our capacities for improving it. We are forced to care. The race to stimulate the healthy and rapid growth of the underdeveloped countries in a nuclear era, the almost overwhelming awareness of the overpopulation threat, the impact of automation with its consequent ills are only slightly more demanding than our recognition that our educational system has hardly kept pace with the demand for an educated citizenry. Mental health has recently captured the nation's imagination. If possible, this problem area is more dependent upon and is based upon even less basic information about man than are these others.

Two generations ago social scientists complained with reason that their knowledge, their warnings, and particularly their solutions went to waste in a "practical"-minded world. Administrators, whether in business, government, education, or medicine, had little time for scientifically oriented ruminations about man. Traditional pessimisms and optimisms about man, however superstitious and however unsupported by experience, provided a sufficient and popular rationale for planning and decision-making in their expanding hard-goods world. However, two wars, cyclical depressions, and the impact of life in a planet-sized world combined with the incomprehensible advancements in the physical sciences shook the administrators' uneasy contempt for theory. With McCarthy as shaman, the nation put the intellectual through a massive rite de passage. [1] From a position of being toler-

---

[1]Joseph McCarthy, an otherwise undistinguished senator from Wisconsin, headed a senatorial investigating committee during the early 1950's. Following dramatic public ceremonies he was exorcised by a competitive governmental agency. "McCarthyism" is a term used to describe attack through unsupported charges.

ated and patronized, the intellectual was, for a period, feared and hated, and finally was graduated into his present position of impersonal support and adulation. The social and behavioral scientist now finds himself sought after. He still complains that he speaks unheard, but at least, every self-respecting organization now has slots in its table of operations for him to fill.

It would be easy to say that there has been no real change in the position of the behavioral scientist and his relationship to the "practical" world. Even a cursory review of the past decade reveals that while billions of dollars have been poured into the solution of recognized technological problems in government, education, and medicine, only pennies have been invested in the anticipation of the impact of these developments upon man. But money is an attractively visible answer. A great deal has recently been said about the difficulty of administering research funds toward effective research. It would be unprofitable to repeat this discussion here. "Bureaucracy" is an easy they upon which the uneasy and over-respected scientist can displace his anxiety and guilt. The fact of the matter is that the administrator is eager for his researchers to produce, and the behavioral scientist feels pregnant and overdue. Yet both are deeply disturbed and dissatisfied by the present rate of productivity.

As an anthropologist engaged in full-time research, it seems to me that there are two central and interrelated processes that impede and frustrate human behavioral research. We need fundamental ideas about man's behavior, and we need trained men to test these ideas. Much that passes for research today is little more than the reworking of exhausted lodes by miners whose training is out of time, if not out of date. If we are to take advantage of public acceptance, we must learn more basic geology and minerology; social science strip mining is insufficient. If we are to comprehend man in his new world, we must look at man and nature in a fresh way. And we must find researchers trained to be willing to take the risk of making new surveys, motivated to look for the unknown and supported consistently in expectation of the likely failure of this search.

About ten years ago, anticipating the need for a different approach to research in mental health, a farsighted governor and legislature in the Commonwealth of Pennsylvania established Eastern Pennsylvania Psychiatric Institute for the purpose of stimulating both basic and applied behavioral research. A great deal of effort has gone into the attempt to provide a productive setting for original and fundamental research. The results thus far have been noteworthy but always limited by problems of adequate personnel. We have had great difficulty in locating young researchers broadly trained in the behavioral sciences, or even young men and women who can or will invest in being trained as original researchers. Relatively liberal salaries and good working conditions can not make up for the shortage of trained investigators. For instance, neither we nor, I am told, anyone else can find young graduate students or recent Ph. D. 's who have the foggiest notion of how to observe or interview about human behavior. Whizzes with a table of random numbers or in the preparation of questionnaires, experienced with a Holarath punch or a Rorschach card, elegant in programming, and expert at running rats or cockroaches, are totally unprepared to do disciplined observation of human interaction and are so dependent upon a schedule that they couldn't conduct an open interview with their own families. Herein, it seems to me, lies the arena of our problem. The academy is not providing the research center with trained, disciplined, but flexible investigators. And where such wonders can be found, they are often wasted re-exploring exhausted territory.

It would be easy to rationalize the limited contribution of the behavioral sciences as a function of their very short life history. Youth, for Americans, is always a suspiciously easy explanation of poor or erratic performance. To be fair, in the case of these disciplines directly concerned with man and his behavior, as experimental or observational sciences they are less than three generations old. With the exception of psychology, the behavioral sciences have produced only a few trained men as compared to the physical sciences. Only a very small proportion of these, once they got their degree, have had either the time, the resources, or the inclination to devote themselves to research. Most of them have been teachers of teachers of teachers; their research, part of their initiation, is an aspect of the rite de passage of the Ph. D. Psychology has produced large numbers of Ph. D's, but a review of the literature reveals that there is no clear relationship between the number of practitioners in the field and significant results in productive basic research activity. Many of these graduates have been drained off into the clinic as testers or therapists. Demonstrated utility in these areas as well as in other applied fields has put a tremendous demand on the graduate schools of psychology to produce practitioners, clinicians, or psychic engineers rather than scientists. It is true that some clinicians engage in research, but they are usually so overloaded that research is at best a bootlegged pursuit.

Experimental psychology, unfortunately, as it pulled away from philosophy and religion, became cursed by scienticism. To extend the old saying about the trees and the forest, many psychologists can no longer see the trees for the twigs. Even the kindest reviewer of the progress of experimental psychology must regret the increasingly sterile preoccupation of psychological experimenters with method. No critic can carp about concern with method. However, all too often methodological discussion among the experimentalists is so encumbered by the need to prove that psychologists are scientists that results are adumbrated by rituals of design and presentation. Preoccupation with minutiae elegantly studied, however of much concern to themselves, has severely reduced experimental psychology's contribution to its fellow behavioral scientists.

Anthropology, the smallest in numbers of the behavioral sciences, has produced out of this small number relatively few basic researchers. Teaching, applied activity, and shortage of research funds have combined with a romanticized self-image to limit the activities of even the few inclined to undertake a research career. As in the case of the other social sciences, much of the research done by anthropologists has been limited to the field work directed toward the Ph. D. However, anthropologists have produced a wider range of research data than have their fellow behavioral scientists. Part of this heterogeneity of research object and design seems owing to the kinds of people recruited into anthropology; more important, probably, is the fact that the graduate school morality among anthropologists weighs against the dissertation's being merely an extension of the professor's work. The young anthropology graduate student is encouraged to prove himself as an independent researcher. Thus, as anthropology matured, it has broadened (some would say beyond recognition) rather than narrowed as a discipline. Furthermore, anthropology, a direct descendant of and still self-consciously related to, biology, has not been cursed by devotion to a single procedure as THE scientific method. Already confident that they are scientists, anthropologists have less need to be resistant to methodological eclecticism. Often they are negative toward quantitative methods, but review of the literature demonstrates that they have used such techniques when they seem appropriate. (See, particularly, the work in anthropological genetics.) Whatever the advantage of its tradition, the fact remains that, while anthropologists train general anthropologists, anthropological researchers, with the possible exception of the anthropological linguists and the archaeologists, are largely self-selected, self-made, and self-motivated. As a cynical colleague of mine, a psychologist, put it, "I enjoy anthropologists on a research team; they are such charming amateurs."

Sociology lies somewhere between psychology and anthropology in all these respects. Probably somewhat more productive than either in the proportion of major theoretical advances based on research, it remains true that sociology, like its sister behavioral sciences, has produced, compared with the physical sciences, relatively little in the way of basic science. Long attracted by indirect methods of examining man's behavior, sociology in many centers today threatens to become increasingly scientistic and to move even further away from its data. The computer room may well become the sociologist's cloister, his haven from contact with mankind. Regretfully, as I look at recent developments in sociology I cannot help but recall the story about the astronomer who petitioned the National Space Administration to move the moon into a more distant orbit so that he could examine it with the too-powerful telescope provided on a National Science Foundation Grant. Presbyopia is, in all three fields, too often mistaken for perspective.

Even taken seriously, these remarks about current trends in the three central behavioral sciences deal only with the contingencies of the situation in the behavioral sciences today. It seems to me that the problem with which we must deal has its inception in certain directions taken by the behavioral sciences some seventy years ago. The behavioral sciences achieved separate status late in the history of the development of science. Sired by the physical sciences, they tore themselves from the jealous maternity of the humanities, of philosophy and religion. Blinded by the brilliance of the successes in mechanics, chemistry, and physiology, few could attend to the importance of the maturational history of these fields. Sophisticated men, they saw little need to repeat the mistakes of their fellow scientists. But the visibility of these errors adumbrated the importance of more positive propaedeutics. To say it simply, they leaped the natural history stages of their sciences. Appropriately convinced that man was subject to a materialistic, deterministic approach, they seized upon the tools and the philosophy of their scientific contemporaries, but failed to gain perspective upon the experience which had given birth to these theories and methodologies. Gratified by the plethora of new insights provided by a rationalistic and relativistic approach to man, they were not forced to see how anthropocentric, how ethnocentric was their fundamental preconception of their subject matter, man.

The physicist turned behavioral scientist, Boas, weary with the philosophism of the late nineteenth century, inveighed against armchair investigations and demanded intensive and extensive descriptions of man's behavior before his nature was overgeneralized or particular pieces of his behavior overparticularized and literalized. The American ethnographer, the linguist, and the archaeologist attended to these instructions; the reliability of a half-century of data collection and organization by these scholars attests to the validity of his perspective. Unfortunately, his sound advice had too limited an audience, its appeal too restricted to those already convinced of the necessity for long-term building. He spoke in a period flush with short-term intellectual profit. Limited academic and research budgets, the exigencies of reputation-building and academic promotion, weighed against long-term investment. And to be fair about it, human nature, revealed by Mendelian extension, explained by Watsonian or Pavlovian formulae, made interesting by cross-cultural exotica and somehow made real by census tract quantification, was promising and attractive. Only during these past few years have we become restless under the increasing sterility, shallowness, and dulling repetition of the research descendent from the seminal approaches of the first quarter of the century.

This restlessness comes from two directions. The larger community now demands, in its faith in us, more than promises. The society, as represented by government, by industry, by education, and by medicine is petitioning us for help in the form of talented, skilled, and even adventurous social scientists. These institutions have met our pleas of poverty with offers of support. That social conscience, which has been one of the sustaining virtues of most behavioral scientists, demands reappraisal, reassessment, and reorganization of our educational and training programs; the leadership of the behavioral sciences is unequivocal in its refusal to drain society's energies in aggrandizement through simple expansion. Sociology and anthropology departments, in particular, are engaged in sober self-examination. Long devoted to principles of planning for others, they are beginning to accept their own best advice.

Pressure, whether exerted by the market place or by guilt, has never been sufficient to reorient intellectual direction. The antithesis to established research ways is coming from within the intellectual stream. From my perspective as a full-time researcher, professional research consultant, and avid conference attendant, I see reason to be genuinely optimistic about recent developments in the behavioral sciences. In a free society new ideas and new data dissolve old concretions, albeit sometimes at a painfully slow pace. Series of developments in intricate feedback with each other are more than promising; the revolution they have occasioned is already in motion.

It was said previously that the behavioral sciences skipped the natural history stages of their development. Recent developments in ethology, comparative psychology, information and systems theory, combined with communicational research, are forcing us to relook at man and at society. We are being forced to build a foundation and a framework under the roof and around the interior decoration that has characterized much of behavioral science research. Pioneers in the social and behavioral sciences flushed with early successes, had become experimental and variable-manipulative, and often even quantitative, before they knew enough about their subject matter, man, within his natural context to measure the damage done when they ripped him out for experimentation. Seizing upon techniques and building laboratories appropriate for chemistry and physics, they fell upon data which had not been comprehended in their natural setting. New data and new approaches are forcing us to put man back again, to examine him both as a biological and as a social and cultural being, to comprehend him in context.

The ethologist and, at times, the comparative psychologist are forcing us to face the fact that society preceded man; indeed, social organization was an imperative of existence long before the emergence of Mammalia. When combined with the work of the communicational investigator and assessed by models provided by systems and information theory, we are becoming painfully but jubilantly aware that we must re-examine established certainties that have dominated the behavioral sciences from genetics to ethnology. Cognition, emotion, learning, planning, teaching, group formation and disintegration, social and individual health and pathology all are open to reinterpretation and investigation. As an anthropologist interested in communicative systems, animal and human, I have been forced to realize that there are a series of "simple" givens of human interaction about which I have accumulated only a revitalizing recognition of ignorance. There is space here to list but a few.

The fact that animals transmit information from one to another within a group is now evident. Every indication is that this is a systematic, and a learned and transmitted process. Yet we have not yet decoded any nonhuman species' communicational system. We can domesticate certain animals (and, perhaps, be domesticated by them), but we have been unable to comprehend their system or teach them ours. Geoffrey Bourne recently asked me what, if we were able to crack Chimp (language), I'd like to ask this intelligent primate. Ruefully, I replied, "I'd like to ask him (or her) what size enclosure, what furnishings, and what companionship would he require to tell me the truth about chimpanzee life." We know that normal children in every society, regardless of the structural complexity of their language, learn to speak that language within the first few years of life. But we haven't the foggiest idea what portion of their total experience can be transmitted through that medium. In fact, the truth of the matter is that while we know children learn to talk, we have little comprehension of the mechanisms or the contexts which contribute to the success or failure of this necessary task. Kinetics has given us instructive hints about the importance of ordered, visible body motion behavior in human and animal interaction. Yet we do not have more than the most heuristic of constructions to rationalize the relationship between vocalic and body motion communication. Preliminary investigations point to the importance of other sensory modalities in communication, but we remain ignorant about both the mechanisms and the structures of olfactory, tactile, gustatory, and proprioceptive sensory communicative activity. It seems theoretically sound to see communication as necessarily a multimodal system, describable subsystem by subsystem, but our knowledge of the relationship between this emergent system and the remainder of social activity remains below the level of sensible conjecture.

It is popular, even trite, to say that in this complex world man must learn to communicate on purpose or he will destroy himself by the forces of atrophy if not by raw power. Yet it is not extravagant to say that unless we do the basic and fundamental research necessary in this area of human existence, we must be pessimistic. Language-learning, translation machines, philosophy, logic, grammar, rhetoric, and good intentions are not enough. Until we can, though in preliminary terms, describe how man accommodates to man, we are not going to do very much about improving his interaction with other men, whether this interaction is exemplified in the parent-child, the doctor-patient, the governor-governed, or the ruler-ruled relationship. And we are not going to get this information, we are not going to do this research, until we can get trained behavioral scientists.

Modern man has become a powerful giant—he can do things faster, more powerfully, more constructively or destructively than ever before. But he can plan his actions or understand himself but little better than his preliterate forebears. With the present knowledge of himself and his society, man can either plunge enthusiastically forward, blind to the dangers of his violent manipulations, or, in recognition of his ignorance, withhold his strength—a muscle-bound giant.

My friends in the physical sciences, weary of my nagging jeremiads (the content of which they are already too aware), point to the shifting emphasis in government grants and say that this will surely help overcome the discrepancy between man's knowledge of his technology and his understanding of himself. And, if we consider the existence of money _in itself_ as evidence of an emerging awareness of the need for research in the behavioral sciences, their optimism is justified. However, if one looks at the way in which this money is being spent, there is less reason to be optimistic.

Americans and their government are turning almost religiously to the scientist and have, at great sacrifice, made phenomenal amounts of money available in his name. But at this point something happens; from the flood poured in above, droplets are devoted to _basic_ human research. And often, when projects are appraised, it is abundantly clear that laboratories, equipment, funds, and even good research designs are wasted if the personnel is chosen with an eye to their academic degree rather than to their experience and preparation for the particular project. Competency is not contagious.

Our recruiting devices are not getting us sufficient talent to train, our graduate schools are not designed to prepare broadly trained basic behavioral science researchers, and the available research money is being distributed with more expediency than wisdom. Unless we develop new methods for training behavioral scientists and behavioral science teachers (and we survive), the behavioral sciences may, in the next hundred years—at the present rate of production—equip us to describe this survival. More likely, the society will revolt against the small return that it is getting for its tax dollar and turn to tested coercive methods to control a restless and frustrated citizenry. We already know how to use war, jails, drugs, propaganda, and superstition to handle dissident man. Unless the behavioral sciences can supply new methods, theirs will be a sorry role in the future. Even Joseph could only predict the drought. He couldn't stop it, but he was able to outline the steps for survival during the crisis.

REFERENCES

1. Boas, Franz, The Mind of Primitive Man, New York, Macmillan, 1938.
2. Radin, Paul, Primitive Man as a Philosopher, New York, Appleton, 1927.

Part III

RESEARCH:
NATIONS, WOMEN, CHILDREN

*"Those Macedonians," said he, "are a rude and clownish
people, they call a spade a spade."*
                                                    Plutarch

Many of the theoretical papers in the two previous sections
stressed the importance of research to the advancement of knowledge
about human survival. Part III is devoted to just such investigations.

Psychiatrist Bryant M. Wedge reviews the problems of international communication that became apparent during his stint with the
Foreign Leader Program of the State Department, in which leaders
from abroad were brought here for the express purpose of improving
their understanding of our country. Effective international communication, he concludes, necessitates that we recognize the distinctive nature of national communication patterns. This observation is in accord
with some of the ideas on understanding the opponent's perception of
the conflict, expressed by both Professor Osgood and Professor Rock
in Part I.

How can tension resulting from intergroup conflict be reduced?
Psychologist Muzafer Sherif reports on the results of a series of fascinating studies wherein individuals, previously unacquainted, inter-
acted under conditions favorable for the formation of groups. Thereafter he studied conditions that led to hostility between groups and those
effective in reducing hostility. In an experimental situation that simu-
lated real life, he developed the equivalent of Cold War and then the
measures for achieving peace.

Were we to achieve such peace, or even just large-scale disarmament, great benefits could accrue to the nations of the world. Those
that would take the form of advances in social welfare are examined by
the Director of the Division of Research and Statistics of the Social
Security Administration, Ida C. Merriam. The distress of the large
segment of Americans suffering from poverty could be sharply allevi-
ated were the vast funds pouring into the bottomless barrel of arma-

ment production used instead to alter the economic condition of the poor.

These incentives for peace, and especially the dread of nuclear war, motivated thousands of Americans to join in one or another of the organizations that constitute "the peace movement." Perhaps the largest, the most vocal and influential has been the Women Strike for Peace, which is the subject of a study by sociologist Elise Boulding. She wanted to know what kinds of women composed the group and what drove them to engage in the varied activities of their organization.

The last two papers, by two psychologists, report on the attitudes of children and adolescents to nuclear dangers. In the first, Sibylle K. Escalona presents findings of a questionnaire study in which children were asked their opinions about the world and the future, but not specifically about war and peace. In the second, Milton Schwebel obtained written answers to pointed questions about the war dangers. In both instances the children revealed acute awareness that danger exists and concern for the future of the world. Both authors comment on the implications of their findings.

Nationalism and International Communication

_____ BRYANT M. WEDGE

The research on which this discussion is based was carried out for the special projects division, Research and Reference Service, United States Information Agency; the observations and interpretations are entirely those of the writer and do not necessarily reflect the views of any branch of the United States Government.

The Problem of International Communication

This is an age of nationalism (7). About a third of the world's people are being mobilized in the framework of newly independent nation-states, and another third live in older states which are undergoing radical modernization with acute nationalistic fervor. Even the established and advanced nation-states, despite—and perhaps in response to—their growing collaboration, show every evidence of continued sovereign vigor (9).

National—and nationalistic—societies zealously emphasize their own distinction from all other nations, develop their own viewpoints and styles and value these highly (4, 5). As a consequence, nations and their nationals tend to interpret the world, particularly the extranational world, in their own distinctive national terms, a process which we shall term ethnocentric perception. The ethnocentric perception of information from extranational sources creates special problems for international communication; each participant in such communication is apt to assign unique and special national meanings to items of information, whether these are being presented or received.

At the same time, this is an age of growing interdependence of nations. The technological revolution of this century and the aspirations of all peoples to share its benefits have led to increasing specialization of production, to dependence on trade for vital materials and products, and to economic interdependence of a high order. Communication and transportation systems have shrunk the world, and the ideological bipolarity of world political organization has driven nations together in defensive alliances. Even the conflicting power blocs find themselves strangely interdependent, for the advent of nuclear weapons and practically instantaneous delivery systems requires a most careful balancing of risks and interests to avoid the kind of collision in which everybody loses (8).

The stuff and substance of interdependent relationships is the ability to communicate effectively. Agreements among allies and trading partners must be made, understood, and kept; technical information and political intent must be communicated in the interests of reconciling national needs with common interests. Conflicting parties must somehow convey to each other an accurate understanding of their vital positions so that the level of conflict can be contained in the common interest of avoiding war. So it is that while the processes of nationalism complicate international communication, the requirements of interdependence demand more effective communication between nations. Effective communication implies the ability to convey one's own intentions and views in ways which will be correctly understood. In view of the problems in communication posed by the age of nationalism, it is vitally important that those sciences which are concerned with communication, perhaps particularly those concerned with communication with alienated minds, apply their knowledge and methods to the systematic study of international communication. This is a brief report of one such study.

An Instance of International Communication

The Foreign Leader program of the Department of State represents a particularly intensive and concentrated effort at international communication. Foreign leaders, men of substance and sophistication in their own countries, are invited to the United States, singly or in groups, to improve their own understanding of this country. Their tours, usually lasting from thirty to ninety days, are designed to provide a wide exposure to the United States, its people and institutions, as well as to carry out discussions and interchanges relevant to their fields of technical competence (2). Since such visits have the avowed purpose of conveying information about the United States, each visit may be said to represent an experiment in international communication.

As it happens, this experiment is often observed and mediated by escorts and interpreters (henceforth termed escort-interpreters) furnished by the Language Services Division of the Department of State. These escort-interpreters assist such visitors in their problems with language and in interpretations of the observations which they have made. One hundred escort-interpreters were systematically interviewed concerning their experiences as participant-observers in this international communication process (11). The sample was weighted toward experience with African, Latin American, Japanese, and Soviet visitors. We will report here on some of the problems in communication which they have observed and on techniques which have proved useful in overcoming them. Finally, we will suggest some general principles which we believe to be useful in improving international communication.

Some Problems in International Communication

The ideas that "seeing is believing" and that "the truth speaks for itself" are decidedly erroneous in international communication. Escort-interpreters report instance after instance in which visiting leaders have interpreted their observations in the United States in terms of their particular national viewpoints. In order to exemplify this, I will report instances drawn from several levels of communication, for it is obvious that words and sentences are merely one source of information.

The "language barrier" does, of course, offer some problems, but in the opinion of the majority of our informants, language as such is not a principal source of misunderstanding; first, because it is so apparent that remedies are obvious—interpreters can be found and languages learned—and, second, because nonlinguistic communication has impact at least as profound as the spoken and printed word. It is in the nuances and connotations of words, the feelings which they arouse, the patterns of thought, and the whole conceptual systems which they represent that misunderstandings arise.

Connotations   Innumerable instances of semantic difficulties were reported—some, at least, representing specific local interpretations. Africans, for example, are prone to understand "segregation" as the equivalent of South African apartheid, with undertones of oppression and exploitation of slavelike classes; even well-read leaders may arrive in this country literally expecting to find Negroes in chains. After visits to the southern states, provided they are offered information framed to acknowledge their own views, such leaders often come to a completely new understanding of the qualities of social segregation in the United States as a condition which, regrettable though it may be, is a temporary, historically understandable social problem which is being worked out by Americans, both Negro and white. They still think that segregation, in the American sense, is wrong, but they understand it differently and less critically.

Customs   Information about social customs in the United States, when interpreted in terms of the social systems of other countries, is

frequently perceived in strikingly incorrect ways. Latin American
leaders, and again I emphasize that these are sophisticated and well-
educated men, often expect to find widespread sexual amorality in the
United States—an expectation based on information about the American
system of dating. For in the Latin American social system, it is assumed that improper consequences are certain to follow when a young
man and a young woman are alone together; extensive systems of chap-
eronage and social sanction prevent this impropriety. Thus, the facts
about American dating, particularly the knowledge that this has parental
approval, lead to a decidedly false conclusion, for there is no basis
for understanding the kind of self-restraint and personal responsibility
in these matters which is expected in the dating system. Such a misunderstanding is apt to persist and even be reinforced by observations
of the American scene (American youngsters kiss, a custom which in
Latin America would lead to even more inevitable consequences) unless
explanations are offered which draw distinctions between the moral
customs of Latin America and the United States. Even then the Latin
American is apt to be unbelieving until he has opportunity to test the
explanation from his own observation and experience.

Thought Patterns   Differentiated societies utilize differing methods of arriving at conclusions, of bringing order out of the chaos of
everyday observation and experience. Americans typically "build up a
case, " starting from facts and arriving inductively at conclusions about
them. Russians, as has been shown by Glenn and others, tend to derive their ordering of facts from general principles or definitions (3).
Thus, when the English historian Seton-Williams empirically demonstrated the development of social class distinctions in the Soviet Union,
the Soviet publication New Times hotly replied that it was impossible
to speak of social classes in the Soviet Union since social class depends
upon private ownership of the means of production. It appears that this
argument was based on different preferences for the way in which facts
are to be explained.
    Escort-interpreters repeatedly encounter instances in which dif-
ferences in thought patterns impede the communication of information.
For example, a French economist asked, "What is the state of mind
behind the Peace Corps?" This kind of question is difficult for Americans to understand, much less to answer, for in the interpreter's
opinion the Frenchman was requesting an articulate statement of the
philosophy which preceded the proposal to establish the Peace Corps.
While such philosophies have been devised, it proved difficult, even
for Peace Corps officials, to explain the probable origins of the Peace
Corps idea as a product of pragmatic response to national and international problems of the United States rather than as the outgrowth of
some kind of abstract cerebral process. Yet such explanations prove

important because they demonstrate how the United States tackles its problems.

Concepts Within each nation the way of perceiving the world is apt to be largely determined by the concepts institutionalized in the national system. If one has always lived in a society where citizens are subject to state control in many details of life, it becomes difficult to conceive even the possibility of independent decision-making in such matters as a choice of career. Escort-interpreters for Soviet leaders report that this presents genuinely puzzling problems; many of them cannot conceive of how workable societies can be organized on a basis of extensive individual autonomy. Nor, so far as their grasp of this notion goes, is it so much a source of envy and admiration as Americans, who value their liberty, are prone to suppose. Thus, statements concerning American freedoms have sometimes been noticed to be more conducive to ideas concerning "hidden ruling circles" than otherwise. It is only when some technical problem is being approached, such as the problems of distribution of tractor parts, that meaningful comprehension of the genuine differences of the American system in this respect become comprehensible.

An extreme example of this kind of Soviet assumption was provided by some visitors who were sent unescorted on a commercial airline on short notice. They congratulated their escort on the speed with which the American Secret Service had been mobilized to exercise surveillance. This does not appear to have been a paranoid idea, but rather the expression of an assumption which it would have been too painful to revise.

Emotional Expectation The emotional set or expectation which characterizes the attitude of one national society toward others seems to color the interpretation of information coming from those nations. This was nicely illustrated during Khrushchev's visit to the United States when, as I have reported before, his gesture intended to represent the clasped hands of friendship was interpreted as that "of a victorious prizefighter's" (it is notable that the identical gesture was interpreted in the American press as friendly when offered by a ship's captain whose vessel was carrying missiles back from Cuba), or when his remark that "We will bury you" was persistently taken as an active threat rather than as the milder assertion that "our system will outlive yours," which experts in Russian idiom insist would more accurately represent the intent. (Incidentally, interpreters have to be very careful of American idiom. When a host said recently that he'd "love to visit Minsk before he died," the guest understood this as meaning that he'd rather die than see Minsk and was insulted.) This is not to suggest that Mr. Khrushchev had particularly friendly intentions toward the United States, but to illustrate how emotional expectations may influence perception, especially of ambiguous information.

This exemplification of problems in international communication which arise from the peculiarities of national ethnocentric perception is intended to illustrate the general nature of the problem. Put most simply, this is that people tend to perceive and interpret the world in terms of assumptions built out of their own experience, in terms of the only world they know, as has been most ably demonstrated by Cantril and his colleagues (1). When one's social world has been formed in the context of national existence, all international information tends to be interpreted in national terms. In the face of this tendency it can well be asked how, in an age of nationalism, can information be conveyed internationally with any accuracy at all?

The Improvement of International Communication

Despite all the difficulty involved, the Foreign Leader Program is remarkably effective in conveying information about the United States to representatives of other nations. Almost invariably, such leaders acquire new understanding of the United States, and this is almost invariably conducive to improved relations. How is this achieved?

Escort-interpreters report with great regularity that understanding depends very heavily on the ability to present information in ways which "make sense" to the alien national. Americans, who are quite used to diversity within their own country, are relatively good at such shaping of communication, but it is often the task of the escort-interpreter to assist in rendering information understandable to the visitor.

The biculturality of escort-interpreters is the basis for their special contribution to the conduct of international communication. However, since there will never be enough such persons to satisfy the vast needs of the present age, it is necessary to learn as much as we can from them, which will improve our ability to communicate directly. Their recommendations and experiences suggest four principal requirements for effective international communication. The detailed requirements for communication in a given area of the world would seem to follow from the deliberate and conscious applications of such principles as these:

I. Recognition of Distinctive National Communication Patterns: The most basic principle of international communication insisted on by escort-interpreters is that effectiveness in communication depends upon an adequate recognition of the specific and distinctive qualities of social communication within the communicant's country. It is because this is so fundamental that I have outlined in some detail the problems of ethnocentric national perception of information in the preceding section.

It is never safe to assume that information is being perceived in precisely the way in which it was intended. Interpreters who have worked with Latin Americans, for example, repeatedly emphasize that even an excellent command of language and general Latin culture does not preclude the occurrence of substantial and sometimes serious mis-understandings in attempts at specific communication with given countries. The same message may be quite differently perceived in Bolivia and in Chile, for instance. It is true that a broad level of discourse may be suitable for the generality of Latin America, but on specific questions—where the meat of operational communication lies—it is essential to recognize the existence of critical national differences and to recognize that these are the objects of a great deal of emotional investment.

The implications of this point of view for the conduct of international communication are very broad. Certainly this provides support for the idea of conducting basic communication on a country-by-country level and of making maximum use of current expertise on the communication patterns of a given country. More importantly, however, awareness of this problem allows the international communicator to be continuously alert to the possibilities of communication failures and to be ready to correct them. Failures are not so damaging in themselves except as they go unnoticed and are not compensated for.

No interpreter, however experienced, claims to have a complete knowledge of the current communication pattern of the several countries with which he must deal in a given language area. Furthermore, interpreters are aware that these patterns change in unpredictable ways. Consequently, interpreters are wary of fixed rules and prefer to regard the communication process as a dynamic one, making use of the relatively stable elements of languages and culture which, however, shift in kaleidoscopic patterns.

II. The Shaping of Communications: The kind of information which can be presented and the way in which it must be presented if it is to be understood obviously depend upon the interest and understanding of the audience country. In one circumstance, philosophic texts may be communicative; in another, technical manuals successfully convey information; while in a third, personal contact as exemplified in Peace Corps activities may provide the most effective means of conveying information. The appropriate language must be chosen, and this is not so simple as might first appear—there have been suggestions that Russians acquire more information from English than from Russian language broadcasts for reasons of Russian psychology, a question which I won't attempt to evaluate here. It is a pertinent question whether international communication in Africa is best mediated by native dialects or by the European second languages of a good many countries. But even though it involves many details in an individual case, the issue is a clear one—communication depends upon being understandable to the audience.

The implication of this recommendation is, of course, that one who wishes to communicate must also wish to understand the nature of his audience. This kind of knowledge is cumulative; it grows from experience with a given audience and permits some accuracy in any initial offering of information. For example, experience accumulated with African visitors over the last few years has shown that they tend to be more responsive to information geared to vision and touch, as well as to personal relationship, rather than to the ear and to the abstract or ideologic.

III. Feedback and Correction: A further essential element in international communication is the capacity to assess the way information is being received and understood. Such feedback information permits a process of correction of misunderstanding and a clarification of issues. Cues to the level of understanding may vary, depending on the nature of the audience, from the kinds of questions which are asked about or spontaneous comments which are offered to results of surveys and polls on specific issues.

Rather than belaboring this point, I will only mention the experience of a "college" administrator from an African country whose interests were evidently not immediately grasped. These became clear only after arrangements had been made for her to meet a dean of one of our leading universities who expatiated at some length upon the organization of American higher education. This led the visitor to inquire, "And how many children do you have?" The program was revised and the visit was highly successful.

IV. The Specification of Differences: We live in a world of diversity. The main characteristic of this age of nationalism is the differentiation of national forms of social organization. As a consequence, the aim of international communication has to be understanding of each other but not necessarily agreement with each other. Fortunately, this rests well with the tolerance for diversity and the respect for self-determination which is characteristic of the United States (6). However, for purposes of communication it is especially important that such differences be specified wherever they may be a source of misunderstanding.

In reporting their experiences escort-interpreters frequently related episodes in which the drawing of distinctions between American social styles and values and those of the visitor's home country led to highly fruitful new understandings.[1] For example, some Soviet visitors were upset at seeing the words "Russki Go Home" chalked in Russian on a wall of an industrial plant which they visited. They felt they were being harassed with the sanction of the United States government. The interpreter acknowledged that the appearance of such a sign in the Soviet Union would be most unlikely without some kind of government sanction. The government of the United States, however, no matter how much it might be distressed by such bad manners on the part of its citizens, could do nothing about this, since the Constitution guarantees freedom of expression and so on. The United States and the Soviet Union are, in this respect, simply different: it is not a question of right or wrong, but of the nature of the societies.

The response of many visiting leaders to the specification of difference is one of "Aha, at last I understand the Americans." And such a response usually occurs after the foreign person has become genuinely puzzled by some aspect of the society he is considering. Characteristics of the American scene such as federalism, autonomy of local government, and voluntary associations for practical purposes are foreign to the concepts and practices of a good many other countries, consequently they cannot be understood readily. When these are presented as peculiarities of the American society and not necessarily as any kind of model for any other societies, they can be grasped. Peculiarly enough, when presented in this way, such institutions become considered worthy of partial emulation. Many a visiting leader has returned to his home country determined to attempt the mobilization of volunteers for his particular purposes.

The instance of international communication which I have discussed here suggests that a principal problem in this area is posed by the distinctively differentiated communication patterns which accompany nationhood in an age of nationalism. Since this is also an age of interdependence, when communication is particularly necessary to the conduct of relations among nations at every level, from the framing of treaties and the conduct of trade relations to the relations between persons, it becomes essential to find means for understanding and minimizing these problems.

---

[1]This formulation is that of the writer's and was rarely articulated by interpreters. Specification is often used but seldom mentioned. This appears to represent a consequence of biculturality—interpreters may be reluctant to emphasize conflicts in social systems of communication which they have incorporated into their own personalities; indeed, it often appears that they are especially highly motivated to reduce such conflicts between representatives of these social systems, a strong and fortunate motive for the improvement of communication.

166

It is suggested here that fundamental principles for the conduct of effective international communication center around the recognition of distinctive national communication patterns. If the problems of communication with alienated societies are reminiscent of those encountered in offering professional assistance to alienated persons, this may be because substantially similar processes are involved.

It may be added that few clinicians have concerned themselves with international communication; it is high time that we offer some part of our viewpoints and skills to the investigation of this critical human problem with the aim, which all clinicians must have, of the improvement of real-life human conditions.

REFERENCES

1. Cantril, H. and Free, L., "Hopes and Fears for Self and Country," American Behavioral Scientist, Vol. VI, Supplement, Oct. 1962, No. 2.

2. Elder, R. E., The Foreign Leader Program: Operations in the United States, Brookings Institution, Washington, D. C., 1961.

3. Glenn, E., "Semantic Difficulties in International Communication" in The Use and Misuse of Words, S. I. Hayakawa (ed.), New York, Premier Books, 1960.

4. Halle, L. J., Men and Nations, Princeton, N. J., Princeton University Press, 1962.

5. Jacob, P. and Flink, J. J., "Values and Their Function in Decision Making," American Behavioral Scientist, Vol. V, Supplement, May, 1962, No. 9.

6. Kennedy, J. F., Special Message of the President to the Congress, May 25, 1961. New York Times, May 26, 1961.

7. Kohn, H., The Age of Nationalism, Harper and Brothers, New York, 1962.

8. Rock, V., A Strategy of Interdependence, New York, Scribner, 1963.

9. Ward, B., The Rich Nations and the Poor Nations, New York, Norton, 1962.

10. Wedge, B., "Toward a Science of Transnatural Communication," Symposium No. 7, Group for Advancement of Psychiatry, New York, 1960.

11. Wedge, B., "Nation-to-Nation, A Study of Cross-Cultural Communication" (to be published).

Superordinate Goals in the Reduction of Intergroup Conflict: An Experimental Evaluation

MUZAFER SHERIF

Research centers, interested action agencies, and men in policy positions are engaged in appraising and instituting measures for the reduction of intergroup conflicts. These thriving activities reflect the overriding urgency of problems of intergroup relations today as they loom grimly in labor-management relations, interracial or interethnic frictions, and above all, in highly sharpened frictions between nations and two giant ideological systems.

As a result, we are confronted with various proposals for reducing the intergroup prejudices and conflicts as I shall specify later. Each of these proposals has an associated formulation of the underlying dynamics, even though these underlying dynamics are not always made explicit.

A program of research was instituted fifteen years ago, prompted by three interrelated objectives:

1. Clear delineation of the common denominator in problems of intergroup relations regardless of the area (ethnic, racial, labor-management, internation). This clarification of the characteristic problem of intergroup relations revealed the inadequacy of various theoretical treatments and action directions because of their inadequacy in delineating the problem on the level and scope it requires (3, Chapter 1; 5, Chapter 9).

2. An evaluation of measures proposed and application steps attempted to reduce intergroup prejudice and hostility through critical survey of these measures and actual results over a time span (4, Chapters 2 - 4). These proposed measures include:

   (a) Dissemination of information through lectures and other face-to-face media, and through mass media of communication.
   (b) Emotional catharsis of pent-up frustrations.
   (c) Conferences of leaders.
   (d) Balance of power.

167

(e) Programs insuring contact among members of parties in conflict or prejudicial towards one another, such as exchange of persons, meetings of students from various groups on social occasions, entertainments, etc.

3. Experimental testing of leads derived from the foregoing surveys over several years, under conditions simulating the naturalness of actual intergroup encounters. This experimental testing required, first, formation of groups themselves with definite organizations (structures) and sets of values or norms of their own, these being the minimum properties of any group of any description. There must be two or more groups to have intergroup relations (4, Chapters 9 - 10; 6).

Our surveys of the literature and empirical findings led us to the conclusion that it is impossible to assess the effectiveness of these measures as isolated factors in the social complex. The characteristics of interaction between groups and the identification of their members as parts of these groups are always the framework affecting the measures. Therefore, it is our position that the contribution of these various measures to the formation and change of attitudes can be appropriately evaluated only within the framework of the characteristics of interactions between groups and the reference group identifications of individuals involved in the intergroup relations. For this reason, the directive base of departure in our experimental project has been the analysis and clarification of the problem of intergroup behavior (point one). Only by clarifying the nature of the problem of intergroup behavior can we proceed to a realistic evaluation of the conditions under which the various measures can contribute.

The hypotheses of our experiments, their design, and their procedures were inspired by the nature of the problem of intergroup behavior, whether this behavior is friendly or hostile. Because of the nature of the problem, we began our experiments with individuals who were unacquainted, had them interact in conditions suitable for the formation of groups, and then (and only then) proceeded to study conditions conducive to hostility between them and measures effective in reducing hostility. The introduction of superordinate goals proved to be effective in reducing hostility between groups. However, superordinate goals are not an alternative to other measures in the reduction of intergroup friction. Superordinate goals are defined as goals that encompass all parties caught in dispute or conflict (e. g., mutual survival), which cannot be fulfilled by the resources and energies of the parties separately, but require the concerted efforts of all parties involved. But if such concerted efforts are to be effective, they should not be a one-shot affair. The effects of superordinate goals are cumulative, as elaborated in detail in our Intergroup Conflict and Cooperation (6). That book gives the full account of the formulation of the problem, the hypotheses derived from existing research and theory, the techniques, the procedures, and the results. Superordinate goals serve, therefore, as the broad motivational base on which conferences or negotiations between leaders, contacts (e. g. , exchange of persons), and the dissemination of hitherto unheeded information can be utilized to good advantage.

Because of the conviction that our understanding of hostile and friendly attitudes between peoples has been clouded by ambiguous and inadequate assumptions, I turn to a brief statement on the nature of the problem of intergroup relations. Obviously, intergroup relations refer to states of friendship or hostility, cooperation or competition, alliance or enmity, peace or war between two or more groups and their respective members. But not every friendly or unfriendly act toward others, not every state of cooperation or competition is necessarily a case of intergroup behavior. We have to differentiate those actions which can be properly called "intergroup" behavior.

Let us start by specifying the main concepts involved. This specification must begin with an adequate conception of the key term, "group" itself. We define a group as a social unit which, one, consists of a number of individuals who, at a given time, stand in interdependent status or role relationships with one another, and two, which explicitly or implicitly possesses a set of values or norms of its own regulating behavior of individual members, at least in matters of consequence to the group. Shared attitudes, shared sentiments, shared aspirations and goals are related to and implicit in the common values or norms of the group.

The term "intergroup relations" refers to relations between two or more groups and their respective members. Whenever individuals belonging to one group interact, collectively or individually, with another group or its members in terms of their reference group identification, we have an instance of intergroup behavior.

The appropriate frame of reference for studying intergroup behavior is the functional relations between two or more groups, which may be positive or negative, depending primarily upon the harmony or conflict of their major interests and goals—in the past, present, and future.

The relationships between groups whose members perceive them as their reference groups have properties of their own—apart from any characteristics the groups may have separately. These properties are a product of their histories of interaction with each other.

Though not independent of the relationships within the groups in question, the characteristics of functional relations between groups cannot be deduced or extrapolated solely from the properties of relations prevailing among members within a group itself. Prevailing modes of behavior within the groups (in the way of cooperativeness and solidarity, or competitiveness and rivalry among members) need not necessarily be the prevalent modes of behavior in their relations with other groups. Hostility toward out-groups may, at times, be proportional to the degree of solidarity within the in-group. Democracy at home need not imply democratic attitudes toward out-groups.

Our research was guided by the conception of the intergroup problem just presented in a nutshell: this conceptual formulation required an experimental design in three successive stages:

Stage 1. Stage of experimental in-group formation. The purpose of this stage was to create two groups to have intergroup relations. When you do have groups, each has a structure or organization and a set of values or norms peculiar to it. These are essential features of any group.

Stage 2. The stage of intergroup competition and conflict. This second stage, which resulted in unmistakable attitudes of hostility and clear-cut acts of conflict and aggression between groups, was not undertaken to create groups in an actual state of hostility, to the point of their preferring to forego many desired activities if they were put in a position of being with the members of the detested group. This was necessary so that the difficult task of reduction of intergroup hostility could be undertaken.

Stage 3. The third stage, namely the stage of reduction of intergroup conflict, was initiated with the conviction that the crucial intergroup problem is not to make already friendly groups more friendly. The urgent intergroup problem is to create optimal motive conditions for the reduction of friction between hostile groups. Until this optimal motive condition is created, attempts to disseminate correct information, conferences of leaders, exhortations to take every man for what he is rather than seeing him through the darkening influence of negative images or stereotypes, and intergroup contacts on pleasant occasions prove to be rather futile (7, 5).

The time allotted does not allow me to specify in detail the criteria for subject selection, the techniques and procedures used, the problem situations introduced experimentally, and the problem-solving alternatives available to the groups. They are reported in detail in the accounts of these experiments (4, 6).

The experiments were carried out in locations altogether under experimental control, excluding all influences not intended in the design and procedures. The subjects of groups were male youngsters from homogeneous racial, social, economic, religious, educational backgrounds. They were initially unacquainted with one another in order to eliminate the possibility of group formation on the basis of existing friendship clusters. They were academically successful, well-adjusted youngsters, both in school and at home, who came from settled, respected families with parents who did not exercise unduly authoritarian control over their youngsters. There were no broken-home situations. Thus, these criteria of subject selection, which were strictly observed, rule out the explanation of our conclusions on the basis of unfortunate family circumstances or other severely frustrating influences in the lives of our subjects.

Problem situations were elaborately devised that embodied built-in goals, without any verbal exhortation, such as getting a meal when all were hungry in the group formation stage or, in the second stage, situations that were competitive or mutually frustrating, without any exhortations to be competitive and excel over their rivals.

To insure naturalness of interaction, the subject was at no time aware that these were experiments in group formation and intergroup relations. Therefore, no observation notes were taken in the subjects' view, no procedure was introduced to clutter the flow of interaction in exchange of conversation and action. What was lost in completeness and reliability of data was remedied, at least to a considerable extent, through the use of a combination of methods adapted to the situations.

The following hypotheses, which were specified, are presented as embodying the essentials of the conditions introduced in the three successive stages of the design and predictions for each stage derived from surveys of literature and previous empirical work.

Stage 1: Experimental Formation of In-groups

Hypothesis 1 (Stage 1)

A definite group structure consisting of differentiated status positions and reciprocal roles will be produced when a number of individuals (without previously established interpersonal relations) interact with one another under conditions (a) which situationally embody goals that have common appeal value to the individuals, and (b) which require interdependent activities for their attainment.

Hypothesis 2 (Stage 1)

When individuals interact under conditions stated in the first hypothesis, concomitant with the formation of group structure, norms regulating their behavior in relation to one another and in practices and activities commonly engaged in will be standardized.

Stage 2: Production of Unfavorable Intergroup Attitudes

Hypothesis 1 (Stage 2)

In the course of competition and frustrating relations between two groups, produced by goals whose attainment by one group precludes their attainment by the other, unfavorable stereotypes will come into use in relation to the out-group and its members and will be standardized in time, placing the out-group at a certain social distance. In other words, the rudiments of prejudice will result.

Hypothesis 2 (Stage 2)

The course of relations between two groups which are in a state of competition and frustration will tend to produce an increase in in-group solidarity.

Hypothesis 3 (Stage 2)

Functional relations between groups which are of consequence to the groups in question will tend to bring about changes in the pattern of relations within the in-groups involved. For example, we found that leaders who had been successful in peaceful activities sometimes lost their standing when intergroup conflict became focal for a group.

Stage 3: Reduction of Intergroup Friction

Hypothesis 1 (Stage 3)

Contact between groups does not in itself produce a decrease in an existing state of intergroup hostility, even though the conditions of contact may be pleasant in themselves. (We found that such occasions were utilized to spite and harass the other group.)

Hypothesis 2 (Stage 3)

When groups in a state of friction are brought into contact under conditions embodying superordinate goals whose attainment is compellingly desired by each group, but which cannot be achieved by the efforts of one group alone, they will tend to cooperate toward the common goal.

Hypothesis 3 (Stage 3)

Cooperation between groups, necessitated by a series of situations embodying superordinate goals will have a cumulative effect in the direction of reducing existing conflicts between groups and unfavorable attitudes of individual members.

In concluding, I venture to state some of the things that we have learned from those experiments about the reduction of intergroup conflict. It is true that lines of communication, that is, contact, between groups must be opened before prevailing hostilities can be reduced. But if contact between groups takes place without superordinate goals— that is, goals which are urgent, compelling, and highly appealing for all groups involved—the communication channels and the contacts serve as mediums for further accusations and recriminations. The discussion or the negotiation gets bogged down in direct and indirect reference to the fruitless question of "Who's to blame?" for the existing state of tension.

When contact situations involve superordinate goals, communication is utilized in the direction of reducing conflict in order to attain the common goals.

In regard to dissemination of information, favorable information about a detested out-group tends to be ignored, rejected or reinterpreted to fit prevailing stereotypes. But when groups are pulling together toward superordinate goals, true and favorable information about the out-group is seen in a new light, and the probability of information being effective is enormously enhanced.

When groups cooperate toward superordinate goals, leaders are in a position to take bolder steps toward bringing about understanding and harmonious relations. When groups are directed toward goals which are mutually incompatible, genuine moves by a leader to reduce intergroup conflict may be seen by the membership of his own group as out-of-step and ill-advised. He may be subjected to severe criticism and even loss of faith. When compelling superordinate goals are introduced, the leader can make moves toward further cooperative efforts, he can more freely delegate authority, and representation processes can proceed more effectively. The decisions reached are more likely to receive support from other group members. Release of emotional tensions is achieved in the course of give-and-take with members of the other group in constructive activity. This is in marked contrast to the results of catharsis while the groups were in conflict.

The catharsis of members served to stir up each other and to heighten group solidarity and actions directed against the other group and its members.

In short, various measures suggested for the reduction of intergroup conflict, such as dissemination of information, increasing social contacts, conferences of leaders and representatives, even catharsis, acquire new significance and new effectiveness when they become part and parcel of interaction processes between groups oriented toward superordinate goals which have real and compelling value for all groups concerned. Superordinate goals are not an alternative measure per se. Rather, superordinate goals provide a motivational directionality along which communication, information, contact or exchange of persons, as well as other specific measures, acquire new significance for recasting the prevailing intergroup relations.

Over a period of time the interaction of groups toward superordinate goals which have genuine and compelling value for all groups concerned should assume organizational forms. If the tasks of building such organizations seem formidable, they are no more formidable, I think, than those which a modern war might impose. And surely there can be no doubt that man's potentialities can be better realized in the course of such efforts than in preoccupation with assigning blame for the state of affairs, in pursuits of old fears, old hostilities, old conflicts with their awesome possibilities in this present world.

Finally, it should be emphasized that the utilization of superordinate goals for the reduction of prevailing intergroup prejudice and conflict is not proposed as just another measure, as some authors who reviewed this work seem to interpret it (1, 2). The utilization of superordinate goals is proposed as the necessary motive condition which prepares the ground for rendering effective dissemination of information, catharsis, conferences of leaders and other negotiators, contacts through exchange of persons, meetings, and other specific but piecemeal measures when these are used, separately or in combination, in appropriate intergroup contexts.

REFERENCES

1. Blake, R. and Mouton, J. S., "The Intergroup Dynamics of Win-Lose Conflict and Problem-Solving Collaboration in Union-Management Relations," in M. Sherif (ed.), Intergroup Relations and Leadership, New York, Wiley, 1962, pp. 94-140.
2. McNeil, Elton B., "Waging Experimental War: A Review," Journal of Conflict Resolution, 6, 77-81, March 1962.
3. Sherif, M., Intergroup Relations and Leadership, New York, Wiley and Sons, 1962.
4. Sherif, M. and Sherif, Carolyn W., Groups in Harmony and Tension, New York, Harper Brothers, 1953.
5. Sherif, M. and Sherif, Carolyn W., Outline of Social Psychology, New York, Harper, 1956.
6. Sherif, M., Harvey, O. J., White, B. J., Hood, W. R., Sherif, Carolyn W., Intergroup Conflicts and Cooperation: The Robbers Cave Experiment, University of Oklahoma, Norman, Okla., University Book Exchange, 1961.
7. Williams, R. M., Jr., "The Reduction of Intergroup Tensions: A Survey of Research and Problems of Ethnic, Racial, and Religious Group Relations," New York, Social Science Research Council, Bull. 57, 1947.

Social Welfare Opportunities and Necessities
Attendant on Disarmament

_____ **IDA C. MERRIAM**

One can approach the question of alternative uses for the human
and material resources that would be released by disarmament from
two different and largely opposite points of view. One approach focuses
on unmet social needs and the opportunities that additional dollars and
manpower could open up. The other focuses on the problems of transition and adjustment and the necessity for rechanneling production and
employment in such a way as to avoid major wrenches to our economic
system. From either point of view, social welfare programs and objectives should have a central place in any discussion of the implications of disarmament.

Unmet Social Needs

There have been a number of attempts in recent years to project
social needs over the next one or two decades and to compare these
needs with potential resources (1, 2, 2a, 3). The dollar figures developed differ, depending on individual judgments of adequacy and of
social priorities and the desirable role of government, and on specific
assumptions about the achievable rate of growth of the economy and
the amounts of money that will continue to be diverted to armaments
and defense-related activities.

A few general conclusions stand out from these studies. We now
have the technological ability to provide for the minimum needs of the
entire population—with "minimum" defined to include a reasonable
number of modern conveniences. We are not now doing so, however,
in spite of large unused resources of plant and manpower. The proportion of the population living in poverty has declined over the past three
decades, but the distance between the rich and the poor remains very
great. Since about 1944 there has been no appreciable change in the
share of total income going to the lowest fifth of the population ranked
by income. Finally, unmet needs in the public sector, needs for goods

and services that can best, or only, be provided through mechanisms other than that of the market place, are greater than the aggregate of unmet private needs.

Wiping Out Poverty

There has also developed within the past few years a renewed awareness of the extent of poverty remaining in the United States. In a study prepared for the Joint Economic Committee of the Congress, Robert Lampman estimated that in 1957 there were 32 million persons, or just under one-fifth of our total population, living in poverty. He used as the definition of poverty an annual income of less than $2,500 a year for a family of four persons, and comparable amounts for other families and individuals. He notes that if the poverty or low-income line were drawn at $4,000 for a family of four—close to the budget requirements for urban wage earner families in 1957 as calculated by the Bureau of Labor Statistics—an additional 28 million persons or, in all, 36 per cent of the population, were living below minimum adequate levels (4).

A more recent analysis by the Conference on Economic Progress, using somewhat different definitions and methodology, arrived at essentially similar conclusions. In 1960, according to this study[1], 38 million persons, or a little more than a fifth of the population, were living in poverty, and an equal number in deprivation (3). Michael Harrington, in his forceful indictment of our indifference to The Other America (5), preferred to talk of 50 million persons living below reasonable levels.

The most recent major study of poverty in the United States was carried out by the Survey Research Center of the University of Michigan (6). It leads to essentially the same conclusions. In the Michigan study family income was defined to include, in addition to cash income, important sources of income in kind, such as imputed rental income on net equity in a home. Families or adult units with inadequate incomes were defined as those with less than nine-tenths of their budget requirements as determined on the basis of a budget developed by the Community Council of Greater New York, which allows for variations in size and composition of each unit.[2] So defined, 28 per cent of all

---

[1]Poverty is defined in this study as annual income of less than $2,000 in the case of an individual, and less than $4,000 for multiple-person families; deprivation is defined as annual income of less than $3,000 for an individual and less than $6,000 for families.

[2]For a description of the standard see: A Family Budget Standard, Welfare and Health Council of New York City, 1955. (The budgets are repriced annually.)

adult units (including single person units) and one-fifth of the nations families were living in poverty in 1959.

Who are the poor? All the studies show the same concentrations of poverty. About a fourth of the poor are aged 65 and over (Lampman) and 14 per cent of all poor families have heads aged 65 and over (Michigan survey). Broken families are another large group—one-third of all poor families are headed by women (Michigan) and one-fourth of all the individuals living in poverty are in such families (Lampman). These groups, together with the disabled, the unemployed, rural migratory and other casual and unskilled workers and, cutting across all the other categories, nonwhites and persons with little education, largely fill up the ranks of the poor. In 1959 one-fourth of the nation's children[3] were in families with incomes below the taxable limit set by the federal income tax laws (7, 8). About half of the poor live in the South (Michigan survey and 1960 Census data). In the country as a whole, slightly more than half live in urban areas, almost a third in rural nonfarm areas, and about one-sixth in rural farm areas (1960 Census data: 1959 incomes below federal income tax limit).

To what extent could resources released by disarmament fill in these shortfalls in individual and family income?

It is relatively easy to calculate the number of dollars that would be required to bring up to the poverty or minimum adequacy line, however defined, all those now living below it. In 1960 about 10 billion dollars would have been sufficient to give every family at least $2,500 and every person living alone at least $1,000. To bring all families up to $4,000 and persons living alone to $1,500 would have required about 30 billion dollars. Such calculations show that the problem of wiping out poverty is of manageable size. They do not answer the question of how additional income can be so distributed as to reach the poor.

It may be noted that full use of idle plant and manpower would have increased the 1961 output of the economy by 25 billion dollars to 30 billion dollars.[4]

Undoubtedly if our economy were growing at a satisfactory rate and job opportunities were available without discrimination, many of those living in poverty today could move out by their own efforts. Others would need special help—basic education, training or retraining, rehabilitation, help in moving from depressed areas or in adjusting to

---

[3]See also Orshansky (8). Using a measure of poverty based on the relation between total income and the Department of Agriculture low-cost food budgets, this analysis found between 17 and 23 million, or from one-fourth to one-third of all children living in poverty in 1961.

[4]Economic report of the President 1962, p. 7.

urban life, special placement services, possibly health care.[5] The potential use of resources for these purposes is discussed later.

A sizable proportion of today's poor, however, are not, and should not be, in the labor force. For these groups, the adequacy of our social insurance and public assistance programs largely determine whether or not they will live in poverty.

Improving the Public Income-Maintenance Programs

Gerald Piel has suggested that if our economy is to adjust successfully to disarmament and automation, the government must "directly and indirectly... certify a growing percentage of our consumers with purchasing power. " (9)

Social insurance is the institutional mechanism by which all developed countries, and most of those in the process of industrialization, certify large groups in the population to receive regular continuing incomes. The retired aged, the permanently and temporarily disabled, the unemployed, and orphaned children and their mothers are the groups ordinarily protected. In many countries all children, or children in large families, receive small subsidies from public funds.

Let us look for a moment at the general level of income we are providing under our social insurance programs. Most important is the national Old Age, Survivors and Disability Insurance program. The average benefit for a retired worker under this system in 1963 was $76 a month or about $900 a year, and for a couple who are both over age 62, the average payment is $127 a month or $1,525 a year. Some beneficiaries have savings; in 1962 three-fourths of the couples and more than two-fifths of the other beneficiaries owned their own homes, usually mortgage-free. The value of all assets other than a home was, however, less than $1,000 for two-fifths of the couples and more than half of the nonmarried beneficiaries. Even fewer had financial assets that could readily be drawn on in an emergency.

More than one-fourth of the beneficiary couples and about one-eighth of the nonmarried beneficiaries aged 65 and over received a payment under some other public or private retirement program as well as their OASDI benefit. But about one-fourth of the beneficiaries had little or no cash income other than OASDI. Of the couples, including couples in which a younger wife or husband was still employed full-

---

[5]The Michigan study includes a very interesting multivariate analysis which suggests that many families whose incomes are inadequate should earn considerably more than they do on the basis of their education and other characteristics. "The discrepancy may arise from psychological dependency, lack of motivation, lack of intelligence and a variety of other factors that were not studied." (6)

time, one-fourth had less than $500 of money income other than OASDI; almost half of all aged widow beneficiaries had less than $150 (including public assistance) other than their OASDI benefits (10). At least 5.5 million aged OASDI beneficiaries had retirement incomes below the poverty level and 7.6 million below a modest but adequate level (11).

At the present time the OASDI benefit for a worker with average earnings represents a little less than a third of his preretirement earnings, and for a couple who are both aged 65 and over, the benefit is about 48 per cent of the husband's previous earnings. Workers who had very low earnings in their working years may receive benefits equal to 80 per cent or more of those earnings. The minimum benefit is $40 a month. These persons are unlikely to have any other income except public assistance. A man who had been earning $7,500 a year, not a luxurious level, would get a benefit equal to only one-fifth, and he and his wife together would get less than one-third, of his previous earnings. These are rather sharp drops in income, even when decreased income tax liabilities are taken into account.

To illustrate the general magnitudes involved, one might ask what it would cost to raise the level of benefits under OASDI so that the average worker got a benefit equal to 50 per cent and a couple 75 per cent of pre-retirement earnings (retaining the same general relationships among types of benefits, benefits for low and high earners, etc.). The increased benefit payments in the first year, according to the Chief Actuary of the Social Security Administration, would amount to about 9 billion dollars. If eligibility were somehow broadened so that 90 per cent of the population aged 65 and over qualified for these higher benefits (compared with the 70 per cent who qualify today), the total increase in benefits would be about 11.5 billion dollars. Actual benefit payments in 1962 were between 14 billion and 15 billion dollars.

There is room for increasing the amount of purchasing power certified to consumers through other social insurance programs as well. For example, to provide cash sickness insurance for all wage and salary workers in private industry, with benefits amounting to two-thirds of previous earnings after a one-week waiting period and for up to twenty-six weeks in duration, would require current expenditures of about 2.2 billion dollars, or 1.5 billion dollars more than the amounts actually received by such workers in sickness benefits and paid sick leave during 1960. Comparable levels of adequacy in workmen's compensation and unemployment insurance would with today's levels of unemployment result in increased expenditures of close to another 2 billion dollars above present levels.

If we want to move most of the aged, the disabled, and survivors out of poverty, we have the mechanism at hand. In raising the level of benefits under OASDI or our other social insurance programs, we

would also increase the incomes of persons above the poverty line.
This is a desirable outcome from both the social and economic point
of view. Our primary concern should be to improve the lot of those
who are now worst off. The most effective and possibly the only way
to achieve this objective, however, is through economic and social
policies and measures which affect the whole society—full employment,
nondiscrimination, basic health and educational services, and more
adequate social insurance programs.

There will remain individuals and groups whose minimum income
needs are not met by such programs and measures. One example is
the large group of poor families headed by women. Some of these women are widows, but the great majority have been deserted or divorced
or were never married. Insurance does not cover these risks, and employment, even if available, may not be the best answer. For them,
and for unskilled and marginal workers, certification of purchasing
power on the basis of an individual test of current need—that is to say,
public assistance—may be the solution.

In theory, public assistance should take care of all current need,
coming into play when all other sources of income fall short of socially
acceptable minimum levels and underpinning all other income maintenance programs. How far short of this standard our existing public assistance programs fall can be measured in several ways. One recent
study (12) used as a standard of need twice the amount of a low-cost
food budget as calculated, with regional variations, by the Department
of Agriculture. Certainly a standard under which 50 per cent of total
income must go for food is minimal indeed. Yet in 1958, to meet this
standard, assistance payments for families on the Aid to Families
with Dependent Children rolls would have had to be increased by 72
per cent for the country as a whole. There was considerable variation
by state and by region. In the West, actual expenditures would have
had to be 27 per cent higher to meet the standard; in the South, 149
per cent. Old-age assistance payments were far less inadequate, 6 per
cent below this standard for the country as a whole. It was estimated
that to provide an income of twice the cost of a low-cost food budget
to all persons on the public assistance rolls in 1958 would have required expenditure of 1 billion dollars more than the 3 billion dollars
actually spent for public assistance by all levels of government in that
year. [6]

No estimate was made of the number of additional persons who
would qualify as "needy" if standards were raised, nor of the amounts

---

[6] A subsequent rough updating showed an even larger deficit for aid to families
with dependent children in 1961. See Perkins, E., "How Much Is Enough?", unpublished paper presented at Biennial Round Table Conference of the American Public
Welfare Association, Washington D.C., December 6, 1963.

of money that would be required to meet their needs. The Michigan study, referred to earlier, found that less than one-fourth of the families living in poverty in 1959 were receiving public assistance.

Because public assistance is a federal-state program, with levels of assistance and conditions of eligibility determined by the individual states, the raising of standards is a far more complex and difficult problem than in the case of a national social insurance program. It must be noted also that federal financial aid is available only for selected categories; general assistance is financed entirely by state and local funds and in many places wholly by the latter. It is important to keep in mind these structural barriers to the transfer of resources released by disarmament.

Public Services

I have not attempted to quantify the needs for increased spending for public services—education, health, public housing, community development, water supply, mass transportation, social services such as day-care centers for children and adults, homemaker services, special training and employment services, rehabilitation, etc. These are obviously large, but it is difficult to find a common basis for measuring needs or opportunities. A few examples will suffice to illustrate orders of magnitude. By 1970 educational expenditures will need to be 75 per cent larger than today (an increase of 20 billion dollars), at today's price and wage levels, merely to provide the same level of education to a growing population. Improvements in performance—fewer high school drop-outs, more post-graduate training, more kindergartens, more specialized attention for children with special problems— could increase expenditures well above these amounts (13).

The Twentieth Century Fund Study of America's Needs and Resources estimated that to meet minimum needs, personal consumption expenditures in 1960 would have to be about 4 per cent higher than they were likely to be, but government expenditures for all purposes other than defense would have to be raised by 20 per cent. This general relationship would probably hold today using somewhat different standards of need.

Problems of Transition

What are the forces that would lead to use of resources released by disarmament for social welfare pruposes? After all, as a nation we could afford to meet most of these needs today if we really wanted to and were willing to be sufficiently inventive about methods.

There are several factors that would, I think, be of some importance. In discussing the transition from a high to a low level of military spending, reference is frequently made to the ease with which the economy adjusted at the end of World War II. Several circumstances contributed to that outcome. There were tremendous unfilled consumer needs and also a large volume of liquid assets in the hands of the consumers. Lower hours of work for civilians and the holding of large numbers of veterans out of the labor market while they made use of their veterans' educational benefits helped keep down unemployment levels. Governmental fiscal policy, including tax reduction, large bonus payments to veterans, and general monetary ease, and a general atmosphere of dynamic optimism were also important. Under these circumstances, the necessary structural changes were made much more easily than might otherwise have been the case.

What parallel circumstances could we look for today? Especially if the tax cuts and reforms proposed by the Administration are put into effect within the next few years, before disarmament reduces military spending to any appreciable degree, there will not be any such volume of unfilled consumer demand as existed at the end of World War II. The real unfilled consumer needs will be among the very low income groups who pay no income taxes. An increase in the level of social insurance benefits and of public assistance may thus appear highly desirable as a means of sustaining aggregate demand. Scholarships and training or retraining, not only for veterans but for all young people and all others affected by automation or other changes in technology, may come to be seen as a desirable permanent feature of our economy. New types of income maintenance programs, such as special relocation grants or loans, could be developed. And public spending for health and housing and social services could well come to be recognized as an essential balance for decreased public spending for military purposes.

It is significant that the funds, as distinguished from the economic resources, released by disarmament would be federal monies. There could thus be a direct transfer of funds from one part of the federal budget to another. Increased federal spending for social welfare purposes could occur without either additional tax revenues or deficit financing. And the situation would encourage reliance on federal programs, although some new devices for channeling federal funds to state or local programs—hopefully with federal program standards—might be developed. Fortunately, many of the federal programs that would be needed are either in existence, as in the case of OASDI, or in process of coming into being now.

Finally, it seems to me not unreasonable to hope that the beginnings of disarmament would release social energies and social inventiveness that today tend to be suppressed and frustrated. Some of the

pressure for disarmament is the pressure of fear. But there is also
an ethic of concern for others and a moral realization of the meaning
of interdependence that must increasingly permeate our thinking about
international relations and our willingness to change established institutions before we are likely to achieve either disarmament or greater
abundance for all. Disarmaments and a more equitable society must
go together into mankind's future.

REFERENCES

1. Dewhurst, J. F. and Associates, America's Needs and Resources, A New Survey, New York, The Twentieth Century
   Fund, 1955.
2. The Challenge to America: Its Economic and Social Aspects,
   Special Studies Report IV, Rockefeller Bros. Fund, New
   York, Doubleday, 1958.
2A. Goals for Americans, The American Assembly, New York,
   Prentice-Hall, 1960. (This document states goals in qualitative terms and is notably lacking in data or quantitative
   estimates.)
3. Poverty and Deprivation in the U.S., Conference on Economic
   Progress, Washington D. C., April, 1962.
4. Lampman, R. J., "The Low Income Population and Economic
   Growth," Study Paper No. 12, Joint Economic Committee,
   86th Congress, 1st Session, Washington D. C., Govt. Print.
   Off., 1959.
5. Harrington, M., The Other America, New York, Macmillan, 1961.
6. Morgan, J. N., David, M. H., Cohen, W. J. and Brazer, H. E.,
   Income and Welfare in the United States, New York, McGraw-
   Hill, 1962.
7. Epstein, L. A., "Some Effects of Low Income on Children and
   Their Families," Social Security Bulletin, Washington D. C.,
   Govt. Print. Off., Feb., 1961, pp. 12-17.
8. Orshansky, M., "Children of the Poor," Social Security Bulletin, Washington, D. C., Govt. Print. Off., July, 1963,
   pp. 3-13.
9. Piel, G., "Can Our Economy Stand Disarmament?" Atlantic
   Monthly, Sept., 1962, pp. 35-40.
10. Epstein, L. A., "Income of the Aged in 1962: First Findings of
   the 1963 Survey of the Aged," Soc. Sec. Bull., March,
   1964, pp. 3-25.
11. Research and Statistics Note No. 2—1964, Div. of Research and
   Statistics, Soc. Sec. Adm.

184

12. Perkins, E. J., "Unmet Need in Public Assistance," Soc. Sec. Bull., April, 1960, pp. 3-11.

13. The Economic and Social Consequences of Disarmament, U.S. Arms Control and Disarmament Agency, U. S. Govt. Print. Off., Washington D. C., July, 1962.

Who Are These Women? A Progress Report on a Study of the "Women Strike for Peace"

ELISE BOULDING

Women Strike for Peace is a new social phenomenon. Born during the Berlin crisis of 1961, it moved to the national scene on November first of that year when an urgent call went out from the "Washington housewives" to the women of America to go out and "strike for peace." Because of the prized spirit of continued spontaneity and local autonomy, this has been an "unorganization" variously known as Women for Peace, Women Act for Peace, and the like. Yet despite its unorthodoxy as a movement, this new force for world order was surely one of the considerations that led to the following statement in a RAND report: "The Peace Movement is finding new advocates for its ideas while retaining its initial supporters... its support is spreading among different groups of the society, and it is beginning to influence influential people" and "has a large potential for generating powerful political influences on military strategies and programs. "[1]

Who are these women? And why did they turn toward peace action? These are the central questions of this study. Why did they begin to move in 1961 when, in fact, an older generation had been trying to arouse a concern for world affairs in the female sex for a quarter of a century? Did nuclear testing produce this action and organization? And how will these women react over the long haul? What will happen when world disarmament is not forthcoming? Will the movement then disintegrate, perhaps with a few final angry demonstrations? Or are the motives of these women characterized by greater vision and flexibility than that?

And who are they? Are they really young mothers with small children at their skirts, inexperienced in community affairs but driven by the one burning thought—to rid the world of arms? Or are they old pros in social action with a well-defined idea of some kind of world social order?

---

[1]Wessel, A.E.. The Peace Movement. Rand Booklet p.2679, Dec. 1962.

This study was first conceived in May, 1962, when the movement was seven months old, and when it had come of age to plan a national gathering of local groups. Speed was essential in conducting the investigation if questions directed to the women were to be answered out of the freshness of the original experience of arousal, and if knowledge about what had brought those first cohorts into it was to be obtained before the movement itself had changed.

Procedure

With the aid of the extremely able local WSP in Ann Arbor, Michigan, and several experienced social scientists from the Survey Research Institute,[2] two questionnaires were put together (and pretested) in record time: one for steering committees, to learn how the informal organizational machinery of local groups was working, and the other for individual women. The mechanism for distribution of both was through the key contact list developed by the Washington WSP group for the country as a whole. Out of 100 steering committee questionnaires sent out, 19 were returned completed in full by local steering committees, 1 in part. At the same time, letters were sent out to each of the key contacts asking for cooperation in the distribution of individual questionnaires to find out more about the women already in the movement and perhaps, from them, how to interest still more women in it. They were asked to send in estimates of the number of women on their local mailing lists. Forty-five localities responded, and on the basis of the 14,000 names reported, each group was instructed to mail out questionnaires (all sealed, stamped, and ready for addressing) to every eighth name on their mailing lists. A total of 1,770 questionnaires were distributed by the end of June. By fall a total of 279 questionnaires had been returned from 37 localities in 22 states, a 16 per cent return. For a seven-page, fifty-question document this is not a bad return without follow-up, though we had hoped for better. We counted on a high motivation level in the respondents for finding out about their movement so they could make it even better. For the most part, the

[2]Of the Ann Arbor WSP, Jean Converse, Elizabeth Converse, Marcia Barrabee, and Theresa Wescott should be mentioned in particular. Mrs. Wescott has continued to act as a research assistant throughout the study and did a remarkable job of coding what others said would be uncodable. Philip Concerse, Sybil Stokes, Herbert Kelman, and Edith Pelz of the Survey Research Center all helped with the questionnaire at the formative stages, and John Sonquist of the same Center supervised the machine tabulation. Without his personal interest the present report would have been impossible, since the research grant which was to have financed this study was denied. .Special thanks are due to the Center for Research on Conflict Resolution and its executive secretary, William Barth, for making a small emergency grant for the study at a critical time.

women who did answer the questions exceeded our expectations by the quality and content of their answers.

The Questionnaire[3]

The questionnaire is divided into three parts: (a) Participation in Women's Peace Group, exploring how the respondent became involved in WSP, what activities she has participated in, and how centrally involved with the group she is; (b) Goals and Activities of WSP, exploring respondents' perceptions of the group's goals and activities and their effectiveness; (c) Background Information, eliciting data on age, education, occupation, parental, family, and childhood experiences.

Preliminary Analysis of Background Information

What follows is a simple statistical summary from the straight runs on the coded data. These have just come off the machine, and there has been no time to digest implications for future analysis of this first material.

It might be well to ask at the outset how typical of the total sample are the 279 who sent back questionnaires. It has been said that one needs a college education to be able to fill out—or to <u>want</u> to fill out— a questionnaire. This seems to be the case here, since 65 per cent of

Table 1. Education: Highest Grade Completed

Grade school through some high school	High school graduate and non-academic training	Some college	College graduate	Advanced degree	No answer	
2%	7%	24%	44%	21%	2%	= 100%

the respondents had a bachelor's or higher degree, and only 9 per cent had had no college at all. Compare this with the 6 per cent of the female United States population over 25 years of age which has a BA or more. Did we only hear from the leaders of the movement, then? No, since on a WSP activity measure 38 per cent rated very active, 10 per cent rated active, and 42 per cent rated themselves as not active or only slightly active. In terms of hours per week put in on WSP work, the respondents range from the 6 per cent who put in no time, and the

---

[3]The preliminary analysis of the steering committee questionnaires has been ably done by Marion Carson of Iowa and will not be discussed here. Eventually the two analyses will be written up together.

22 per cent who put in an hour or less a week, through the 29 per cent who put in from one to six hours, up to the committed ones who work from six hours weekly up to "all the hours there are," as one woman said. In other words, the respondents vary considerably in their personal degree of involvement in WSP and in their views of its effective-

Table 2. Hours Spent Per Week on WSP-Related Activity

None	1 hr. or less	1 - 6 hrs.	6 - 15 hrs.	over 15 hrs.	DK & NA	
6%	22%	29%	17%	6%	20%	= 100%

ness. (Eight per cent, in fact, are not members of WSP, but are members of other peace groups, such as the 48-year-old Women's International League for Peace and Freedom, who happen to be on a WSP mailing list. This group has been separated out for later analysis, and the current summary refers only to those who gave WSP as their primary reference group, for questionnaire purposes at least.) Since we particularly asked that the random sampling in each locality be done on the basis of the total mailing list so that inactives would be picked up in the sample, our returns give reasonable confirmation of the fact that local groups were conscientious in their randomizing. We have, then, a fairly representative sample on the basis of extent of involvement in in the movement, but unrepresentative to an unknown degree as far as extent of education is concerned. We will try to find ways later to check on this, but as we will see, there is some reason to suspect that the sample is not too badly biased even in this respect.

The proportion of suburb and city dwellers (71 per cent) to medium, small town, and farm (26 per cent) is as the national contact list would lead us to expect. We compared place of residence of non-WSP respondents to see if WSP seemed more or less of an urban movement than other peace groups, but the percentages are identical for both groups. The regional distribution seems to reflect, to some degree at least, that of current activity in Women Strike for Peace, with highest concentrations in the East Central States, the West Coast, and the Midwest, and low participation in the Mountain States and the South.

One of the questions of great interest has been, How many of these WSP people are really the younger women who haven't been active before? Here a comparison of WSP with non-WSP is again useful. Sixty-six per cent of the WSP's are concentrated in the 25 to 44 age bracket. (If you want too many refinements on that, you will have to brave the wrath of the women. Even in an anonymous questionnaire they protected the age-old secret of their years with remarks like "Now, really!" instead of a number, or a coy "Let's just say over 40, shall we?") Only 52 per cent of the non-WSP's are in that age bracket, and the bulk of the over-65's are in the non-WSP group. (Two of them worked with Jane Addams in the early Women's International League for Peace and Freedom.) The spread, nevertheless, goes from 18 to over 90 in both groups, indicating that neither WSP nor older peace groups have any monopoly on either youth or age. From this point on, all figures refer to the WSP group only.

Only 5 per cent of the group are never-marrieds. Of the married women, 43 per cent have from 1 to 4 children under 6, 49 per cent have from 1 to 4 or more children between the ages of 6 and 18, and 20 per cent have children over 18. As one might expect of a group largely busy with child-rearing, 61 per cent are not employed outside the home at present. Nearly 70 per cent of their husbands are professionals. Furthermore, a majority (62%) of the husbands are themselves active in the peace movement, which points to the presence of happy nonconformist middle class families united in their goals in a conformist sector of society!

Table 3. Age of All Respondents

	18-24 yrs.	25-34 yrs.	35-44 yrs.	45-54 yrs.	55-64 yrs.	65 and over	No answer	
WSP N=226	5%	34%	32%	13%	8%	4%	4%	= 100%
Other N=53	4	26	26	13	8	17	6	= 100%
All N=279	4	32	31	13	8	7	5	= 100%

Table 4. Per cent of Respondents Having Children in Each Stage of Family Life Cycle

Under 6 yrs. of age	6-18 yrs. of age	Over 18 yrs. of age
43%	49%	20%

Are the respondents "organization women"? Not necessarily. While 24 per cent of them are active in other peace or world affairs organizations, 38 per cent either say they do not belong to any other organizations or do not write down any organizations in response to the question concerning other community activities. If we combine civic, race relations, civil liberties, peace, and political activity in one category, this accounts for 40 per cent of the women; church activities account for 11 per cent, hobbies 7 per cent, and professional organizations for 4 per cent. We do not have a count of the number of other organizations to which each woman belonged in this preliminary analysis, and the number of no-answers makes the question of at least doubtful value, but the evidence from the respondents who have answered this question completely points to the fact that a few are very active, but many are non-joiners or only nominally active in other orzations.

Table 5. Other Organizations in which Respondent is Active

Civic, race relations, civil liberties, peace, political	Church	Professional	Social-civic, hobby, special interests	No answer	
40%	11%	4%	7%	38%	= 100%

The roughly one-third segment of respondents who do not feel deeply involved in WSP also show up in the 35 per cent who have not experienced much change in their life pattern as a result of WSP. Forty-nine per cent, however, put in more hours into work for peace, do fewer of the things they used to do, have changed their social circle, sometimes their whole social outlook. A reading of the questionnaires indicate that the younger women for whom WSP represents a significant change in their life patterns have usually found meaningful social relationships for themselves and their family through it.

Perceived Goals of Movement

The answer to the question of the most important goals of WSP came as a surprise. Only 55 per cent of the women gave abolition of war or multilateral disarmament as the primary goal of WSP, and 22 per cent gave the nonviolent solution of all conflicts, political and social, as the primary goal. The remainder chose varieties of world government or limited international controls. The non-violent solution of all conflicts is traditionally the pacifist credo, and one of the major attractions of WSP for nonpeace organization women was supposed to be that it was a place for nonpacifists to oppose war as an impractical instrument of policy in the nuclear age, without getting tangled up in what many consider irrelevant social issues. It may turn out on further analysis that most of the 22 per cent simply represent the pacifist element in WSP, but a look through some of the questionnaires which list this as top goal indicates that some of the women do not have any commitment to pacifism or to any other peace organization, but rather a well-thought-out intellectual position. There is ample evidence in answers to other questions on goals that the women are not simply saying "Stop! stop!" but are thinking out alternative patterns for society. To the question, "How would you state the fundamental purpose of your group?" only 10 per cent replied "to stop testing"; 23 per cent answered in general terms about working for peace and disarmament; 33 per cent in terms of educating and arousing the community; and 21 per cent in rather specific terms of developing United Nation-type machinery to control conflict, or political action directed at a change in foreign policy.

Table 6. Purpose of WSP

Peace, disarmament	Stop tests	Education, arouse community	New international machinery, new U.S. policy, political action	No answer	
23%	10%	33%	21%	13%	= 100%

When the women described what spurred them to participate in WSP this same impression of a well-thought-out concern holds up. While 28 per cent did join because of concern about fallout, testing, and civil defense, and another 4 per cent because of the Berlin crisis, 41 per cent were responding to an increasing sense of urgency about the total world situation and a feeling of need to make a declaration of personal responsibility (a phrase used by several women).

Table 7. Spur to Participation in WSP

Urgency of world situation	Testing, etc.	Berlin	Appeal of WSP group	Long-time peaceworker	Other	
41%	28%	4%	10%	9%	8%	= 100%

WSP was born out of a nationwide rush of demonstrating women and in the first months gathered its rapidly multiplying membership chiefly through this dramatic mass communication device. It is therefore interesting to see where demonstrations rank in the list of WSP activities participated in and enjoyed by respondents. Sixty-six per cent of them have participated in demonstrations. Most of them were, however, unable to use the categories of "enjoyed" or "not enjoyed" to describe either demonstrations or any other experience. "We do it because it must be done," they write sternly. Of the demonstrators, 19 per cent were able to say they enjoyed it, 17 per cent frankly stated they didn't. Probably the woman who wrote, "I feel that I look like an idiot, although in a way I like to affirm my position publicly," spoke for many. Also, it was the only activity to which many of the respondents gave high marks for effectiveness.

Table 8 gives a complete listing of per cent of respondents engaging in each of the major types of activities of WSP. By far the largest proportion have engaged in letter-writing—the least nonconforming act open to them. Next comes public education and distribution of literature, and again the holding of public meetings and making literature available is a well-recognized form of community action. Self-education, enjoyed by many, was not considered "effective." Visits to officials were not much enjoyed, probably because these were often highly frustrating experiences, and of the 74 women who engaged in economic boycotting (mostly the milk strike in the spring of 1962) only 2 either enjoyed or "disenjoyed" it, and only 4 thought it effective. Political action and civil disobedience, the two extremes of action to effect social change, were both almost entirely absent. Peace research came out fairly well, though there is no way of being certain what respondents meant when they checked this. Remarks indicated many thought in terms of supporting the Arms Control and Disarmament Agency.

Table 8. WSP Activities Participated in by Respondents

Letter-writing	80%
Education of public, literature distribution	69%
Demonstrations	66%
Self-education	40%
Economic pressure	33%
Visits to officials	30%
Peace research	21%
Political action	4%
Civil disobedience	2%

Table 9. Respondents' Reactions to Activities

Activities most enjoyed*	Activities least enjoyed*	Activities groups should do more of*
Demonstrations, self-education, organizational work	Demonstrations, organizational work	Public education, organization work

*Three most frequent mentions.

The category "organization work" refers to organization of WSP, and did not appear in the activities chart respondents were asked to check. It appeared so often in the answers about which activities were enjoyed and thought effective, however, that it needs to be noted. Women obviously feel ambivalent both about demonstrations and about organizational work. They may not enjoy them, but many feel the success of the movement depends on both. This is particularly interesting in the light of the high value they place on unorganization," as they have themselves frequently termed it. Answers to the steering committee questionnaire indicate that many women are realistically aware that unorganization can only work if a number of women take active responsibility and spread work widely; otherwise, a small authoritarian clique results. Hence the attention given to organizational work.

Another approach to women's feelings about what is effective action was through the check list offered them of ways in which the peace movement might influence Presidential decisions. They were asked to rank-order them in terms of effectiveness. Here demonstrations drop way down, educating the general public holds its own, and political action comes noticeably to the fore for the first time.

Table 10. Most Effective Ways of Influencing Presidential Decisions

Demonstration	Educating general public	Peace research	Political action, lobbying	Indirect influence	Economic pressure	
5%	42%	9%	30%	8%	6%	= 100%

In a sense, we have captured the thoughts of these women as they are in an interesting transitional stage. The sense of accomplishment which the earlier demonstrations had engendered has now worn off, but the sense of purpose has jelled; the concern for organization, political action, and continuing education of the public foreshadows the actual developments of recent months toward a central (though loosely) coordinating office with paid staff.

What kinds of women do the respondents feel are attracted to WSP, and what kinds do they feel it should attract? There is no question but that this group of respondents perceives the movement as attracting largely intellectuals and civic-minded people, mostly of the middle class, and many feel that more effort must be made to get working-class and uninformed, unaroused people into the group. Unless their perceptions are grossly distorted, this may be taken as some evidence that the respondents themselves are not hopelessly atypical of women for peace generally in being well educated.

Table 11. Kinds of Women Now Attracted and To Be Attracted by WSP

Intellectual civic-minded humanists	Rebels	Conformists Uninformed Apathetic	Working Class	Middle-Class professionals	Mothers	All Kinds	Other	No answer	
				Now attracted					
56%	10%	0.5%	0.5%	8%	5%	4%	10%	6%	= 100%
				Should attract					
10%	1%	19%	13%	6%	4%	12%	20%	15%	= 100%

Ideas of the Future

What do these women see as happening to society in general, and to their movement in particular? Nearly half are not sure what will happen. Of the remainder, only 6 per cent see the movement as merged with other groups or disbanded; 5 per cent see it staying just as it is.

The rest believe it will grow, become more influential, undertake more political action, and work for world order in a variety of ways.

The women are a little more sure of the world's future than of their own as an "unorganization," since only 20 per cent fail to give a concrete picture of changes in the world in which their children will

Table 12. Women's Peace Movement in Five Years

Bigger, more influential, larger scope	Same	Merged, disbanded	Contingent, don't know	
46%	5%	6%	43%	= 100%

grow up. Thirty-one per cent answer primarily in terms of world community, foreseeing various developments in world government and increased international cooperation in a variety of fields; a few see leveling of economic differences between haves and have-nots and ideological mistrusts between major power blocs. Thirty-two per cent see improvements in the United States, democracy more "perfectly realized," more welfare services rendered by state, more opportunities for minority groups. Only 2 per cent fear there will be an undesirable increase in government control of lives of citizens.

These questions regarding the future were all open-ended and left up to the respondent whether the national or the international society was emphasized, and we are here reporting the "first mention" for each respondent. On several of these questions the respondents tend to fall into three roughly equal groups: those who do not have any well-defined ideas about the future and either say so or simply abstain from answering; those who answer primarily in terms of the international community; and those who answer in terms of the national community. For neither of these last two groups does answering in one set of terms preclude also mentioning the other. This tabulation only indicates what was uppermost in their minds at the time. One of the tasks for the future will be to analyze these answers further in terms of other responses of the same individual. Now they can only be enumerated.

Table 13. Changes in Future World Order

International		United States			
Sense of world community World government More international cooperation	Improved democracy More social services	Too much control	Other	No answer	
31%	32%	2%	15%	20%	= 100%

When asked what the main stumbling blocks to world peace are, the "don't knows" finally melted down to 7 per cent. Here is something nearly everyone has an opinion about! Forty-three per cent of the women saw the main obstacles as lying directly in the international sphere itself, 30 per cent thought in terms of United States government policy and United States publics, and 20 per cent thought in terms of "people" of any country. Again, it must be emphasized in studying Tables 13, 14 and 15 that the mention of any one item in the table does not preclude mentioning other items, and about half of the respondents did give second mentions; a third gave third mentions. The wide spread of items mentioned only underlines the problem sooner or later faced by all organizations concerned with peace and disarmament: that the achievement of disarmament depends on a complex pattern of events taking place at many levels. At what points in that pattern, and at what level, should an action organization put forth its main effort?

Table 14. Stumbling Blocks to World Peace

International

| Fear .... 15% |
| Nature of man .... 8% |
| Power struggle, economic |
| struggle, ideological |
| struggle .... 20% |
| Total 43% |

United States

Government policy
| Military-industrial complex ..... 16% |
| Other .... 2% |
Public opinion
| Fear, hatred of Communism ..... 5% |
| Total 23% |

Publics, any country

| Irresponsible press, other... 7% |
| Fear .... 8% |
| Other .... 12% |
| Total 27% | No answer: 7% | = 100% |

There is an interesting shift between Tables 14 and 15. When thinking of stumbling blocks to world peace, the respondents have naturally thought to a considerable extent in terms of their own country, since this is where their own efforts have been concentrated. But when asked to imagine what changes might take place which do not necessarily involve their personal efforts, they think more in terms of changes at the international level. International mentions go up from 43 per cent to 66 per cent, and national mentions go down from 23 per cent to 15 per cent. In a final question in this section on what kind of international machinery might be needed to keep peace if disarmament were to be achieved, 84 per cent think in terms of some kind of United Nations machinery, 11 per cent in terms of other types of arrangement, and only 3 per cent think that only "education" and "understanding" will be needed.

It seems, then, that the women who went out on strike for peace on November 1, 1961, and stayed on to work for peace in the following months, are a more complex and sophisticated group than the "buggy-pushing housewife" image conveys. Allowing for the fact that it was the most articulate (though not the most active) who answered the questionnaire, we see reflected through their eyes an earnest, thought-

196

Table 15. Changes Which Will Help Bring Peace

International			United States		
More cooperation, more communication between U.S.S.R. and U.S.		9%	Government policy		
Disarmament, stop testing		36%	Convert to peacetime economy		4%
World government, world law, strong U.N.		12%	Changed foreign policy		3%
Settle hotspots		9%	Public		
Total		66%	More informed, responsible		8%
			Total		15%

Other: 8%

No answer: 11%   = 100%

ful group of society's favored ones, the educated middle-class professionals and wives of professionals (who are also trying hard to attract their less-informed and less-concerned sisters). They are all ages, many have children still at home, and they have been aroused to such a keen sense of the urgency of the state of the world that they are willing to break out of usual behavior patterns and do odd things, such as demonstrating in public. The effort to nonconform to that extent is great, however, and they are quickly driven on to the next stage of thinking out what the task lying ahead really is, and how to be effective in working for it.

Why These Women?

One important questions remains. Why these women, and not the others? For every aroused middle class mother there are hundreds of unaroused ones. The question takes considerably more research and thought than can even be hinted at here, and there are many different kinds of basic research into nonconformity and alienation which throw some light on it, ranging from small-group experiments in manipulated perception to the depth-analysis type of interview undertaken in the authoritarian personality studies. At present, I can only quickly summarize the answers to some questions included in the questionnaire of a highly personal nature, about the respondent's personal "awakening" experiences, religious and political beliefs, her parents' beliefs, and the extent to which the respondent felt she obtained a significant part of her world view and concern about peace from her family. Frankly, a number of respondents resented these questions and could not see their relevance, but fortunately most of them answered anyway.[4]

---

[4]To all you women for peace who grumbled your way through the fifty questions as best you could and finally exploded on the last page, I take this opportunity for saying thanks for having answered anyway; I have a strong stomach for grumbles! And the code number on the last sheet was an area code only. Your anonymity has been preserved despite your suspicions to the contrary!

The unspoken question behind the question which followed is this: How important is the family in giving a child his world view? By looking into the childhood of this generation's mothers, perhaps we can get some clues for the recognizing and providing of relevant experiences in the lives of our children that will expand their sense of world community. And when a child grows up without such experiences at home, where do these experiences come from? This is important to know in working with teen-agers and adults.

Religious and Political Preferences

Fifty-three per cent of the women expressed a religious preference. This is about as expected in a group as intellectual as this one, and the direction of shift from parents' beliefs in very interesting and indicative of the times. There has been much more second-generation movement out of the Protestant churches than out of the Jewish, and substantial movements of Protestants into nontraditional sects (Quakers, etc.) and non-Christian groups as well as into the "none" category. Political preferences indicate an even greater movement away

Table 16. Religious Preference of Respondent and Parents

	Catholic	Jewish	Protestant	Non-traditional Sects	Other; qualified; non-Christian	None	No answer	
Respondents	1%	19%	9%	23%	13%	27%	8%	= 100%
R's parents	4%	33%	35%	5%	8%	7%	8%	= 100%

from parents' political preference. The heaviest movements has been away from the Republican party, but among the 53 per cent of women who call themselves Democrats, many wrote in parenthesis "an unhappy Democrat" or "an unsatisfied Democrat," or "used to vote Democratic," indicating there is no other affiliation which attracts them but that they are far from content with the party they are in. Thirty-five per cent call themselves independents, but with the new wave of political awareness sweeping over WSP it will be interesting to see whether they remain independents, form a new party, or return to one of the old parties. From the point of view of family identification, I find it interesting that fewer of the mothers than fathers of the respondents were Republicans. It points to an unusual degree of independence on the part of the mothers, since women traditionally vote with their husbands (not only in the United States but the world over).

The question of how much of their world views comes from their family divides the group three ways. A little more than a third have a

Table 17. Political Preference of Respondents and Parents

	Republican	Democrat	Independent	Liberal Radical Socialist	Other, & No answer	Apolitical	
Respondent	4%	53%	35%	4%	3.5%	0.5%	= 100%
Respondent's father	35%	40%	7%	5%	11%	2%	= 100%
Respondent's mother	26%	41%	6%	3%	16%	8%	= 100%

mild to strong feeling of continued similarity of views. A little less than a third feel their views are very dissimilar to those of their family, and the remainder do not mention their family at all. More women have a particular sense of closeness to father's views than to mother's views, and siblings loom a little larger, both positively and negatively, than either parent (confirming that "outnumbered" feeling mothers of large families are prone to have)!

Table 18. Degree of Family Influence on Respondent's Views

	Strong to Some Identity	Strong Difference	Split Among Siblings	No answer	No mention	
Undifferentiated family	33%	24%	--	12%	31%	= 100%
Mother	9%	3%	--	8%	80%	= 100%
Father	15%	5%	--	8%	72%	= 100%
Siblings	17%	12%	4%	7%	60%	= 100%

Where did those women who feel their views are strongly different from those of their family get their concern for world affairs? And even those who have a world affairs-oriented home, could they remember any particular time when they began to feel a strong concern about war? Seventy-five per cent of the women could pin point a special time in their lives when they began to feel a concern about war. For most of them it came in their teens, but there were mentions of every age from preschool to middle thirties.

Table 19. Age of Awakening to Concern Over War

Always	6-12	13-18	19-23	24-29	30 +	Don't know	No answer	
3%	17%	33%	18%	9%	14%	0	6%	= 100%

The two major types of awakening experiences described were based on intellectual insights that must have had a strong emotional reinforcement at the time: The experience was either the solitary one of reading a book or seeing a movie, or it was a classroom experience or discussion in a club or church group that presented certain questions very vividly to the mind and emotions. One woman described hearing "The Battle of Blenheim" read to her in school when she was between eight and ten. "But 'twas a famous victory—I remember my disgust." The third most important category is personal experiences of suffering and loss, ranging from losing a family member in the war or having actually lived overseas and seen war devastation, to having been the means of having killed or hurt a beloved animal. Next comes the range of reactions to Hiroshima and all the consequent chain of Hot and Cold War events (reactions to persecution of Jews are included here too); the point at which one of these events really got inside a respondent and started making her think things through differs enormously from woman to woman. The highly personal awakening at the birth of a child is found too, as are, finally, the comments, "I have felt this way ever since I can remember."

Table 20. Experience of Awakening to Concern for War

Independent reading, movies about war (I, II, Korea)	28%
School, college, church group experience	23%
First-hand experience of loss, suffering	16%
Atomic war, Cold War, persecution of Jews	15%
Birth of child	5%
Always concerned, gradual awakening	4%
Other and no answer	9%
	100%

The significance of the kinds of awakening experiences described for the kinds of views and activities the respondents adopt remains to be explored in further analysis.

In conclusion, we have glanced through the superficial "who" of these women, and we close with a confrontation of the still-elusive question Why? There will be much more to be said about both the who and the why after more time has been spent examining the thoughtful answers provided by these 279 women. I think there is little doubt that they represent a new potential worthy of RAND's serious consideration, and this same potential is probably also emerging in all parts of the peace movement, including the parts where the old-timers are! The merging of a concern intense enough to make middle-class women willing to look foolish in public with a trained intellect and social sophistication which makes them seek both for long-run solutions and for immediate political effectiveness is the mark of the new woman. By failing to include the analysis of the non-WSP women I have done a potential injustice to groups like the Women's International League for Peace and Freedom, which have carried on their half-century-long task of working for disarmament with undiminished vigor in the face of public apathy and scorn, and are now finally experiencing the renewing lift of working in an atmosphere more friendly to their concerns. A fuller report of our findings in the future will be able to document what is already clear from the first glance at the responses—that many WILPF members came to the aid of the Women Strike for Peace group and helped get it started, in addition to carrying on their own work. They perceived instinctively that this generation had to make its own movement and did not try to be possessive about the new spirit abroad in the land. They have, in fact, been richly rewarded by a great increase in their own strength and vitality too.

We may venture to remark in closing that never has the unique combination of <u>individuals</u> with particular qualifications and <u>times</u> "ripe for change" been so auspiciously presented to a social movement as at present. At a time when most thinking people the world over are seriously questioning the adequacy of existing national rituals for preserving human security on the globe, we find released into the stream of history a large group of well-educated women able to take time to participate in national and world affairs, and aroused to the necessary pitch of intensity to help them overcome their historical preference for the quieter activities of nest-building. This is something new under the sun!

Children and the Threat of Nuclear War

SIBYLLE K. ESCALONA

I intend to discuss the impact of the nuclear danger upon aspects of personality development in children. We know that environmental factors, specifically the social environment, play a large role in determining not only attitudes and patterns of behavior, but also psychological structures, that is, the development of character. The nearly universal recognition of a potential or, as many of us think, an actual threat to the continuity of human civilization and to the integrity of our biological habitat is a change in the social environment which ought to make a difference in the mental content and, thus, the psychological experience of children. On the basis of preliminary observations I am convinced that the profound uncertainty about whether or not mankind has a foreseeable future exerts a corrosive and malignant influence upon important developmental processes in normal and well-functioning children as well as in those who are in any case vulnerable to additional stress, owing to pre-existing psychopathology. In my view, the subtle and pervasive effects of the present social climate upon all children are a far more serious hazard than is the incidence of heightened anxiety and of fear which children share with the rest of us at moments of political crisis. In this paper I shall present some facts and some ideas in support of this conviction.

Before turning to the data, I want to make it clear that the exploration of the psychological consequences of the present crisis, important as it may be, is a secondary response to the actual threat to survival. If there is a real possibility that nuclear weapons will be used, with disastrous consequences for people everywhere and for all future generations, a preoccupation with the psychological aspects of the matter is trivial. It is as though a family in a house afire were to spend their time reassuring the children instead of putting out the fire. In our role as professionals and in our capacity as citizens, the primary task is social action to forestall a nuclear war and to work towards a livable world. I believe that it is possible to combine a primary commitment to necessary social action with an interest in identifying and counteracting malignant psychological aspects of the immediate situation.

There is strong evidence to show that children are aware of the

201

existence of nuclear weapons, of political tensions, and of the apprehensions felt by the adults with whom they live. We know less, however, about what this information means to children and about whether or not it makes a significant difference in their lives. An informally constituted group of colleagues in New York City, which calls itself The Committee on Children, decided to obtain factual data on children's conscious awareness of the world situation and on their attitudes toward it. Since the spring of 1962 this group has been at work developing a questionnaire which we hope to administer to large numbers of children in many parts of the country. At this time I can report only on what we have learned from pilot studies. We experimented with four different versions of the questionnaire, and samples were drawn from the greater New York area alone. Data were collected during the summer of 1962, well before the Cuban crisis, and during October and November, 1962, as well as February, 1963. Because of the variation in the form of questions and the inadequacies of sampling, no generalizations can be made on the basis of our material, not even about New York City. However, it remains of interest to know what children did say when asked their expectations of the future.

The present report is limited to the responses of 311 children between the ages of ten and seventeen years. (We also have 130 responses from younger children, but these are more difficult to evaluate and are here omitted). These 311 children were drawn from widely different socioeconomic groups. More than 100 questionnaires were obtained from schools and community centers serving grossly underprivileged areas and including a very large proportion of Puerto Rican and Negro children. Another third of the sample was obtained from schools and camps drawing on lower-middle- and middle-middle-class groups. And the remaining 100 questionnaires were obtained from private schools, one of them under religious auspices, which represent intellectual upper-middle-class cosmopolitan families.

We wanted to find out whether children's spontaneous and overtly conscious expectations in relation to the future are significantly affected by the nuclear danger. We know that unconscious expectations or fears may be potently at work and that children may not communicate conscious but anxiety-laden thoughts about the future. But I am among those who consider that conscious and communicable aspects of mental life carry a great deal of weight and are important. The effort was to get children to express their rational expectations about the future, and to ask our questions in such a way as not to suggest a direct reference to war or to the political situation.

The kinds of questions we asked were: "Think about the world as it may be about ten years from now. What are some of the ways in which it may be different from today?" Also: "How would you like it to be different?" "If you had three wishes, what would they be?"

As you can imagine, we obtained perfectly fascinating material on children's vision of expanded space and of an automatized world. Interplanetary travel, space stations, trips to the moon, flying cars, machines for all possible purposes (including one in which, as an 11-year-old suggested, "you push a button and it tells you what you should do that day"), and robots loomed very large. The universal wish for a long life or immortality, and for lots of money, was expressed by nearly all children. A great many spoke of miracle cures for fatal diseases, of better living conditions, of an end to discrimination, of better education and housing, and of more kindness in the world. Among the underprivileged city children there was a surprisingly strong emphasis on beauty and cleanliness. These children want beautiful houses, clean streets, flowers, country life, and contact with animals, not to speak of urgent concerns about jobs, health, school grades, bicycles, and enough food.

How much room did all of this leave for larger concerns in behalf of the future? Of these 311 children, 219 (or 70 per cent) mentioned the issue of war and peace. In all but a few instances this was more than a pious wish for world peace included among the three wishes. As you shall hear, these children often spoke of what war would mean, of how and why they thought the world would arrive at a peaceful existence, and of the main obstacles to peace. As one would expect, the undereducated children from marginal social groups were neither as articulate, nor as a group were they as preoccupied with the danger of war, as were the middle-class children of comparable ages. With the exception of a small group of twelve- and thirteen-year-olds from a Harlem district, who were the most pessimistic of our samples, the frequency with which the problem of war was discussed was lower for the poor children. Of the underprivileged groups (excluding the Harlem sample), 39 per cent mentioned the possibility of war in speaking of their future. For the lower-middle-class group the corresponding value was 62 per cent, and for the middle-middle- and upper-middle-class groups the corresponding values were 75 per cent, 79 per cent and 100 per cent.

However, if one turns to what these children have to say about the topic, how pessimistic they are once they do mention war, it turns out that the underprivileged groups are at least as pessimistic as the others. Of those who mention war, 35 per cent considered a destructive war very possible or even a certainty. Slightly more often than most other groups, they saw it as a decisive alternative. As a twelve-year-old put it, "We may have gone to the moon. We would maybe have a new way of transportation. Maybe we will not even be here 10 years from now. Maybe there will be no such thing as a world. Maybe there will be a world war III. We don't know." Or, as another has it, "I think I would be all broken up because of the war which will come. The war destroys New York."

The over-all impression from comparing the responses from the deprived group with those from the middle-class group is as follows: That many of these children are so preoccupied by immediate pressing concerns, such as poverty, worry about school grades and jobs, and hostile elements in the immediate situation such as gangs, that there is less house-room for the contemplation of more remote dangers. Not unrelated to this is the circumstance that many of these children are cognitively impoverished, and the future is not envisaged except in immediate terms. But also, once such children do recognize the danger to future existence, they are more inclined to view it fatalistically and pessimistically. They express a wish for peace, but express no notions of how it might come about and little expectation of a positive solution.

Before describing the variation of expectation and of attitude encountered among these children, I would like to make one more general observation. As already mentioned, some of the data was obtained before the Cuban crisis, the remainder shortly afterwards. One would expect that the tension during that October week would have greatly reinforced children's awareness of the possibility of war, and in many ways it must have done so. However, of the 55 children who responded while at summer camps, 79 per cent discussed the problem of peace and war, and of these, 34 per cent envisaged a destructive war as a wholly possible and, in some instances, a probable alternative. You will remember that during the summer of 1962 the question of shelter-building received much heated discussion. In New York City, at any rate, it is my impression that throughout the shelter controversy, and throughout the simultaneous public stir about fallout levels as the result of atmospheric testing, children were strongly impressed with the possibility that they and their own homes might be endangered by powerful atomic weapons. In any case, for the children in our sample the concern was as great before the Cuban crisis as it was afterwards.

By and large, those 218 children who mentioned the possibility of war also committed themselves to a probability statement. I have already cited some examples of the extreme, namely a firm expectation of war or, more frequently, a decisive either-or statement. I shall supplement these by giving you other examples of how such views are expressed by different children. A twelve-year-old answered a question about whether anything could be done about keeping the bad things from happening thus: "No, because all of the people will die and the world will blow up." A fourteen-year-old speculates that ten years from now the world could be "completely united—and have no danger of war. If there was war before then, the world could be almost completely destroyed with no certain power but just poverty-stricken countries. " Another fourteen-year-old: "Either complete peace or total destruction. " A thirteen-year-old: "Red China is going to become more powerful than any other country, and they'll probably find the atom bomb and bomb the world. " That this child connected these anticipations with survival becomes clear in some of her other answers. For instance, she also writes, "I feel that man has enough trouble surviving on earth and why should they (literally) seek for more problems. " An eleven-year-old thinks the world would be "more modern (if we aren't wiped out by the bomb first). " And last, a thirteen-year-old: "I think if there is a world ten years from now, it will be horrible and full of fear from war (with whatever weapon they have invented by then). "

Many of the children who do not consider that a war may well occur, nonetheless envisage a remarkably unpleasant future. Here are some examples. A fourteen-year-old: "The people of the world never change, but the atomic powers will still be expanding and the threat of war and complete destruction will hang as a cloud of fear over the world. And people will have to live with the fear of death eventually by the instruments of war. " An eleven-year-old: "In ten years countries will still be quarrelling—larger countries will be preparing bombs to wipe out the world. " Another eleven-year-old writes: "The people will be living underground, and they would have to have a lot of light or I think the children would not be very strong as they are now. But I really hope it will be a lot better than I think it will be. " And a ten-year-old says, "There wouldn't be any schools or houses and they would live in the ground. People would be different colors and have long feet and long hands. That's what I think the world will be ten years from now. " This child, too, is quite serious; in response to the question of how she would like it different, she writes that "it would be peaceful and happy. " The older and well-educated children displayed their pessimism in sophisticated ways. A fourteen-year-old first described medical advances and continued, "Yet as far as the world situation is concerned tension will be much worse. " He explains that Red China will have the bomb and will expand, that Russia will be unable to control China, and that the underdeveloped countries will turn to Communism. American politics, he thinks, would turn more to the right as the world situation worsens, and he concludes with, "Great powers would continue to pollute the atmosphere with test bombs. " A large proportion of the questionnaire answers obtained, especially from the private schools, turned into essays of this sort which, in totality, touch upon every aspect of the problem. Disarmament, the United Nations, a World Federation and World Court, the economics of conversion to nonmilitary production, the changing balance of power among nations, ideological conflict, moral and religious aspects, and the psychological roots of aggression all are mentioned, and frequently discussed very sensibly.

Another interesting aspect is what these children say and imply about the causes of danger and about the changes required to make peace possible. Only 11 children (or about 3 per cent) gave evidence of a mechanism surely more common in other groups, that of externalizing the danger on Communism (or on Khrushchev and Castro personally). And even these few expressed sympathy with the people in Communist countries, hoping that they will become free. The vast majority see the problem as the necessity for nations and people to get along, and always include this country in their demands for finding peaceful solutions. The younger ones, and many of the children from depriving backgrounds, seem to treat it as a matter of personal friendliness and intention. A good many children write the equivalent of a ten-year-old's plea, "I wish Russia and Cuba be our friends." The older and more sophisticated children recognize conflicting interests and the need for legal and military mechanisms to maintain peace. Most are critical of the power needs of large countries and appear to include America. Here are some examples. During the second week of October, 1962, an eleven-year-old said: "I would like Kennedy and Fidel Castro to become good friends and both countries start to live together and we shouldn't have war—and there will be no more fighting and that we would not have to live underground." Another eleven-year-old answered the question, "Is there anything that can be done to keep the bad things from happening?" "Yes, by making friends with other countries, that's why we have United Nations." A fourteen-year-old: "I would like to see the 'big 5' sit down and discuss the world situation with good results... and we could all live with no threats of bombs hanging about our heads." A thirteen-year-old would like: new leaders and "a peace organization better than the U. N." "If East and West cooperated," he continues, "medicine and space science would improve and warfare would fall into the past." Or again, a fourteen-year-old: "I would like to see the U. S. and U. S. S. R. friendly and all their scientists working together for the good of mankind." You should know that all of these quotes about cooperation come from public school children. The more sophisticated private school youngsters expressed the same sentiments, but were far more knowledgeable about disarmament, negotiation, peace movements, and the economic sources of conflict.

It would be tempting to continue with the questionnaire material, for the powerful impression of troubled and wistfully hopeful children has a cumulative effect as one reads dozens and hundreds of these answers. In particular, it would be well to survey the answers obtained to the question of "How would you like it to be different?" This question seemed to invite the indirect expression of fears and dissatisfactions. It is here that children spoke of hoping that there would be no more fear of bombs and radiation, that people might not be hurt, that there would be less fighting, less poverty, better treatment of Negroes, and all the rest.

However, the time has come to say a few things about the implication of these and other observations for the development of children. Developmental psychology has begun to make explicit some of the ways in which children internalize and make part of themselves what they learn from adult models. We think that certain patterns of adaptation characterize each major developmental stage. And by the same token, we think that each phase of development is especially vulnerable or sensitive to particular aspects of the outer world. For the school-age and adolescent stages, to which this discussion is limited, the central developmental processes revolve around the mechanisms of identification and of the establishment of personal identity. As I use these terms, they are related but not interchangeable. Identification is a dominant mode of middle childhood, whereas identity formation is the integration and synthesis of all past identifications into a cohesive sense of self and of one's place in the scheme of things. Much of adolescent development can be understood, as Erikson has pointed out, as the struggle to achieve a sense of personal identity. I propose that nuclear danger necessarily weakens and impedes the most useful and constructive processes of identification in school-age children, and that it distorts normal processes of identity formation in adolescents. It goes without saying that patterns of family living and the broader social scene have always contained disruptive elements. Long before nuclear weapons had been dreamed of, both constructive identifications and an acceptable identity were hard to come by—and the psychiatric clinics, the hospitals, the schools, and the courts are witness to the many, many failures of development which our society has produced. My hypothesis is merely that the changes in the social milieu and within individuals that occur in the wake of the nuclear crisis are of such a kind as to make still more difficult developmental progress in these two areas.

To be specific, though necessarily schematic, school-age children are profoundly aware of their status as children. This means to them both that they are as yet dependent and unable to compete with adults, and also that they are in the process of growing and of learning to become adult. Their image of what there is to be learned, of what it means to be an adult, of the attitudes, skills, and attributes of successful living all come from what they see and sense in their elders. As we know to our cost, they identify not only with that which makes a powerful positive impression—courage, lovingness, skill, and learning—but also with painful and hateful components in the personalities of those who loom large in their lives. The sons of ineffective fathers may desperately strive for strength and masculinity and

seize upon teachers, public heroes, or any other models as identification figures. Yet, at the same time, they may come to feel unconsciously that in becoming a man and a father, one is doomed to become
as weak and ineffective as one's own father was. In short, those identifications that have adaptive value and that are strengthening to the child
are derived from models who actually possess useful virtues and successful kinds of competence. An oversimplified version of a change in
identification figures that occurs as a result of the nuclear crisis is
as follows. Children know that an overwhelming danger exists. But
what they see also is that parents, teachers, in fact, all adults feel
inadequate to cope with this danger. Even the most affirmative sup-
porter of action for peace cannot assure children of his complete confidence in a livable future. This is an unalterable fact, as long as nuclear weapons are allowed to exist. But most children see, most of
the time, more than that there are destructive forces which even adults
cannot control. They see in their elders evasion or lethargy based on
underlying fear and fatalism—and children are known to be sensitive
to underlying feelings and to unconscious defenses that operate within
adults. And other children see helpless anxiety and manifest despair in
adults who have become keenly concerned. Only rarely can children
see what is so rare on the social scene, namely, a resolute facing of
the problem and clear-cut convictions as well as deliberate action,
even without assurance of success. Many of those children who do
observe a firm stand in their elders—and this group was apparently
not sampled by our questionnaire—are given a demonstration of hatred
and scapegoating as the only solution. To judge by the newspapers and
by some public utterances, the way to stay alive is to trust no one and
to destroy your opponents. These are also far from optimal patterns of
identification. And while they may serve as a protection against anxiety on one level, they generate anxiety on another. For surely such an
image of the world and how to survive is, to say the least, ugly and
uninviting.

An equally oversimplified formulation in relation to the adolescents must attempt to reconcile strong impulses from within, with all
they have learned about themselves, about reality, and about the larger
social framework in which they live. Inevitably, their better acquaint-
ance with the adult community, with adult values and adult traditions
leads to disappointment and rebellious criticism. However personal
and immature the reasons for adolescent scorn may be, young people
have a keen eye for the shortcomings and inconsistencies of adult society. The hypocrisy and selfishness and emptiness of which adolescents have complained since time immemorial really exist. And if it
were not for young people, and for those who in their youth acquire
enduring altruistic attitudes, society would lack a most important im-
petus for progress. Under ordinary circumstances, adolescents be-

come young adults and achieve a more objective perspective largely in response to the realistic opportunities for satisfying experience which society offers. There are opportunities for learning and teaching, scientific advances are exciting, happy relationships among people are possible, there are jobs, and sexual partners, and opportunities of many kinds. It is not required that these satisfactions be guaranteed. Young people come to terms with the adult world as long as it holds out a reasonable promise for the fulfillment in some spheres of living. Adolescent growth is largely a matter of the pull exerted by the prospect of maturity pitted against remaining needs for dependency and the security of childhood. But if there is no future to look forward to, or if it seems chiefly disastrous, where is the pull for maturity to come from? Had there been space to tell you more of what adolescents wrote, you would have no doubt that the recognition of the threat to survival is of vital moment to children at that stage. And what was said about identification figures for middle childhood is now extended to adult value systems. Adolescents find more than ordinary cause for profound distrust of adult standards of thought and behavior. It is as though the wildest adolescent phantasies of adult insufficiency had suddenly come true. For they feel that it is we who brought things to such a pass and who are not going to better them. I have elsewhere discussed another adolescent reaction to the world crisis, which has also occurred. It consists of an alliance among young people and those elements of adult society that do assume an active and consistent stand in relation to the issues of peace and of human betterment. The formation of personal identity can, under some conditions, find its focus in this issue.

There are no conclusions, but the alternatives that emerge are well expressed by two of our young respondents. One of them was laconic in replying to the question about the world ten years from now. He wrote "we be dead." The other, an adolescent, gave as his first and foremost wish: "Valid reasons to believe in future progress, not regress and destruction for myself and the world."

Let us listen to the children.

Nuclear Cold War: Student Opinions and Professional Responsibility

MILTON SCHWEBEL

In the aftermath of the 1961 Berlin crisis close to 3,000 students most of them in high school, were asked to write their answers to questions on war and civil defense. The crisis had been fraught with danger. Fear was rife in the nation, and its people were engaged in a debate on the adequacy of deterrent force and of fallout shelters as solutions. But what of the children? Were they a special breed inured to crisis because they had lived their entire lives in the shadow of thermonuclear mushrooms? Even this June's high school graduates were born after Hiroshima, and most college undergraduates first became aware of a world beyond their threshold only after the world had unlocked the secret that gave it the power to destroy itself. Do they take it as a matter of course and of no concern that crises will occur again and again? Are they freer of fear than we who grew up in an era when our land was beyond reach of a potential enemy's might? More specifically, do they expect war or peace? And do they look with favor upon fallout shelters?

Sample and Design

Three simple questions were prepared. They were designed to be intelligible to the young and backward pupils and meaningful to students at all levels. The questions are: I) Do I think there is going to be a war? II) Do I care? Why? III) What do I think about fallout shelters?[1]

Through the cooperation of principals, counselors, and teachers, the questions were answered anonymously by about 3,000 students from grade three through first year college, with a heavy con-

---

[1] A fourth question, "What do you think will happen if there is a war?" was asked. Because responses tended to duplicate those given to Question II, they were not analyzed.

centration at the junior high school level. Various social strata are represented, including working-class children in very depressed areas, e. g. , Williamsburg in Brooklyn, and upper-middle-class, e. g. , Westchester and Park Avenue. The ability range is from extremely slow classes (IQ range on group tests from 70 to 90) to classes of very able students, and the language range is from the level of near illiteracy to that of literary talent.

Geographical representation includes three different types of areas, each having a potentially different immediate fate in the event of nuclear war: urban (New York City); suburban (the environs of New York and Philadelphia); mountain (Upstate New York). The responses of about 2, 200 students, almost all of them in the junior and senior high school, have been analyzed. Because the sample is "Middle Atlantic State" in nature and is not stratified, it is impossible to make projections for all students in the U. S. However, the size of the respective subsamples is such as to permit reliable subgroup estimates and intergroup comparisons.

A simple form of content analysis was employed to determine direction of response to each of the questions. One class, randomly selected, was scored by three scorers. Agreement by all three was achieved in more than 90 per cent of the papers for each of the three questions.

Responses

The written responses of the students reveal that as a group they present the complete array of reasons for the probability of war and peace and of arguments for and against the use of fallout shelters. A summary of typical responses to each of the three questions will convey a sense of the tone and the affect:

I. Do I think there will be a war?

Those who expected war gave reasons like the following: tension between nations, especially the U. S. and the U. S. S. R. ; crises such as Berlin, Laos, Cuba; competition for power between the U. S. and the U. S. S. R. ; nuclear testing, and stronger and stronger weapons the danger of an accident; the greed of men; humans have fought and always will; Communism, Russia, China, Premier Khrushchev; President Kennedy; all the shelter talk. *

Those who expected peace gave as their reasons: all nations and peoples will be destroyed; no one can win; nobody wants to die;

---

*Editor's Note: This paper was written in 1962.

the President will prevent it; the Communists don't want it; it hasn't happened so far with all the crises; people's greed won't permit them to see their wealth destroyed; the Soviet Union has developed too much to want to see itself destroyed.

II. Do I care? Why?

"Yes, I care," was almost invariably the response, with such occasional additions as, everybody does; anyone who doesn't is insane (or crazy or inhuman); a naïve question; it's insulting even to be asked this.

Some of the typical reasons cast in personal terms are : I will die; my parents, brothers, sisters, friends will die. My family and I will be separated. If my family dies and I live, I'd rather be dead. I am young and want a future to live, marry, have a family, work, create, paint, etc. My father will be drafted. I will be drafted. The U. S. S. R. is strong and will win. Even if I survive, what will there be worth living for, with millions dead?

Other reasons for caring, in somewhat less personal terms, are: The world will be destroyed, the earth thrown out of axis. Civilization will be destroyed. My country will be destroyed. Innocent people and babies (even on the enemy's side) and my generation who had nothing to do with bringing it on will die. Peace is beautiful. God meant for men to live in peace and be brothers. What will war solve? Will people then begin to fight again, this time with sticks and stones?

In some instances intense anxiety was revealed, such as: I worry. I cry. Sometimes I am disturbed at night. I don't like to think about it, it's so terrible.

"No, I don't care." The reasons given by this small percentage of respondents can be subdivided into three types: a) If I began to care and think about it, I wouldn't be able to enjoy life anymore. b) I can't do anything about it; I'm helpless, impotent; if it happens, it will be God's will. c) Why worry—you've got to die some day. Anyway, I think we'll win.

III. What do I think about fallout shelters?

This summary of typical responses is subdivided into "Yes," "Yes, but....," " "No, but...., " and "No" groups. Many of the "but" responses were identical except, of course, for the conclusion that the individual drew from the contingencies he presented.

"Yes, I favor shelters:" They are very good; just what we need to save some people for future generations, to save some to rebuild democracy, to save my family. They're better than nothing. I'm for anything that might save life.

"Yes, I favor shelters, but"—not if you're in a direct hit, or in a target center, or poor and don't have a shelter, or if you're separated from the family or the family gets broken up, or if you must kill your neighbors, or if there are not community shelters. Yes, but what then, if you live and animals are dead and there's no food?

"No, I'm against shelters, but"—some could be saved by shelters but then there'd be riots and panic; what good is it to be saved with family separated and maybe some dead? What about afterward, with no food? Rather be dead than come out and find a desolate world, bodies all around. If God wants the world destroyed, shelters won't help.

"No, I'm against shelters"—they are stupid, a farce, a money-making proposition; they just are preparing people for a horrible war. It's like building your own tomb; they won't work; radiation will seep in; food and oxygen shortage; and what afterward? There's no future in them. Work for peace, instead. Pray, instead.

Findings

During the fall and winter of 1961, junior high school students were about evenly divided in the expectation of war (Table I-a). Senior

Table 1

"Do I think there will be a war?"

Distribution of Responses (per cents) and Chi Square

	Sample	(N)	Yes	Ambivalent[1]	No
I-a	Junior High	(1711)	45	9	46
	Senior High	(164)	42	6	52
I-b	Junior High[2]	(1330)	44	8	48
	Senior High	(164)	42	6	52
	$x^2 = 1.885$	2 d.f.	$0.50 > P > 0.30$		
I-c	Average/slow	(122)	52.	12	36
	Bright students	(134)	36	7	57
	$x^2 = 11.047$	2 d.f.	$P < 0.10$		

1. This category also includes a small number of no responses.
2. For the analysis of difference between the two distributions, the New York City students were eliminated from the junior high sample because these students were not represented in the senior high sample.

high school students were slightly more optimistic. The difference be
tween the junior and senior high school students was not statistically
significant (Table 1-b). When brightness was introduced as a factor
in the junior high school sample, with each of five classes of brighter
students matched with a class of average/slow students in the same
school and grade, bright students were found to be significantly more
optimistic about peace than average/slow students (Table I-c).

About 95 per cent of the students said they cared about a war,
usually because they saw death, destruction, and separation from their
families as the consequences. For the most part, the other 5 per cent
handled their concern by such mechanisms as denial, e.g., "If I allowed myself to care, I would not be able to enjoy life anymore."

Junior high school students were about evenly divided concerning
the use of fallout shelters, whereas senior high students were strongly
opposed (Table II-a). The difference between the two levels (junior and
senior high) was highly significant (Table II-b). Likewise, a majority
of bright junior high students opposed the use of shelters while average/
slow students favored them; the difference between the two groups was
statistically significant (Table II-c).

Table 2

"What do I think about fallout shelters?"

Distribution of Responses (per cents) and Chi Square

	Sample	(N)	Yes	Ambivalent[1]	No
II-a	Junior High	(1711)	48	12	40
	Senior High	(164)	21	10	69
II-b	Junior High[2] (excluding N.Y.C.)	(1330)	45	12	43
	Senior High	(164)	21	10	69
	$x^2 = 41.560$		2 d.f.		$P < 0.01$
II-c	Average/slow	(122)	62	12	26
	Bright students	(134)	33	12	55
	$x^2 = 24.230$		2 d.f.		$P < 0.01$

1. This category also includes a small number of no responses.
2. For the analysis of difference between the two distributions,
the New York City students were eliminated from the junior
high sample because these students were not represented in
the senior high sample.

When high school students in a mountain community were compared with those from metropolitan suburbia, the two groups were not significantly different in their expectations of war or peace. However, on attitudes toward shelters the junior high mountain group was significantly different from its suburban counterpart (Table III). Surprisingly, in the mountain area, where shelters would have greater immediate value, they were less favorably regarded. It is possible that uncontrolled demographic factors were responsible for the difference; yet even the absence of difference between these two groups would suggest that at least some of the students were responding to something other than the realities of survival.

Table 3

Comparison of Response Distributions (per cents) of Suburban and Mountain Students on Fallout Shelter Question

Sample	(N)	Yes	Ambivalent[1]	No
Junior High[2]				
Suburban	(1183)	46	12	42
Mountain	(147)	35	12	53
$x^2 = 7.58$		2 d.f.	$0.05 > P > 0.02$	
Senior High				
Suburban	(79)	11	14	75
Mountain	(85)	29	7	64
$x^2 = 9.05$		2 d.f.	$0.02 > P > 0.01$	

1. This category also includes a small number of no responses.
2. For the analysis of difference between the two distributions, the New York City students were eliminated from the junior high sample because these students were not represented in the senior high sample.

Although both senior high school groups were clearly opposed to shelters, the mountain group was less so, and the difference between the distribution of the two was statistically significant. Possibly this reversal reflects the greater knowledge of the senior high school groups and an awareness of the relative immediate advantage of their respective locales in the event of war.

Cuban Crisis Week

During the first week of the Cuban crisis about three hundred high school students answered the same questions. Two hundred junior high school responses were written by students who were roughly comparable[2] to a large segment of the post-Berlin crisis sample. The President addressed the nation Monday evening; these papers were written on Wednesday, Thursday, and Friday. Analysis of the responses showed that at this critical time the students were considerably more optimistic about peace than their counterparts had been a year earlier (69 per cent expected peace as opposed to only 48 per cent in 1961—Table IV-a). They were more strongly opposed to shelters than students had been a year earlier (66 per cent were rated as opposing shelters as opposed to 43 per cent in 1961—Table IV-b).

Table 4

Comparison of Response Distributions (per cents)
Post-Berlin Crisis and Cuban Crisis Week
Junior High School Samples

	Sample	(N)	Yes	Ambivalent[1]	No
IV-a*	Post-Berlin	(1330)	44	8	48
	Cuban Crisis	(200)	23	8	69
IV-b**	Post-Berlin	(1330)	45	12	43
	Cuban Crisis	(200)	30	4	66

1. This category also includes a small number of no responses.

* "Do I think there will be a war?"
** "What do I think of fallout shelters?"

Once again, the brighter students were found to be more optimistic about peace than their less able classmates (with 80 per cent of the bright students expecting peace); and the brighter students were more strongly rejecting of shelters (with 80 per cent seeing little or no value in them in the event of nuclear war).

Discussion

Whatever else may be said about "our younger generation" it seems clear that in so far as it is represented by the sample in this study, it knows and cares about the threat of thermonuclear war. From whatever source they derive these facts, and whether they live in a

---

[2]Both samples (post-Berlin and Cuban crisis week) were suburban and junior high school level. However, comparability of brightness level was difficult to establish.

metropolis, or a suburb, or in a mountain town, the students know that widespread death and destruction are in store for them and the world in the event of war. [3] And they describe the nightmarish horrors with such vividness one would think they had read the recently published book, Children of the A-Bomb (1), which contains the compositions written by children between ten and eighteen who, in Hiroshima on a hot August morning six years earlier, had seen their world collapse about them. (2) If at times the students introduce such anomalies as "father might die at the front," they are very likely echoing some of the confused thinking of an older generation still bound to the concepts of traditional warfar.

Nor can this generation be accused of selfishness. Hundreds of students were concerned with the fates of others, of family and friends, infants and the unborn, strangers and foreigners. Many were saddened at the thought that the great progress of mankind, its culture and civilization itself were endangered. Of course, they were worried about their own survival, bitter about the possible deprivation of the satisfactions of adult life, anxious about mutations and monstrosities. Perhaps their strongest emotions were reserved for those adults who advocated shutting the door of a shelter on strangers and neighbors and, if need be, shooting them down. They were horrified at the suggestion and demanded that if shelters were built they must be available to all people, rich or poor.

Of all the concerns, none seemed more acute than that of separation from family and siblings. While experiences in Great Britain during World War II, e.g., as reported by Freud and Burlingham, [4] might have predicted this for the youngest school children, it was surprising to discover a similar reaction among high school students as well. This could, in part at least, explain some of the negative attitude toward shelters, for many of the respondents expressed their dread at being in a shelter without knowledge of the safety of a parent

---

[3]This is almost as true of the children in the intermediate grades (whose responses have not been included in the analysis) as of the adolescents in high school. In a questionnaire study of about 200 parents of *elementary school children* (suburban and rural), the evidence was clear that such children did sometimes think about war and shelters.. Seventy per cent of 140 parents indicated that children commented about these issues. The children were especially interested in learning about protecting themselves and their families, but 35 per cent did comment about protection for people other than the immediate family.

[4]A. Freud and D. Burlingham observed nursery school children found the war of little significance as long as only their comforts and food were affected or their lives threatened. But war "becomes enormously significant the moment it breaks up family life..." (3)

or brother or sister, and their preference for death to survival in a decimated family. [5]

Fear appears to be a determinant in the prediction of peace. Those who are most knowledgeable about the consequences of thermonuclear war and who clearly differentiate its probable consequences from those of past wars are most likely to fear it. The brighter students and those in the upper grades, who are probably better informed than the average or dull students, or those in lower grades, respectively, were more optimistic about peace, a finding comparable to that of Withey in his study of adults. [6] Furthermore, the immediate threat posed by the Cuban crisis elicited responses that paradoxically were more expectant of peace.

These same subgroups of students, presumably the more knowledgeable ones, tend to reject shelters as a worthwhile instrument of survival in the threat of war; and during Cuban crisis week their opposition to shelters was even greater. Something more than shelters is at stake here. These students now find their beliefs in conflict with official policy, and some of them perceive the pursuit of the shelter program as irrational behavior on the part of adults.

Many other investigations of theoretical interest can be made with the students' responses to the questions, such as the modes of handling fear, and differences between the sexes and social classes. But the essential information for the purposes of the study has already been evaluated. And through it all—through all the papers and the analyzed data—runs the theme, clearly and consistently, that children know and fear the dangers of nuclear disaster; that the more they know it, the more they fear it and wish for, pray for, and insist upon peaceful solutions. And when they have no hope, they live in dread of the future.

The analyses that have been made offer no valid measure of the degree to which mental anguish has been converted into pathology. In most instances the responses do not indicate the extent to which the students are preoccupied with these concerns; they do not indicate the intensity of the students' feelings at times other than that spent responding to the questions, or their defensive maneuvers. The question of the effects of cold war on mental health is difficult to research, just as it is difficult to assess the somatic pathology caused by radioactive fallout. Only epidemiological studies some years hence will be

---

[5]The late Ralph Linton described the family as the bedrock of human relationships. "In the Gotterdammerung which over-wise science and over-foolish statesmanship are preparing for us, the last man will spend his last hours searching for his wife and child." (4)

[6]Stephen B. Withey found that adults with higher education found war less likely than those with less education. The same was found when the variable, information about world affairs, was assessed. (8A)

able to give us more definitive, but even then perhaps not conclusive, answers to questions about the effects respectively of test fallout and of the fears induced by Cold War. Yet in the absence of conclusive empirical data we hardly need suspend judgment and avoid professional encounters with the problem. Wars, hot or cold, like depressions, unemployment, poverty, give rise to social problems that are incontrovertibly related to individual behavior.[7] They influence morality and hence interpersonal relations; they shake security and thus shape perceptions of the social scheme and expectations for the future. Time and again the students described their universe as a highly uncertain one, its people greedy and irrational, its future questionable. Their great hope lay in the fact that no nation could win and that rational people would not choose suicide, or that, at least, conflict would be postponed until they had had a chance "to live," i.e., to work, marry, have children.

An insecure world is bound to take its toll of health. For the disturbed child, like the students in the study who wrote that they cried themselves to sleep terrified by thoughts of war, the extra burden of fear may be more than he can bear. For the normal child, the uncertainty of the future is not in the forefront of his thoughts, but it probably has its eroding effects in more indirect form. High school girls are frightened by the danger of having deformed babies, and boys and girls are cynical about preparing for a future of which they say they are being cheated.

Some of the students, like those who said they did not permit themselves to think about the world, are defending themselves against stress by the mechanisms of suppression, avoidance, and denial. These mechanisms can be effective, but only at a price, and the more efficient a child becomes, the greater the price he pays. To keep the danger of nuclear war out of his mind, he must avoid thinking of world conflict and of everything else that might remind him of war. Current events in school, the news reports on television and radio and in the daily papers can unsettle him. To defend himself he avoids reading and listening to the news, and to play it safe, gradually extends this to other listening and reading matter. Of course, he must carefully censor his thoughts, lest they bring the dangerous threats to mind. So, to defend himself from the disturbing effects of the times, he

---

[7]Writing about the long-run effects of disaster on mental health, Wilson notes that little is known. "There is no reason to think that stress promotes only dramatic change, instantly perceptible to the observer—or indeed, to the subject." Because of the enduring quality of stress, he recommends follow-up studies, tracing the covert consequences. (5)

sacrifices some of his powers to read and to listen with comprehension, and to think. [8]

These are, in general, the two paths open to young people: to face the facts of a destructive nuclear war and to pay the price of at least the slow erosive effects of an additional burden of fear, or to avoid the facts and to pay the price in denying themselves at least partial use of their most human characteristics, the abilities to think and to understand.

Which of these two paths children and adolescents take depends in large measure on their adult models, among them, their teachers. They see us as persons who have mastered the problems of life, and their security depends in part on their confidence in adopting our attitudes toward threatening events and our problem-solving techniques. By participating in our adaptive measures they acquire or modify their problem-coping techniques. If they see us act ostrich-like and deny the existence of threat, they will do the same. If they see us hysterical or blind with rage, they are most likely to adopt emotional responses to threat. If, on the other hand, they see us confront the issues in a rational, analytical way, sensitive to human values yet objective about facts, they are likely to acquire these habits of thought.

Perhaps the most effective counter-agent to fear is the recognition that one is not powerless in the face of a threat to survival. It is true of all people, but especially of those of school age, that passive waiting for a dreaded event can be devastating. Students are strengthened when they learn that many groups are striving to solve the problems of survival and of international conflict, and when they discover that they themselves can participate in shaping their destiny.

Jahoda (7) defined the healthy person as one who is able to perceive the world and himself correctly, who masters his environment, and possesses a unity of personality. This last quality may be regarded as a consequence of the other two characteristics; that is, the ability to comprehend the laws of motion of the natural and social world, and the active participation in controlling it, give one a sense of confidence, of integrity and wholeness. If the divergent theories of psychotherapy and analysis have one mutual principle, it is in this criterion of successful treatment, that the executive powers of the patient are now sufficiently strong to permit a greater openness to experience and more autonomy in organizing his life. If there is one over-all objective in formal education, though often disregarded in practice, it is to facilitate the child's understanding of his world and

---

[8]Martha Wolfenstein has elaborated on the use of denial, on its occurrence as a mechanism when an individual feels helpless to cope with a threat, on its compatibility with the need to feel strong which is shaken by impotence. American parents are seen as models who control or repudiate anxious feelings. (6)

to foster his capacities to participate in the social process of mastering the environment.

Knowledge and mastery, the common elements in the definitions, provide a guiding principle in our professional work with children and parents. There are no panaceas, psychological or otherwise, and this principle is not offered as one. We are discussing a complex problem, particularly as we consider variations in individual reaction. [9] A theoretical framework is not intended to imply oversimplification but rather to provide guidance in determining action in concrete situations. The students know about nuclear war. For the most part they go about their daily lives seemingly unaffected, and perhaps for only a handful of children, if that many, can mental health problems be directly attributable to the Cold War. Yet it is clear that many of them have gnawing fears and that at least at crisis times—e.g., Cuban crisis week—these fears are activated. Their responses give reason to believe that their morale has been shaken and their values colored by the reiterations of danger unaccompanied by opportunities to participate in the social act of protecting one's community and achieving peace. It is precisely these opportunities that are presented here as therapeutic. Study that leads to more profound understanding, and action that is perceived as contributing to the maintenance of peace and the security of the community are adaptive behaviors. Mental health includes the ability to cope with life's crises. Young people should not have to rely so heavily upon primitive thinking, denial, and evasion; they do not have to be preoccupied with images of a phenomenon to which some adults, perhaps in their own anxiety, react with a hush-hush response. There need be no mystery about war, no special aura. Man has known untold cruelty and destructiveness; what is different now is only its magnitude and the fact that for once our land is endangered.

This guiding principle—that understanding and action be employed in response to threat—was used in formulating a set of recommended practices for teachers (9). The title headings of the practices are presented as an example of the applications of this approach:

1. Show interest in student views about war, survival, and the maintenance of peace.

2. Aid and encourage them to acquire the knowledge necessary for an understanding of the issues (10).

3. By example and instruction stress the need for an objective and analytical approach to the problems of nuclear cold war.

4. In accordance with their ages (11) and, of course, their interests, help students find constructive actions in which to engage.

---

[9] A schema for the consideration of individual behavior in the face of threat is described by S.B. Withey. (8)

5. Espouse those deeply human values that have characterized our best traditions.

6. Use discussion, among other reasons to detect and correct distortions about the bomb, the dangers, and the efforts to achieve peaceful solutions.

7. Teach the students respect for differing views and particularly dissenting views among themselves.

8. Pitch the content and level to the ages and understanding of the children.

We have been discovering that children have the capacity to learn far more complex concepts than we had thought; we have known for some time that children yearn for independence and responsibility appropriate to their age and suffer crippling effects when these are denied. It is proposed that the encounter with the threat of nuclear war be transformed into a constructive experience wherein youth are given the opportunity to learn about and work for the kind of world that will offer them a future. In some students this will initially intensify or activate anxiety. Studies of the effects of disaster and threat point up the therapeutic and supportive benefits that are derived from the collective act of attacking problems. We do not value disasters or threat, but they occur, and threat exists. We can make the most of the threat of nuclear disaster by making it a focus of therapeutic cooperative action.

REFERENCES

1. Arata, Osada (ed.) Children of the A-Bomb, New York, Putnam, 1963.

2. Allerhand, Melvin E., Kaleidoscope, Committee on Psychological Effects of the Nuclear Age, I, 2 (Jan. 1963), 2482 Derbyshire Rd., Cleveland, Ohio.

3. Freud, A. and Burlingham, D., War and Children, New York, New York Medical Books, 1943.

4. Hill, R. and Hansen, D. A., "Families in Disaster," in G. W. Baker and D. W. Chapman (eds.), Man and Society in Disaster, New York, Basic Books, 1962, p. 221.

5. Wilson, R. N., "Disaster and Mental Health," in G. W. Baker and D. W. Chapman (eds.), Man and Society in Disaster, New York, Basic Books, 1962, p. 148.

6. Wolfenstein, M., Disaster: A Psychological Essay, The Glencoe Free Press, Glencoe, Ill., 1957.

7. Jahoda, M., "Toward a Social Psychology of Mental Health," in M. J. Senn (ed.), Symposium on the Healthy Personality,

New York, Josiah Macy Jr. Foundation, 1950.

8. Withey, S. B., "Reaction to Uncertain Threat," in G. W. Baker and D. W. Chapman (eds.), Man and Society in Disaster, New York, Basic Books, 1962, Ch. 4.

9. Schwebel, M., "Students, Teachers and the Bomb," NEA Journal, 52 (3), 46-48.

10. "Human Survival: A Selected Bibliography," Amer. J. Orthopsychiatry, January, 1963.

11. Escalona, Sibylle, Children and the Threat of Nuclear War, Child Study Assn., 1962.

Part IV
THE PEACE RESEARCH MOVEMENT

There is no truth existing which I fear, or would wish un-
known to the whole world.

Thomas Jefferson

As stated in the Introduction, the papers in this book are but
a sample of the work of behavioral scientists on survival. Although
peace research has only recently captured the interest of something
more than the handful of persons who published articles on the subject during the decade following World War II, the scientific activity
is now considerable and the literature is steadily growing. Part IV
provides a perspective of this international peace research movement
and of some of its products.

It is appropriate that the major paper in this section was written by the Director of the Peace Research Institute of the Norwegian
Institute for Social Research. Sociologist Johan Galtung, a former
UNESCO professor in Chile, reports on programs in many countries
of the world. He discusses the special problems of peace research
organizations, including those of sponsorship and affiliation. Drawing a parallel with the history of medical science, he proposes as
part of the process of professionalization the adoption of a moral
code similar to that of Hippocrates. His final recommendation is the
initiation of a plan for an international peace research year.

What has the peace research movement produced thus far?
The second paper, prepared by the editor, is an annotated bibliography of the behavioral science literature on human survival.

International Programs of Behavioral Science Research in Human Survival

It is the basic thesis of this paper that behavioral science research is one of the necessary conditions that must be satisfied to achieve peaceful relations in the international system without having to pay for them in terms of social justice or social freedom. This type of research is not only intellectually most fascinating, but it also constitutes an untapped reservoir in our strivings for peace. What I shall try to do will be to raise this thesis from the level of the slogan to the level of a proposition backed up by some facts and some theory for the conditions under which the thesis is most probable. To do this I shall not present the usual research list of "what has been done, what ought to be done"—but rather, look at peace research from a "structural-functional" point of view.

What Is "Peace Research"?

Let us first attempt a definition of the field. We mean by "peace research" research that is directed towards the understanding of (a) conditons that may prevent international and intergroup violence, and (b) conditions for furthering harmonious and creative relations between nations and other groups of people. Thus, peace research has two sides, one negative and one positive, corresponding to the two sides of any good definition of "peace": peace as absence of war, as nonwar; and peace as a working, interacting relationship based on mutual exchange for mutual benefit—if desirable, by means of a sufficiently pervasive and strong international superstructure. The field is enormous, and to facilitate the overview the following division may prove useful: on the one hand there is a generalized science of conflict research, ranging through the spectrum of the social sciences from intra-personal conflict all the way through interpersonal and intergroup conflicts to that which interests us most: the international conflicts. Such books as

226

Thomas Schelling's The Strategy of Conflict, Kenneth Boulding's Conflict and Defense and Anatol Rapoport's Fights, Games and Debates are important contributions to this growing interdisciplinary field, not to mention the Journal of Conflict Resolution. Particular interest would focus on the time axis of conflict, to provide us with the fragments of a general theory for conflict genesis, dynamics and resolution.

On the other hand, there is peace research in the sense of doing research on what passes for peace initiatives. Ten fields can easily be recognized here: arms control and disarmament; economic and social development—particularly in its international consequences; intra-psychic organization; intra-social organization; international organization; cross-conflict contact; communication; public opinion; the various forms of nonviolent conflict resolution, and finally, peace research itself. The list does not claim to be exhaustive, and it is certainly not a list of mutually exclusive fields. An important area of peace research like the relatively poorly developed field of conference research, for instance, stands at the intersection of the fields of social contact, social communication, and nonviolent resolution mechanisms. The importance of including peace research as a topic should be emphasized; the present paper is an effort in that direction.

Again, instead of engaging in the usual long lists of what has been done and what should be done, let us focus attention on some simple principles that may seem trivial but have important consequences. First of all, that a field of these dimensions can only be explored by means of cross-disciplinary cooperation is a truism today; most scholars would unite in a reaction against the kind of scientific imperialism that says that this field is really psychology, or sociology, or international relations—at least, they would unite against it except when it is done on behalf of their own discipline.

Second, like all good research, it will have to be invariant of the ideological conviction of the researcher, except when it comes to choosing topics of investigation. This is easily said, but more difficult to do. Today one very often has the feeling that the conclusions of a researcher in the field can be more easily predicted by knowing his institutional affiliation than by knowing his data. It is not a good sign when researchers close to the establishment show an inclination towards arms control while researchers close to the peace movement show an equally strong tendency to conclude with disarmament. But there are organizational ways of counteracting this phenomenon, and we shall explore them later.

Third, the history of science is full of examples of the progress made when researchers have the courage to attack, even if only falteringly, what is commonly held to be not researchable, for moral or other reasons. People like Columbus, Leeuwenhoek, Wöhler, Pasteur, Freud or Kinsey all had this against themselves: they entered forbidden territories. In the history of peace research the decade or so following the Second World War may be seen as the period when the ice was broken, no doubt partly because of the services rendered to various Administrations during the war by several distinguished social scientists. There are still white dots on the map such as some special sectors of high-level decision-making, nonviolent defense in case of military capitulation, some of the functions of diplomacy, etc., but they will gradually be defined as researchable. In short, peace research will never really unfold itself if it stops short of the really controversial—nor will it ever mature if it only considers the controversial really worth while.

Fourth, although peace research, like all other research, should engage in theory construction in developing propositions of gradually increasing complexity and fields of application, it should not leave out of sight its essentially pragmatic nature. For applied science to progress it is not enough that its propositions be tenable. One must also develop research in which the independent variables can be manipulated. For that reason, much of the research on the authoritarian personality will, so far, have to rank low because, as Else Frenkel-Brunswik pointed out, the efforts involved in changing this variable are almost forbidding (1), at least with the insight we possess today. The prospects are more optimistic when it comes to recruitment for a particular purpose such as the Peace Corps in which one does not have to change people but only has to classify them, and for instance, avoid the authoritarians, these favorite scapegoats in so much research. In short, tenability is not enough, applicability comes as an addition requirement. In other words, peace research should not only be good research, it should also be relevant research, it should have short-term or long-term policy implications.

Finally, peace research, like all other research, should be universal in its methodology—given the problem and the method, the answer shall, ideally, be independent of space and time. But not all science is as universal in its consequences as this one is. Peace concerns everyone on earth, that is the consequence of a development that has increased the target distance of a projectile from 2 to 12,500 miles between 1807 and 1954 (2). Thus, research aimed at furthering the interests of one's own nation, if necessary at the expense of other nations, should not be called peace research but something else, perhaps "security research" or "defense analysis." As this field of scientific inquiry is strengthened, as it will be very soon, social scientists will have to face exactly the same problem as the physical scientists since the first atom was split: shall their science be used in the interest of the national or the international order? In times of war the psychological and social conditions so much favor the nation-centered answer because of the obvious contra-argument "What if the enemy does it and we do not?" But in times of peace, even the meager peace we have at present, there may still be time to develop institutional settings strong enough to protect the peace researcher and make him a true contributor to the health of the international system. This will also be explored later.

A Parallel between Medical Science and Peace Research

Peace research is cross-disciplinary, cross-ideological, controversial if necessary, theoretically oriented and concerned with applicability—and should deal symmetrically with the units that engage in war and peace, the nations. There is only one good parallel available in the history of human science: medicine, the science of somatic health. There may be something important to learn from its development as a science, and I shall briefly review some crucial points, mainly taken from an article by Richard Shyrock, "The Rise of Modern Scientific Medicine" (3). There are a number of interesting parallels, and we shall mention six of them here.

Thinking of the fabulous size and expanse of the medical institutions of today it is almost incredible that modern medicine may be said to be less than one hundred years old. What happened in the later half and third of the last century was the alliance between the old art and handicraft of surgery, which of course must be counted in millennia, not in centuries, and quantitative natural science. This was an alliance between theory and practice, personified in the university hospital professor and institutionalized today in the training of medical men all over the world. A rather dismal condition for this was the rapid urbanization that took place during the century in Western Europe, because urbanization meant concentration of people; this in turn meant concentration of deaths, and this implied the existence and availability of relatively large quantities of corpses for autopsies and statistical treatment—and this was a far step from the older days when the interested student sometimes had to go to the churchyard and steal a corpse. I hesitate to draw the parallel with peace science—besides, we already have Lewis F. Richardson's Statistics of Deadly Quarrels. But for the other part of the story the analogy may be good; what we are witnessing now is the growing, if still uneasy, alliance, certainly stronger under some Administrations than under others, of the old art of diplomacy with quantitative social science, with precisely the same debate between the "artists and intuitionists" and the theoreticians and electronic calculators. The former are doomed to lose, but the latter will only succeed to the extent that they are able to understand better than the intuitionists themselves what they stand for. The result, diplomats well versed in peace science, is already emerging.

A part of the lore of this alliance in the medicine of the last cen-

tury was the tendency to <u>dephilosophize</u>. Instead of engaging in armchair speculations about what health really is, one did research and
discovered a web of invariances that form the basis for today's control
of somatic man. We see the same development in our field, away from
the tract, the empirically unguided sweeping speculations and on to the
piecemeal approach—with the danger that we lose the great lines and
the long perspectives. But a typical and important aspect of this is the
willingness to call something "peace research" or "research in human
survival" and just go ahead collecting research experience without having a satisfactory definition and a conceptual framework and a deduc-
tive theory. These formal aspects of science are indispensable in the
long run, but they may be a strait jacket if developed and applied pre-
maturely.

Medicine also was able to detach itself from common folklore
with its strange mixture of wisdom and superstition, at the same time
using this as a reservoir of hypotheses. The same is happening to
peace research—to take an example: "That'll teach 'em" is a dictum
often heard in international relations in connection with the application
of force. Taken as a researchable hypothesis it is a most difficult and
fascinating project in the theory of learning. Taken as an apodictic
truth it will constitute a serious block to progress in the field—and
the same applies to <u>si vis pacem, para bellum.</u>

Most important in the development of medical science was the
ability to detach itself from the two extremes of overgeneralization
and overspecification. One was able to devise a theory in order to
avoid ideas such as "to every symptom its own cause" or "to all symptoms one or two causes." Instead of talking about the "cause of disease," one started to talk about "causes" and then about types of diseases, without splitting so much that all advantages in generalization
were lost. We are on that road in peace research, but we have not
been there long. In common lore one still speaks about <u>the</u> cause of
war, and only few reach the sophistication of developing good typol-
ogies of wars. One is still using common semantics as a guide, in the
belief that what language has lumped together should remain so, but
this will not remain so for long.

Another highly interesting parallel should also be pointed out:
Medical science was long hampered by a strong belief in methodolo
gical singularism—the belief that one could not generalize meaningfully from one person's disease to another's because of the influence
of the differences between the personalities and somatic characteristics of the patients. What today is known as the ideology of individual
treatment was once an impediment to abstracting from the patient the
characteristics of the disease in order to be able to generalize. Medical research would not have made progress if it had confined itself
to the publication of long, detailed reports on the sickness stories of

individual patients. The analogy with the overabundance of completely
unanalytical, highly detailed foreign policy reports with no attempts at
generalization is obvious. But in the eagerness to make good theory it
should not be forgotten that the basis for abstraction and generalization
is detailed and exact knowledge of singular cases, in medicine as in
international relations.

The way medical science is organized today probably points out
the direction in which the science of peace will have to go. The extent
and importance of the field is recognized by giving it the university
status of a faculty, not of an institute or department or a "program."
It recruits scientific personnel from the various contributing sciences
from physics to psychiatry, and medical research is this cross-disciplinary attempt to build negative and positive somatic health. Thus,
it stands in an interesting exchange with the participating sciences: it
defines problems for them to solve, benefits from the pattern of serendipity in the other sciences—sees applications where they see none,
and does original basic research in addition to its own applied research. The mutual exchange for mutual benefit exists, even if relations may be strained at times. The structural similarity with peace
science is so great that it would be strange if this is not also to be the
future status of that science. As Professor Röling, the dean of Dutch
peace science, says: "I am convinced that in ten to fifteen years all
over the world Peace Research Institutes will be blooming as a matter
of course." Maybe in fifteen to twenty years or even sooner Peace
Research Faculties will be blooming—as a matter of course, as a matter of human survival.

There is one final important factor about the development of
medical science which will be commented on later. The time has now
come to look around the world and compare these utopian views with
what actually exists of peace research in the world today.

A Survey of Peace Research Activities

It seems fit to start with the United States since the center of the
movement no doubt is in this country, probably due to the coincidence
in one nation of both the largest military and the largest social science
potentials in the world. Mrs. Elise Boulding of the Center for Research
on Conflict Resolution, University of Michigan, lists sixteen academic
research centers where this kind of research is being carried out (4):
Center for International Affairs at Harvard; Center for International
Studies at MIT; Center of International Studies at Princeton; Center
for Peace Research in Omaha; Center for Research on Conflict Resolution, Ann Arbor; at the Institute for Communications Research, University of Illinois; Institute of War and Peace Studies at Columbia; the
Institute for Policy Studies in Washington, D.C.: Peace Research

Laboratory at Washington University, St. Louis; Research Programs on Economic Adjustments to Disarmament, Columbia; Research Foundation of Colorado State University, Fort Collins; Stanford Research Institute and the Stanford Studies in Integration and Conflict, California; The Program for Graduate Training and Research in International Relations at Northwestern University in Evanston, Illinois; University of Pennsylvania; and the World Rule of Law Center, Duke University, North Carolina. Plotted on a map, there is the traditional concentration in the northeastern part of the United States. But that is no objection; it rather seems to indicate that his movement has been accepted by the center of the United States academic world very quickly.

Further, seven of the professional associations have activities in this field: the national associations for anthropologists, orthopsychiatry, psychologists and sociologists, and The International Studies Association, the Society for the Psychological Study of Social Issues and the American Academy of Arts and Sciences all have programs in this field. In addition, eight foundations and associations can be mentioned, three governmental institutions, of which the most important is, of course, the United States Arms Control and Disarmament Agency, six private research institutes concerned with national defense (but also with nonmilitary means)—the most famous being the Institute for Defense Analysis and RAND—and finally, a number of student peace research activities.

Of more direct interest to people engaged in the more microcosmic side of the social science spectrum are the activities on the East Coast of Current Research Related to Psychological Factors in Peace and War described in a report prepared by the Institute of Communications Research for the Committee on Psychology in National and International Affairs of the American Psychological Association. As many as twenty-two research projects of immediate interest within this field are reported. No doubt there is more going on, and there will be much more fairly soon, for most of these projects were started rather recently as a clear expression of a new research orientation.

The time perspective on this can be grasped when one hears that out of the forty activities reported by Mrs. Boulding from the United States only about ten were in existence as little as five years ago, and among them five are of the more classical type of centers for the study of international relations where peace research in our sense is a marginal activity. The number of researchers in the field is very difficult to evaluate. Kenneth Boulding says in a recent article that "on a strict definition perhaps no more than a few hundred people are engaged in it; on a wider definition several thousands. This is a small effort compared with the massive resources which still go into purely military research. It is, however, a growing movement with great potential for the future" (5).

If this growth is to continue, there will be centers of peace research at all places of academic learning before the end of this decade, and before the end of the twenty-first century there will be more peace researchers than people in the country. However, it is well known that social change, though it may look exponential in the beginning, will tend to level off and produce a more logistic curve after some time. But it can safely be said that the days of less rapid growth are still far off in the future.

Outside the United States the perspectives are less dynamic. In Canada there is the Canadian Peace Research Institute founded in 1961; in England there is the Peace Knowledge Foundation founded in 1960 and the British Conflict Research Society; in France, a group working at Ecole Pratique des Hautes Etudes; in Holland there is the Dutch Institute for Peace Research at the University of Groningen since 1962; in India, the Gandhi Peace Foundation founded in 1958 which, however, does little in terms of research; in Japan, the Hiroshima Institute of Peace Science established in 1962 at the initiative of the president of Hiroshima University and the American anthropologist Dr. Earle Reynolds; and in Norway there is the Peace Research Institute, Oslo, organized as a Section for Research on Conflict and Peace at the Institute for Social Research since 1959. In addition to these there are traces of development in Australia, Belgium, Czechoslovakia, Germany, Ghana, Poland, Denmark, Sweden, Finland, Spain, Switzerland, U. S. S. R., and Yugoslavia—all of which will no doubt emerge, in due time, as in the other countries.

Just a few more words about the development in Norway since it is the country outside the United States that has come furthest along this road. Much of it is owing to the very close cooperation between Norwegian and United States' social scientists, particularly with the sociologists at Columbia, New York, and the social psychologists at University of Michigan, Ann Arbor. There are probably three reasons for this unique situation in Norway: the strong position of social science already mentioned, the traumatic experience of five years of German occupation which presents all Norwegians who went through it with a burning question: "What should we have done?"—and the discrepancy between the official answer to that question, an armament unparalleled in Norwegian history and strong allegiance to the NATO alliance on the one hand, and Norwegian neutralism and general worship of the role of David in the traditional David and Goliath conflict on the other. As an expression of this, the Norwegian government established a Council for Conflict and Peace Research in February 1963, with the following four tasks: to make a survey of the field in Norway, evaluate the possibilities of future development, give priority lists and budgets for the consideration of the Norwegian Parliament, and work for Nordic cooperation in this field. This amounts to a governmental research council in the field of conflict and peace, the first of its kind in the world. It remains to be seen how this experiment in governmental initiative in such an academically difficult and politically touchy field will turn out. The basis for some form of Nordic cooperation was laid in the First Nordic Peace Research Conference, held in Oslo in January, 1963, with about twenty papers and some seventy participants from universities, administration, and peace organizations. In September, 1963, the Peace Research Institute in Oslo organized a European Peace Research Conference with twelve papers and thirty participants.

At the international level it should be mentioned that several international peace organizations have peace research on their programs; some of these are the International Pugwash Conference on Science and World Affairs since 1959; the old and venerable Women's International League for Peace and Freedom (two of whose international presidents have been awarded the Nobel Peace Prize), and the Accra Assembly, a conference of some one hundred and twenty specialists from different parts of the world, which called for the establishment of an independent and International Institute for Disarmament Research.

In August, 1963, a conference was held in Clarens, Switzerland, with the participation of representatives from a number of these national and international peace research organizations, establishing an international Committee for the Organization of Conferences for Research on International Peace and Security (COROIPAS), with a small secretariat in London.

Finally, and most importantly, let us consider the work of the United Nations and its specialized agencies. "At the Second Session of the UNESCO General Conference, held in Mexico City late in 1947, it was decided that one of the UNESCO's main tasks during the following years should be the attempt to discover some of the most important factors underlying tensions among nations and some of the techniques which might be applied to the reduction of such tensions. This program was to be placed in the hands of social scientists who would have the opportunity of applying their knowledge and their techniques to this crucial question. " These are the opening words in Otto Klineberg's Tensions Affecting International Understanding (6). What was then called the "tensions project" would today go under the name of "peace research, " by some considered awkward but, like the "peace corps, " a name that has come here to stay. Klineberg is one of the real founders of this kind of research in the sense that he has actively contributed to its stock of knowledge. This program was certainly not the reason the tensions project became less than one had reason to hope. Today little or no research of that kind is carried out by UNESCO, and there may be a lesson to learn here that will be developed later.

But the United Nations takes an active interest in it, although the much celebrated United Nations report entitled <u>Economic and Social Consequences of Disarmament</u> leaves much to be desired from the point of view of the behavioral sciences, with its 9 paragraphs, albeit very interesting ones, about the social consequences as contrasted with the 156 paragraphs devoted to the economic consequences. Maybe the ratio of prestige between the social and economic sciences is about 9:156, but it is to be deplored that this should be so perfectly mirrored in a document of such crucial importance. It is certainly to be hoped that the coming United Nations Training and Research Institute in New York will show a better balance, and that it will serve as an active catalyst for peace research activities.

However this may be, the representative from Honduras to the United Nations, Sr. Francisco Milla Bermudez, requested the inclusion in the General Assembly Agenda in 1961 of a resolution on the establishment of a United Nations Committee on the organization of peace and disarmament and the study of related problems. It was tabled in December, 1962. Time is not yet mature for this to be developed in the General Assembly, but it is well worth quoting from the speech: "The United Nations cannot remain indifferent to these governmental and private initiatives (for scientific peace research)... which have attracted notice particularly during the current year... but should coordinate and promote such efforts on a world-wide scale and become the focal point for their extension, thus fulfilling its historic function of eradicating the scourge of war by every means in its power." More precisely, he calls for member states to establish government departments or ministerial services for peace and disarmament, requests national and international nongovernmental organizations particularly concerned with peace and disarmament to conduct scientific inquiries on ways and means of resolving conflicts, and asks for the creation of a nine-member committee under the General Assembly to collect documentation and encourage the kind of development already indicated.

This is the factual background. Both outside the United States and at the international level the same clear trend is found, born in the late fifties or the early sixties, to multiply and mature during the rest of the decade. The number of conferences shows the same trend, the exchange of documentation asked for by the Honduras representative takes place without the assistance of the United Nations and periodicals are created almost monthly—like <u>Conflict Resolution</u>, <u>Journal of Arms Control</u>, <u>Disarmament and Arms Control</u> and the <u>Journal of Peace Research</u> (first issue in June 1964, published in Oslo).

Peace Research and Social Structure

To reach an evaluation of all these efforts to come to intellectual grips with the conditions promoting peaceful relations, let us place peace research in the social structure, both nationally and internationally. It is not alone in its concern for the health of the international system. Traditionally, the foreign policy of a country, whether it was only concerned with furthering the interests of one's own country or of the total international system, was always in the hands of relatively few people concentrated at the apex of the social pyramid. It is pathetic to read Nicolson's account of the origins of the British Foreign Service (7): when the Foreign Office was created in 1790 it consisted of an Under-Secretary, 10 clerks, a Latin secretary and a "decipherer of Letters." It is a far step from these 13 people to, for instance, the U.S. Foreign Service in 1953, when the Republicans assumed office: a total State Department staff of 19,405 out of which there were 1,305 Foreign Service Officers serving the 72 diplomatic missions and 198 consular offices of the U.S. (8). Since that time it has increased further, among other reasons because of the 24 new nations in Africa. Even though the background of U.S. diplomats is varied, as has been much commented upon (only 40 of the 72 chiefs of missions referred to above were career men, the rest were appointees mainly from business and political circles) (9), there is nevertheless a solid concentration of the social top center in the diplomacy. As Suzanne Keller's research has shown, President Roosevelt's efforts to disperse the recruitment to a wider basis than the Ivy League colleges and the "private preparatory schools frequented by the children of the metropolitan 400" were largely in vain. For the military elite this is perhaps less true, since the allocation to top positions is more the result of career mobility. Janowitz reports that "recent trends in their social background (the military leaders) supply striking confirmation of the decline in the relatively high social origins of the military, and of its transformation into a more socially heterogeneous group." Thus, in 1950, only 3 per cent, 4 per cent and 0 per cent of the military leaders of the Army, Navy, and Air Force were from the upper class. But this does not mean that the social background necessarily was humble: 47 per cent, 57 per cent, and 30 per cent respectively were from the upper middle class (10).

Of the third official profession dealing with international relations, the technical assistance administration, little is known, although the guess would be that is is solid upper-middle-class in its origin. These three, the diplomacy, the military, and the development agencies share between them the professional responsibility for relations with other states, under the supervision of the executive and the legislative. They represent, and are, the center of society.

On the other hand, there is the peace movement, which may look homogeneous from the outside yet is highly heterogeneous for anyone who knows it from the inside. By and large, the popular movements concerned with international relations and advocating specific policies may be classified according to where they put the balance of blame for the sad circumstances of the Cold War—mainly in the East, mainly in the West, or somewhere in the middle (whether the latter is according to "objective" or what in Marxist terminology is known as "objectivistic" standards, the tendency to distribute blame equally, after the fifty-fifty rule as Izvestia aptly calls it) (11), and according to their stand on disarmament: multilateralism, graduated unilateralism, or total unilateralism.

There are three crucial differences between the three parts of the establishment mentioned previously and the peace movement, in addition to the rather obvious one that the former are in power and the latter is not. First of all, the professional man, regardless of which of the three branches he is in, will necessarily develop a segmental view of the world. There is ample evidence supporting the general thesis that the professional man exaggerates the importance of his own perspective and tends to interpret the world in such a way that it maximizes the relevance of his own skills. Thus, the diplomats defines the world as to maximize the importance of bilateral organization, negotiations, treaties, and conferences; the military man sees the world in terms of power relations, and the development agency in terms of differentials in per capita income. Interbranch rivalries for money and prestige will tend to institutionalize this segmentalization of the perspective. As a contrast, the participant in the peace movement is not, as such, tied to any one perspective. Clearly, there is the tendency for peace organizations to crystallize around a specific one-factor theory, such as the idea of "world law," "world government," "world decentralization," "unilateralism," "education of the masses," "world language," "multiple deterrence," etc., and the same tendency to obtain cognitive balance between what one sees and hears and what one feels to be the condition for world peace to obtain. But the peace movement as a total is much less predictable; it can move in all possible directions and does so, and will always constitute a reservoir of initiative and ideas, some of them ingenious. Except for the few professionals the peace movement can afford to keep on its meager payrolls, there will not be this well-known marriage between occupation and ideology.

The second difference lies in the obvious difference between position and opposition: the three branches referred to have as their task to implement foreign policy; the function of the peace movement is to oppose the official policy, or at least parts of it, and suggest alternatives. Thus a strong peace movement is, like "Her Majesty's loyal opposition," an asset to any country. It can serve as a reservoir of initiatives that, as Donald Michael (6) points out "require imagination, sometimes ingenuity, and only occasionally careful thought.

The implications of an initiative and the detailed procedures for conducting it invariably demand systematic study, and at this stage of the peace movement very often calls for top meetings and conferences, disarmament negotiations, new proposals in current conflicts, and more specific ideas such as the telephone line between the two top bloc leaders, the hostage idea (in its collective form as the exchange of a great number of U.S. and Soviet students to each other's capitals to serve as potential victims of first strikes, preferably sons and daughters of top elites in the two countries — and in the individual form as the suggestion to send a renowned individual, like Pope John, to the foci of conflict e.g., Cuba, late October, 1962), the idea of developing methods of nonviolent defense in case of occupation, etc., not to mention the idea of peace research. Lest anyone belittle the possible value of such ideas, it should be remembered that what today are commonplace, such as the Red Cross, the League of Nations, the United Nations, the International Courts of Justice were conceived and born by such movements. But the transition from idea to reality presupposes thorough research.

Third, there is the difference between center and periphery of the society. We have data in Norway indicating that the participants in peace movements like the Ban-the-Bomb movement are not recruited from society's center. They are not from the periphery either; the periphery is unable to participate and uninterested in such activity, apathy reigns. But from what we know about the sociology of the periphery or the non-center we can deduce this: the peace movement will show a tendency to (a) believe in one-factor theories, (b) have a short-time-perspective, (c) have an apocalyptic theory of social change to the effect that change should be brought about suddenly and completely, and (d) see international relations in terms of complete engagement or complete disengagement, no taste, no choice. From this follows the tendency to advocate total unilateralism here and now and the pendant idea of the radical, peripheral right: the preventive or preemptive war. As ideas, they are unacceptable for a number of reasons, but their relations to the social position of their advocates should be borne in mind. To understand is to forgive, at least a little bit—this should also apply to the narrow, detailed expertness of the professional policy-maker.

To come to the point: it is our misfortune that we, the public, are suspended between these two forces: the narrow, highly specialized and expert but often opportunistic perspective of the professional— and the broad but crude, idealistic but often naïve perspective of the peace movement man, with his queer way of making himself heard and seen: marches, voyages, pickets, full-page ads, etc. What is missing here is precisely a full mobilization of the academic forces, a mustering of man's intellect in the same way as has been done to master the problems of somatic health, of utilization of natural resources, and to some extent also to master the problems of mental health. This kind of research could be interspersed between the power elite and peace periphery, and provide the latter with a much broader perspective and a more theoretically founded knowledge than it is able to develop by itself, in a form it is more likely to take seriously than that which the peace movement has to offer, although it is less likely to understand. On the other hand, peace research can give to the peace movement a sense of responsibility to the development of implications of its own ideas, an impulse to move from the slogan to the propositional level. If a successful symbiosis is established, peace research would receive from the establishment detailed information about problems which the politician has to face but which are only partly perceived by the rest of us; and it would receive from the peace movement its reservoir of hypotheses of bad and good ideas for serious testing and elaboration. Not that academic peace research does not have its own hypotheses, but it does no harm to have additional outside sources of ideas that can be made researchable.

The Organization of Peace Research

Thus, the basis for exchange exists if only the parties can be persuaded that they will gain from it. This is the basis for social organization, and the question is: in what organization structure are these ideas best implemented? By and large, there are three models that have gained a certain currency, and they will be examined.

First of all, there is the idea of building peace research into the three government branches mentioned. In the United States both the Department of State and the Department of Defense have research agencies, and so does the Agency for International Development and, most importantly, since it represents one of the best examples of what intelligent behavioral science can contribute to the design and improvement of a social institution there is the Peace Corps. In Norway, the Norwegian Institute of International Affairs is strongly wedded to the military, diplomatic, and developmental establishments, and in most other countries there are similar arrangements.

Second, there is the idea of building peace research into the peace movement, as has been done to a considerable extent in Canada and also in England. The Canadian Peace Research Institute is financed by funds contributed by the public, with the strong Canadian peace movement an important factor. Similarly, one of the many forerunners of today's peace research movement is the Pacifist Research Bureau in Philadelphia, which has issued some quite stimulating pamphlets.

Third, there is the idea of the institute independent of either, linked to a university or a foundation, recruiting its personnel through the usual academic channels, its hypotheses by the usual, more or less random ways of scientific research, its motivation through a multitude of sources, among which the desire to contribute to peace may gradually decrease at the expense of the desire to contribute to science in general and one's own career in particular—as is the case for most other sites of academic learning.

Now, when the peace research movement is still in its infancy, is the time to choose and decide, and I will strongly advocate the third model. Both models one and two have built into them the danger of two types of persons having corruptive and corrosive effects on each other. The social scientist may become bogged down with responsibility if he becomes a part of the establishment. With all the uncertainties that will exist with the science of peace for the foreseeable future, the researcher will not be given sufficient time for careful examination of methods and postulates. He will soon know too much about politics and be so bound by the rules of secrecy that he will not be able to contribute to policy. For stronger, more established sciences, well-protected by the rules of professional societies, this may be less important, but that stage is certainly still in the future for peace research. Although it may not be so vulgar that the peace researcher receives his pay and in return uses his academic means to prove the policy-makers right, it is almost certain that the governmentally employed peace researcher will be suspected of doing so because of the high variability we will have for some time in determining what constitutes a valid anwer to a question, as well as what constitutes a question.

The peace movement has the same motive to use the prestige of science to receive a sort of academic certificate of validity, but where the establishment may react with fear and hostility at being "researched upon, " the peace movement may feel so obviously right in what they assert that they see peace research mainly as a time-consuming ritual to become more legitimate. This does not constitute the right setting for serious research either. Demands and expectations will be too high and often extrascientific. Science is based on such pillars as intersubjectivity (findings shall be invariant of such extrinsic factors as ideological convictions of the researcher); freedom to define, or at least to redefine, a problem; enough time to go through the process of rejecting some hypotheses for perspectives before one settles on one, etc. If past experience is a guide, these are all necessary conditions for good research, and difficult to create in a setting of ad hoc decision and action or of ideological purity.

But there is also another side of the coin: the damaging influence the researcher can have on both policy-makers and the peace movement. Academic man is neither trained in political responsibility nor in quick decision-making. He can kill both with the incessant: How do you know that? What is the empirical or theoretical support for that belief? Have you done research on that? This will be detrimental for the policy-makers' ability to act and act quickly, if often only on hunches, as well as for the rabid and often immature, but still spontaneous and imaginative inventiveness of the peace movement. However much one may want to change them, they both perform invaluable functions very different from that of research and very important to society.

If the answer lies in independent organization of peace research, how then is contact to be maintained so that there can still be an impact on the center as well as the periphery, in the way mentioned? There are a number of answers to this, all of them well known. In a society with freedom of communication, journals, conventions, and the diluted content of scientific insight that reaches the mass media will do much of the job. But there are other possibilities, such as systems of mutual internships. Just as the peace researcher should spend some time in one or more of the governmental branches, the executives there should at some stage in their careers participate in projects or follow courses and seminars sufficiently much to know the idiom and have some sense of quality. A system of mutual recruitment would be to the benefit of both parties. To temper the influence of the establishment of peace research, it can be similarly argued that institutions of peace research should have a pattern of exchange with the peace movement, both in the sense that their officials are invited to participate and in the sense that qualified participants form a basis for recruitment into that academic field. All of this is actually happening today, and the conference organized by the Institute for Arms Control and Peace Research at Ann Arbor in December, 1962 and in January, 1964, was a good example, since it provided a meeting ground between such diverse groups as scientists (in military hardware as well as in human reaction to them), people from the administration, and peace movement leaders.

Traditionally, the university provides scientific research with the best protection from pressures both from above and from below, both from the administration and from popular pressure groups. Thus, at the University of Oslo there is an initiative to create a position of full professor in conflict and peace research, and such positions are emerging at the universities of Groningeir and Lancaster. Although this seems to be the road one will have to go, developing the science of international health as much as the science of somatic health, this does not mean that one should completely exclude the possibilities of some development of peace research according to models one and two. To the extent past experience is a guide, versatility in institutional basis seems to be a most important asset. What one should be systematically on guard against is too much centralization of this type of research into large-scale institutes. Research seems to indicate that one of the keys to high scientific productivity lies in decentralization, a factor probably not unrelated to the fabulous positions most sciences have in this nation (12). Competition and horizontal as well as vertical mobility among universities are important keys to progress.

At the international level the problem of finding a basis between the international superstructure, the United Nations and its specialized agencies, on the one hand and the international peace movement on the other is not an easy one. Just as on the national level, the problem is that of finding a basis for finance and recruitment. The government and the U. N. may be willing, as the peace movement may be able, but however much one may want the U. N. to be an active party to most international conflicts, this is not a good argument for basing international peace research only on that organization. In general, it is wise to keep a distance between the organization that sponsors the research and the organization on which one does research, and that is not done if all peace research is established as U. N. in-house activity. In addition, there is the problem of having 113 masters and the danger that the researchable topics palatable to all of them will be few, far between, and, in addition, uninteresting is high. This is one of the factors responsible for the low output of UNESCO-sponsored research, and there is no foreseeable end to its importance. Besides, the U. N. will easily be wedded to certain views. Even if they are not partisan along an East-West axis, they may be so along an axis of optimism versus pessimism—and consistently in favor of optimistic views and of de-emphasizing difficulties. However valuable this may be politically, official optimism, national or international, is no basis for research.

But again, even though the solution seems to lie in a more or less loosely coordinated chain of independent peace research institutes with an International Peace Research Institute as a center organized according to some of the principles mentioned in the Accra Assembly resolution, both the U. N. and the international peace movement should certainly be encouraged to develop a maximum of research interest. A versatile and flexible system both at the national and international levels should in this way emerge.

"Peace is Our Profession"

What then, more precisely, is the aim? The analogy between international and somatic health has been mentioned many times. Of course, there is no reason to entertain an illusion that these two health concepts have anything like the same cognitive and normative standing. The somatic concept is based on some kind of cognitive definition, in terms of equilibrium, statistical average, self-realization, etc., and is relatively consensual among physicians—there is a broad basis of agreement as to what constitutes somatic health. Once we move to mental health this agreement decreases, as demonstrated so eloquently by Marie Jahoda in her book <u>Current Concepts of Positive Mental Health.</u> And in the field of international systems there is certainly not much consensus among specialists as to what constitutes "health." But this kind of consensus is not created by decree, only by hard research to know the nature of the international system better. Gradually, a kind of working consensus will emerge, about for example, the desirable nature of most parts of the international superstructure that is constantly growing around us.

As it emerges, it seems safe to predict that we shall get one important development in peace science similar to what we have had in medical science; this is the final parallel, but perhaps the most important one: what I am thinking of is professionalization. A profession is much like a caste with its own rules. Above all, professionals are their own status-judges, they stand in a contractal relationship to the rest of society—a state in the state, with a certain autonomy—but they have to pay for it by rendering to the society services deemed to be indispensable. There are dangers like the narrowness in perspective referred to, but there is the major advantage of <u>esprit de corps</u> and high ethical standards. Thus, professionalzation is a normative, a moral fact with profound implications. The archetype is the oath sworn by physicians all over the world, attributed to Hippocrates. Let us look at it, because the implications are so stimulating.

There are five rules:

The physician shall "prescribe according to ability and judgement and never do harm to anyone." This norm represents the universalism of medical man—he shall be equally at the disposal of everybody, friend as well as foe, and do his best. He is the servant of mankind, not of any particular subgroup. We can be sure that this norm has been called utopian, naïve, blue-eyed many times, and still it persists and is obeyed considerably more often than not—even in times of war, so much so that the horror we all feel in connection with the crimes committed by Nazi "physicians" well illustrates how internalized this norm is in all of us.

Then there is the negative side of this: "To please no one will I prescribe a deadly drug nor give advice which may cause the patient's death." He shall not use his science against the <u>raison d'être</u> of his métier: that of saving life.

One of a more general nature is: "I shall keep myself far from all intentional ill-doing and all seduction, and especially from the pleasures of love with women, or with men." The moral is clear: he shall not use his professional status to obtain gratifications that otherwise would have been blocked to him.

Then follows the famous norm about keeping secret what is revealed to him when he is exercising his profession and, finally, an excellent piece of prescription: when you do not know what to do, call another physician who may know better!

These are model rules; they give the moral basis, just as medical science gives the cognitive basis for the high status of medical man, a rank that is among the requisites for his ability to carry out his functions. On this basis of trust and insight medicine has worked such wonders as doubling the expected life age for great portions of mankind during a period of one century. Thus, it is tempting to project into the future and envisage the time when the peace scientists will form a profession with equally strong norms, placing their knowledge at the disposal of the development of international order much in the same spirit as the United Nations Technical Assistance expert tries to do it today, but on much more burning topics: where they will "prescribe according to ability and judgment, and never do harm to anyone."

The real difficulty is in the field of identification: this is not a question of identifying with his home country or with his host country. He must see world problems in world perspective and look for a symmetric solution that maximizes long-term international health. And since the welfare of nations constitutes a relatively tightly coupled system, he is in a different position from a medical man who can treat one human being at a time. He is more in the position of the gynecologist faced with a mother-fetus systen when the birth of the child may entail the death of the mother. He cannot accept anything similar to the Catholic "Save the child!" (so it can be baptized) or the Protestant "Save the mother!" (she has more human value)—that would be the same as an ideologically partisan attitude. Like a gynecologist, he must devote all his energy to the prevention of such zero-sum or negative sum situations, and that can only be done with a true identification anchored to the international level.

This being said, there are three ways in which a strong peace science can contribute to peace, when by "strong" we mean both in quality and quantity.

First of all the obvious, by being technical advisers on peace. Without elaborating this point I think it should be mentioned that there is a serious shortcoming in the frequently found formula to the effect that "the goals should be set by the politicians, and the means worked out by the scientists." It excludes the important function of science as the provider of new perspectives, of new horizons, and new goals. Thus, one of the foremost tasks of peace research seems to be to contribute to what we so much miss: a real conception of what the peaceful world might look like, of what benefits might accrue to mankind from it. The U. N. report on economic and social consequences of disarmament is a good beginning, but much more should be done to show the potentialities open to man. There is so much experience to the effect that man first needs a utopia in his mind if he is to create a better world, and this is not provided by contemporary international politics with its desperate and ad hoc efforts to tackle the problems as they arise. Peace research should present a number of models of the future world for us to choose among, and in the meantime it must see as its task the contribution of its best knowledge in such fields as the recruitment of personnel to cross-cultural statuses and positions of strain, how to conduct conferences, how to improve channels of communication, how to provide United Nations Police Forces with the best symbolic images, how to distribute international civil servants in order to maximize international loyalty, how to avoid economic development that leads to self-sufficiency, decreased interdependence, and less war-avoiding interlocking between states, how to utilize the potentials for nonviolent defense that will have to be used in a disarming or disarmed world, etc. —to mention some of the fields of research in which we are engaged in Norway. In the short and the long run, there is no doubt that peace research can contribute—to deny that is to deny the function of rational man.

But, and this is the second point, contributions will not only be in terms of concrete proposals. The very fact that peace research is being carried out and is sponsored from above and below is itself a peace-promoting factor, provided it is not used as a foreign policy weapon. If the idea is to develop something "where we are ahead of the Russians," one can be sure that the result will be increased tension, since it will only be perceived as a particularly Machiavellian approach to international politics. But if the idea is as stated, to provide the cognitive basis for a healthy international community, then the very fact that this is being done in great numbers will have a tremendous impact. It will make foreign policy more rational—with the dangerous implications this may have. But more importantly it will produce strong norms against shallow thinking, empirically unfounded and theoretically badly-guided advice. It will create a better sense of quality, and this will, in turn, lead to more quality.

Third, the professionalization mentioned above. Today a considerable proportion of the foreign service of most countries is made up of people with training as lawyers. This means an emphasis on a normative, legal perspective at the expense of theoretically well-guided empirical perspectives. With a gradually emerging profession of peace scientists we shall have a very important basis for recruitment into national and international centers of policy-making. If they can bring with them something of the spirit of the Hippocratic oath, a major peace factor will have been created.

In conclusion, let me be practical about this. In a world that uses more than 120 billion dollars each year on armaments, equivalent to 8 to 9 per cent of the world's production of goods and services and close to 100 per cent of the national incomes of the developing countries, at the same time as around 50 million of the world's inhabitants are attached to military machinery with a well-known overkill capacity, there is little time to lose. We will have to arrive at something similar to the institutional basis of medical science in a much shorter time. Where medical science, with its strong emphasis on universalism in dealing with human beings, needed something like the structure of the nation-state to really unfold itself, peace science cannot do this, since its units of research are nations. It will need some kind of internationalization as soon as possible—if only in the relatively uncommitting form of an international association, frequent conferences, and a couple of international institutes.

But one can hope for and ask for more. Why not an International Peace Research Year, modeled after the International Geophysical Year? Some of its possible functions could be:

1. under the auspices of the United Nations to call for a general concentration of available scientific forces on the conditions for peace,
2. to establish an international, independent institute,
3. to facilitate communication between those interested in this kind of research, across national, professional, and academic barriers,
4. to establish a systematic archive of peace proposals and peace hypotheses,
5. to discuss possibilities of giving at least some peace researchers some kind of protected international status, and to work on an ethical code for the field, and, above all,
6. to do joint research wherever feasible on such topics as economic and social consequences of disarmament, readiness for different kinds of functional internationalization, ability to withstand disappointments in disarmament processes, how extranational loyalties develop, how channels of communication such as press and diplomacy really function, national stereotypes, how technical assistance can be implemented to maximize cross-national and international integra-

tion, etc. There is no limit to this list other than one's own imagination.

All this is eminently feasible, provided one is not intimidated into believing that everything a little bit new is utopian, naïve, and premature. We have to aim high if we are to make progress at all in this field. And progress we must! That is our responsibility as social scientists, our contribution in the fight for human survival.

REFERENCES

1. Frenkel-Brunswik, E., "Further Explorations by a Contributor to 'The Authoritarian Personality'" in Christie, Jahoda (eds.), Studies in the Scope and Method of "The Authoritarian Personality," Glencoe, Ill., Free Press, 1954.
2. Allen, F. and Hart, H. Technology and Social Change, New York, Appleton, 1957, p. 36.
3. Studies in the History of Science, Philadelphia, Univ. of Pennsylvania Press, 1941.
4. International Newsletter on Peace Research, I, 1, Winter, 1963, pp. 13 ff. A more comprehensive survey will be found in a forthcoming repertory prepared for the UNESCO by the Peace Research Institute in Oslo.
5. "Peace Research Trends in America," Council for Correspondence Newsletter, Fall, 1962, p. 26.
6. Social Science Research Council, New York, 1950, p. 1. Also see Klineberg, O., "Psychological Aspects of International Relations," in Personality and Political Crisis, Glencoe, Ill., Free Press, 1951, pp. 228-260.
7. Nicolson, H., Diplomacy, London, Oxford Univ. Press, 1960, p. 203.
8. The New York Times, February 7, 1954, p. 27.
9. Mills, C. W., The Power Elite, New York, Oxford Univ. Press, 1957, p. 207.
10. Janowitz, M., The Professional Soldier, Glencoe, Ill., Free Press, 1960, p. 90.
11. As quoted by TIME, Latin America Edition, February 1, 1963, p. 25.
12. Ben-David, J. and Zloczower, A., "Universities and Academic Systems," European Journal of Sociology, III, 1, pp. 45-84, particularly p. 83.

An Annotated Bibliography

MILTON SCHWEBEL

During World War II and immediately afterward a number of articles and books by behavioral scientists on the causes of war and the preservation of peace were published. Then came a hiatus of almost a decade, partially broken in the fifties by a few social scientists and then shattered by the Berlin crisis of 1961, which had a profound effect on the interests and activities of many scientists and practitioners. Survival had become a professional problem: even if one could apply his knowledge and talents to the solution of the problem only during hours stolen from recreation or sleep, it was no longer an abstract issue or one unrelated to the central concerns of the scientist and the daily professional work of practitioners in social work, psychiatry, and psychology.

The experiences of recent years have stimulated publication of research reports, speculative articles, and recommended programs for the resolution of conflict. In fact, a steady stream of books and articles is coming off the press, and this bibliography was prepared for the purpose of presenting a selected and classified sample of the literature. *

Over the years recurrent themes have appeared in the literature on such crucial questions as the origins of war. Two major categories of theory have been postulated by behavioral scientists, one of them "instinctual, " the other "societal. " As an example, we can recall inquiry about the causes of war and Freud's pessimistic response, in which he stressed man's aggressive and destructive instincts. Only a few years later John W. Fletcher wrote a paper entitled "The Verdict of Psychologists on War Instincts" (Scientific Monthly, 1932, 35, pp. 142-145). "Without raising the issue as to the inevitability of conflicting aims and interests arising among nations, " Fletcher said, "American psychologists are almost unanimously agreed that the traditional opinion that instincts determine the mode of adjustment of such conflicts is without scientific warrant. " A few years later — two years before the Pearl Harbor attack — John Dollard and his colleagues published their now classic study, Frustration and Aggression (Yale University Press, 1939; 1961). They defined aggression as the intent to do damage or harm to another person or thing, and attributed it to frustration. The degree of frustration within a society, they argued, was one of the factors causing war.

These conflicting themes reappear in the recent literature. Man's aggressive instincts are indicted as major determinants of war, and the antecedents of these instincts are said to be found in animal behavior. In sharp contrast is the

---

*Adapted from a bibliography bearing the same title, by M. Schwebel and M. Krim, in *Am. J. Orthopsychiat.*, 1963, 32, 183–191.

view that social and economic factors are pre-eminent, and that men are not prisoners of instinct. Their frustrations and their aggressions are man-made and are subject to control.

As U Thant declared in a paper reported below, history never repeats itself, and if the themes in the current literature are similar to those of two or three decades ago, the variations are very great. One important evidence of change is the shift of emphasis from the study of war to that of peace. In his analytical review of "Psychological literature on the prevention of war" (Bulletin of the Research Exchange on the Prevention of War, 3, No. 3, Jan. 1955, pp. 2-15), Joseph B. Cooper reported that between 1941 and 1955, 68 articles dealt specifically with peace and 1048 with war. Partly this was because the world was at war during some of the time, and partly because we were more knowledgeable about war than peace. Only very recently has a "peace research" movement of any consequence arisen, and this fact has been reflected in the changed emphasis in the content of papers.

"The Black Death" is the title of William L. Langer's study of the plague that killed a quarter of the people of Europe in 1349-50. (Scientific American, Feb. 1964, pp. 114-21.) Here were conditions of universal catastrophe, and Langer wondered what light they might shed on human behavior today. He found striking similarities to our present condition: flight of the rich to places of presumed greater safety; indifference to human life; crime and violence and extreme sensual indulgence, and their opposites in an excess of religiosity and superstition; scapegoatism; momentary economic prosperity followed by serious declines as a result of the great disruption.

But history never repeats itself. The plague was a mystery and men were victims of their own ignorance during that distant prescientific era. Today there is no justification for unenlightened behavior, for flight, indifference, or scapegoatism. If man does not prevail over the threat to his survival, it will not be for lack of knowledge of the causes of war and the roads to peace.

The bibliography consists of the following sections: 1. Nuclear War and Civil Defense, 2. Conflict, 3. Strategies for Peace, 4. Psychosocial Factors in Peace and War, 5. Attitudes and Images, 6. Game Theory in Peace Research, 7. Economics of Disarmament and Defense, 8. Decision-making, 9. Toward a Warless World, 10. Moral Issues, 11. Significant Journals, 12. Peace Research Organizations, 13. Miscellaneous Source Materials.

We begin with a group of publications that antedate the 50-megaton period of international conflict, a few of them written at a time of great hope for the peace of the world.

Sorokin, Pitirim A. 1942. Man and Society in Calamity. E. P. Dutton & Co., New York, N. Y.

Stagner, R., J. F. Brown, R. H. Gundlach and R. K. White. 1942. A survey of public opinion on the prevention of war. J. Soc. Psychol. 16: 109-130.

Wright, Quincy. 1942. A Study of War. University of Chicago Press. Chicago, Ill.

May, Mark A. 1943. Social Psychology of War and Peace. Houghton Mifflin. New York, N. Y.

Murphy, Gardiner, Ed. 1945. Human Nature and Enduring Peace. Houghton Mifflin. New York, N. Y.

Stouffer, S. A. 1949. Studies in Social Psychology in World War II. Princeton University Press. Princeton, N. J.

Klineberg, Otto. 1950. Tensions Affecting International Understanding. Social Science Research Council. New York, N. Y.

Cantril, Hadley. 1950. Tensions That Cause Wars. University of Illinois Press. Urbana, Ill.

Pear, Tom H., Ed. 1950. Psychological Factors of Peace and War. Philosophical Library. New York, N. Y.

Toynbee, Arnold. 1950. War and Civilization. Oxford University Press, Oxford, England.

Myrdal, Gunnar. 1952. Psychological Factors of Peace and War. Philosophical impediments to effective international cooperation. J. Soc. Issues. Suppl. Series, No. 6, 31 pp.

Kelman, H. C. , W. Barth and R. Hefner, Eds. 1955. Research approaches to the study of war and peace. J. Soc. Issues. 11(1).

Gilbert, G. M. , Ed. 1956. Psychological Approaches to Intergroup and International Understanding. University of Texas Press. Austin, Tex.

Wallace, Victor H. , Ed. 1957. Paths to Peace: A Study of War, Its Causes and Prevention. University Press. Melbourne, Australia.

NUCLEAR WAR AND CIVIL DEFENSE

This section includes publications on the probable consequences of nuclear attack and the condition of the nation thereafter, and on the adequacy of proposed civil defense measures. The authors represent medical and physical as well as behavioral sciences.

A National Shelter Program, Its Feasibility and Its Cost. 1962. P. O. P. O. Box 577, New York 27, N. Y. 27 pp. 25 cents.

This report was prepared by a group of independent scientists, among them T. Dobzhansky, O. Klineberg and S. Melman. Drawing upon available information in their respective fields, the specialists deal with the following topics concerning nuclear attack and shelters: structure, heat effects, air supply, cost of shelters, water supply, radiation effects, genetic effects, industrial disorganization, and psychological impact.

The Medical Consequences of Thermo-nuclear War. 1962. New Eng. J. Med. 266(22): 1126-1154.

An analysis of the probable consequences of nuclear attack in the Boston area represents a major contribution. This special section of the journal includes four articles, on the human and ecologic effects in Massachusetts, the physician's role in the period after attack, some psychiatric and social aspects of the defense-shelter program, and a glossary of radiation terminology. The authors of the third of these topics are Harvard psychiatrists P. H. Leiderman and J. H. Mendelson.

Effects of a 20-Megaton Thermonuclear Explosion on Columbus Circle (N. Y.). 1962. Scientists' Committee for Radiation Information. New York Academy of Sciences, 2 East 63rd Street, New York 21, N. Y. Revised ed. Mimeographed. 15 pp.

Basing their estimates on evidence from test explosions and atomic drops, the scientists analyze the effects on the New York Metropolitan area of a single 20-megaton bomb. They describe the explosion and its aftermath, including the following types of hazards: immediate thermal effects, immediate nuclear radiation, blast effects, firestorm, fallout, economic and social disruption, long-term effects.

Biological and Environmental Effects of Nuclear War. U. S. Government Printing Office, Washington 25, D. C.

The Hearings before the Special Subcommittee of the Joint Committee on Atomic Energy, Eighty-sixth Congress, June, 1959. Civil Defense—1961. U. S. Government Printing Office, Washington 25, D. C.

The Hearings before the Special Subcommittee of the Committee on Government Operations, House of Representatives, Eighty-seventh Congress, August, 1961. U. S. Government Printing Office, Washington 25, D. C.

Nordlie, P. G. and R. D. Popper. 1961. Social Phenomena in a Post-Nuclear Attack Situation. Human Sciences Research, Inc. 1408 Fillmore Street, Arlington, Va.

Utilizing present knowledge about individual and group behavior, the authors attempt to predict post-attack behavior and its effects on social recovery.

Kahn, Herman. 1961. <u>On Thermonuclear War</u>. Princeton University Press. Princeton, N. J.
Written by one of the leading exponents of the view that a nuclear war can be won, this book presents the case for a strong civil defense program that would enable the survivors of an all-out war to rebuild the nation.

Hagan, Roger (February 24). 1962. Community shelters: the bait and the trap. <u>The Nation</u>. 194(8): 160-167.
A critical appraisal of the concept of Civil defense and the proposed programs.

Waskow, Arthur I. <u>Civil Defense: Both Red and Dead</u>. American Friends Service Committee. 160 North 15th Street, Philadelphia 2, Pa.
Waskow, Arthur I. <u>The Shelter-Centered Society</u>. Peace Research Institute. Washington, D. C.
Summarize discussions of civil defense at conference of social scientists, including psychologists and psychiatrists.

CONFLICT

War is a special case of conflict. Some of these publications consider a variety of types of conflict; all of them are concerned with the source springs of violent struggle between states.

Boulding, Kenneth E. 1962. <u>Conflict and Defense: A General Theory</u>. Harper & Brothers. New York, N. Y. 349 pp. $7.00.
Theoretical economist and Director of the Center for Research on Conflict Resolution at the University of Michigan, the author examines the theories concerning conflict developed by various scholarly disciplines, such as economic theory about business competition, psychological theories about internal conflict over the choice between unpleasant alternatives, arms race theory on the effects of reciprocally reinforced hostility. He then proceeds to a generalizing of theories and provides a new framework from which to view international relations, one in which sovereign states are compared with competing businesses. Boulding's work contributes ideas on areas for urgent research, serves as an example of a sophisticated approach to analysis, and provides a useful framework for viewing conflict.

McNeil, Elton B. , Ed. 1962. <u>Social Science and Human Conflict</u>. Prentice-Hall. Englewood Cliffs, New Jersey.
Chapters on human conflict from the viewpoint of each of the social sciences, and a summary of current theory and research in the field.

Medical Association for the Prevention of War. July 29, 1961. The pathogenesis of war. <u>The Lancet</u>. Pp. 259-261.

Medical Association for the Prevention of War. Sept. 1961. Bulletin No. 24.
Eleven papers on biological, economic and psychological factors in war, and on the responsibilities of medical doctors in its prevention. These were originally presented at the association's conference, Cambridge, England, 1961.

North, Robert C. 1963. Conflict. <u>International Encyclopedia of the Social Sciences</u>. Free Press of Glencoe, New York, N. Y.

STRATEGIES FOR PEACE (Arms Control, Disarmament)

This section includes titles on arms control and disarmament, and also on more basic means of improving relations between states. A numer of theories on peace-keeping are examined, among them that of "stable deterrence."

Bernard, V. W., J. D. Frank, H. D. Kelman, O. Klineberg, and C. E. Osgood. 1963. Behavioral Sciences and Peace. (Pugwash Continuing Committee, 8 Asmara Rd., London N. W. 2.)
    Report from American psychiatrists and psychologists attending the Tenth Pugwash Conference.

Blackett, P. S. S. 1962. Studies of War. Hill and Wang. New York, N. Y. $3.95.
    The author is a nuclear physicist and a Nobel prize winner, a trained British naval officer, and a military strategist. He reviews much of the published work on nuclear arming and threats of war, criticizes much of the theory on the subject, and makes proposals for ending the arms race.

Boyd-Orr, John, Hermann Joseph Muller, Hugo Osvald and Hugo Boyko. Oct. 1962. Declaration (a letter). World Federalist 7 (6).
    Announcement of the founding of the World Academy of Art and Science, which will function as an informal World University. Its aim is to provide a forum for distinguished scientists and scholars to work on a truly international basis to apply their knowledge to problems of human welfare.

Boyko, Hugo and W. Junk, Eds. 1962. Science and the Future of Mankind. World Academy of Art and Science.
    Collection of essays dealing with beneficent uses of science and with applications to political and economic problems in order to promote peace, economic welfare, and a high level of culture. Included are essays by Albert Einstein, J. Robert Oppenheimer, H. J. Muller, H. D. Lasswell, Bertrand Russell, and others. Foreword by Lord Boyd-Orr. The World Academy of Art and Science, established in 1960, is an outgrowth of the 1956 International Conference on Science and Human Welfare. This book is its first publication.

Bray, Charles W. 1962. Toward a technology of human behavior for defense use. Am. Psychol.: 527-541.
    This paper considers first the future problems of the Defense Department for which research in psychology and the social sciences may help to provide answers. There are the human use problems (for example, command and control systems and missiles), and the complementary social problems (for example, personnel turnover and the effects of inadvertent launch). Six out of 40 possible research programs have been selected for special attention, and these reduced to three major areas: human performance, the adaptations of complex organizations to changing demands, and persuasion and motivation.

Burton, John W. 1963. Peace Theory, Preconditions of Disarmament. Australian National University. Canberra. 1962. Alfred Knopf. New York.
    Deals, among other things, with the problem of how social change can be handled creatively.

Fisher, Roger, Ed. 1964. International Conflict and Behavioral Science. Basic Books. New York, N. Y.
    A collection of papers prepared by anthropologists, economists, educators, historians, lawyers, political scientists, psychiatrists, and psychologists. Their purpose was to consider "Alternatives to the use of force as a means of settling international problems," and the papers considered the questions, "What should the government do?" and "How do we make the government do it?"

Fleming, D. F. 1962. Does Deterrence Deter? (Part of Series: Beyond Deterrence). 48 pp. Peace Literature Service, American Friends Service Committee.
    The deterrence theory and its operation are briefly reviewed for the World War I and II period, and more extensively for the Cold War.

Glagolev, Igor. Scientific Research on the Problems of Peace and Disarmament. Aug. 1963. Extracts from paper sent to Clarens Conference on Peace Research. Fall 1963. International Newsletter on Peace Research. 1(3): 19-21.
    Considerable scientific work on disarmament has been and is being done in the U. S. S. R. ; this work is reviewed by the Director, Consultative Scientific Group on Disarmament, Pugwash Committee, U. S. S. R. He concludes that a new interdisciplinary peace science is emerging. However, it should aim not only for peace, but for social progress.

Melman, Seymour. 1961. The Peace Race. Ballantine Books. New York, N. Y. 152 pp. 50 cents.
    This Columbia professor of industrial engineering, who edited Inspection for Disarmament, shows "the restrictive and defeatist effects of a conventional economic and military policy..." and proposes "the means to win with freedom under peaceful co-existence...." He recommends measures for ending the arms race.

Schelling, Thomas C. and Morton Halperin. 1961. Strategy and Arms Control. New York: Twentieth Century Fund.
    The authors indicate by their analyses the many complex issues involved in disarmament and propose the use of stable deterrents as an alternative to disarmament.

Shore, William X. Factual Investigations in the Maintenance of International Peace and Security. Ph. D. thesis. Columbia University, New York.

Singer, J. David. March 1961. Deterrence, Arms Control, and Disarmament: Toward a Synthesis in National Security Policy. Mental Health Research Institute, University of Michigan, Ann Arbor, Michigan. (Unpublished.)
    Three basic approaches to national security policy, designed to lead from a reliance on deterrence, through arms control, to multilateral and enforceable disarmament, are examined.

U Thant. May 25, 1962. History Does Not Repeat Itself. Address at Carleton University, Ottawa. Copy available from United National Association, Ottawa, Canada.
    The assumption that history repeats itself is fallacious, and has led to disastrous decisions. Chamberlain was desperately anxious in 1938 not to repeat the mistake of 1914, and as a result committed worse ones at Munich. In 1956, Eden, disillusioned by Chamberlain's failure in 1939, embarked on a tough Suez policy which failed disastrously. The U. S. S. R. has an obsessive fear of encirclement, rooted in memories of the 1919 intervention. Fear of a catastrophic surprise attack dominates U. S. thinking because of memories of Pearl Harbor. The other main theme is the need for a true international democracy, and the need for the wealthy countries to distribute their abundance.

Wadsworth, James J. 1962. The Price of Peace. Frederick A. Praeger. New York, N. Y. 127 pp.
    The old way of working for disarmament has failed; a new approach is needed. We need quiet bilateral diplomacy, a strong wave of public opinion, a concentrated program of research, intensive public information. The author gives background on past disarmament negotiations from personal experience. While the U. N. is the "conscience of the world, " it is still the two great powers

who must agree on disarmament. No further progress is likely until there is a much greater relaxation in international tension.

Waskow, Arthur I. 1962. The Limits of Defense. Doubleday. Garden City, N. Y.
   Presenting a reasoned case for disarmament, the author analyzes each of the current theories of strategy (counterforce, balanced deterrence, and a mixture of the two), in the proportions determined by the balance of power in the Pentagon, finds them a national danger rather than a defense, and calls for disarmament plus actions that will enhance democracy.

Waskow, Arthur I. 1963. The Worried Man's Guide to World Peace. Doubleday.
   Anchor. $1.25.
   A review of peace policies and activities, suggested criteria by which they can be judged, and ways in which social science findings indicate effectiveness in influencing policy.

Wright, Quincy, William M. Evans, Morton Deutsch, Eds. 1962. Preventing
   World War III: Some Proposals. Simon & Schuster. New York, N. Y. 436 pp.
   $6.95.
   This symposium on procedures for preventing war consists of 28 papers, many written by behavioral scientists.

Focus on Arms Control and Disarmament. February - March 1963. Intercom,
   New York. (Published by the Foreign Policy Association.) 5(2): 9-72.
   Brief history of arms control and disarmament since 1958. Documents roles of U. S. and U. N. Summary of research activity and centers. Useful ? dresses and bibliography with abstracts.

Peace, 1962. (Spring) 1962. New University Thought. New University Thought
   Publishing Co. , 909 East 55th Street, Chicago 15, Ill.
   A special issue containing articles on the views of Americans concerning war, disarmement, and civil defense, and on the ways in which the public schools are alleged to be preparing the minds of students for war.

The Study of Disarmament, 1945-1962. Disarmament Committee of the Washing-
   ton, D. C., Women's Strike for Peace. 1822 Massachusetts Avenue, N. W.,
   Washington 6, D. C. 80 pp. $1.00. (Also bulk rates.)
   An attempt to present an objective account of both sides of the history of disarmament negotiations. It is designed as a springboard for study and discussion and includes a selected bibliography as well as the full text of both the U. S. and U. S. S. R. disarmament proposals.

PSYCHOSOCIAL FACTORS IN PEACE AND WAR

   The following authors are also concerned with conflict. Their special emphasis, however, is on the psychosocial factors that contribute to the outbreak and the prevention of war, and the psychological consequences of nuclear cold war.

Escalona, Sibylle K. 1962. Children and the Threat of Nuclear War. Child Study
   Association. 9 East 89th Street, New York 28, N. Y. 40 cents.
   The first document of its kind, this pamphlet brought together knowledge available at the time concerning children's reactions to nuclear danger, and provides guidance to parents and teachers in handling the anxieties and fears set off by life in an age of threat from thermonuclear destruction. The major topics are the differences between nuclear danger and other dangers, how children cope with their thoughts about nuclear danger and how parents can help, and special circumstances affecting the schoolchild's response to nuclear danger. The author considers separately the age groups of 4 to 6, 6 to 12 and adolescence.

Frank, Jerome. Sanity and Survival. Acts for Peace. 1730 Grove Street, Berkeley 9, Calif. 16 pp. 25 cents.
The author, a psychiatrist, points out the psychological forces that keep nations trapped in the arms race, and explores as an alternative the nonviolent resolution of conflict.

Klineberg, Otto. 1964. The Human Dimension in International Relations. Holt, Rinehart and Winston. New York, N.Y.
The author, a psychologist, declares there is nothing in human nature that makes war inevitable, and examines a variety of theories and their empirical support and concludes with recommendations for improved negotiations, better international understanding, and research.

Masserman, Jules H., Ed. 1964. Violence and War, with Clinical Studies (Science and Psychoanalysis, Vol. VI). Grune and Stratton. New York, N.Y. $8.75.
1962 Symposium held by the Academy of Psychoanalysis and the American Association for the Advancement of Science, which gives a concise survey of current thought about violence and war.

Meacham, Stewart. The Social Aspects of Nuclear Anxiety. Paper presented at Annual Meeting of American Psychiatric Association, St. Louis, May 6-10, 1963, reprinted by Peace Education Division, Am. Friends Service Comm. 160 N. 15th St., Philadelphia, Pa. 1963.
The commitment to war in today's world is basically irrational. We tend to project the blame for this situation upon others and obscure the issue with delusory visions of our heroic role; we adapt ourselves to the illness. Healthy reactions include helping people and participating in organizations working for peace. The question of the psychiatrist's role is raised: shall it be to help people conform to the war-centered situation, or to discover resources needed to build a new world?

Osgood, Charles E. 1962. Alternative to War or Surrender. University of Illinois Press. Urbana, Ill. $1.45.
An experimental psychologist who has made a major contribution on the nature and measurement of meaning here applies psychological theory to the development of programs for conflict resolution, especially to graduated reciprocation in tension-reduction.

Schwebel, Milton. March 1963. Students, teachers and the bomb. NEA Journal. 52(3): 46-48.
Reports on a study of children's opinions and proposes ways of ameliorating "nuclear anxiety" in the classroom.

Sherif, Muzafer, et al. 1961. Intergroup Conflict and Cooperation: The Robbers Cave Experiment. University of Oklahoma Press. Norman, Okla.
An example of the application of psychological research methodology to urgent problems of the day, this is a highly creative research design wherein behavioral scientists caused, conducted, and concluded peacefully a war between groups of 11-year-old boys in an experimental camp.

Children and the Threat of Nuclear War. 1964. Child Study Association of America. Duell, Sloan and Pearce. New York, N.Y.
The observed, inferred, and expressed reactions of children and adolescents to nuclear crises and ongoing threat, and some recommendations for parents and teachers.

PEACE RESEARCH

The titles in this section collectively provide a history of the peace research movement, proposed goals, current investigations, many proposed topics for research, and one author's evaluation of what has been accomplished.

Albertson, Maurice. Report of Student Peace Research Workshop at Camp Colorado, Summer 1962. Peace Research Newsletter, Research Foundation, Colorado State University, Fort Collins, Colo.
Report contains detailed proposals for research on such topics as: Applicability of Sociopsychological Concepts to International Relations; Live Crisis Analysis; Effect of Other Political Events on Disarmament Negotiations; Sociopolitical Factors in the Transition to a Disarmed Economy; Measurement of Attitudes Toward War/Peace Issues and International Affairs; Ideology of the Peace Movement.

Boulding, Elise. June 1, 1962. The Technology of Peace-Making: A Report on Developments in Social Science Research on War and Peace in the U. S. Center for Research on Conflict Resolution, Ann Arbor, Michigan. 14 pp.
A historical survey of the peace research movement, from the establishment in 1933 by Quincy Wright at the University of Chicago of an interdepartmental curriculum on international affairs, to 1962, when many centers were operating in the U. S. and several in other countries.

Burton, J. W. August, 1963. Peace Research and International Relations. Typescript. Canadian Peace Research Institute. Dundas, Canada. 12 pp.
Compares peace research and international relations study. Peace research is dynamic, oriented to social change, with a bent toward immediate social application of results, and a sense of urgency.

Feldman, Shel. 1963. Report on Current Research Related to Psychological Factors in Peace and War: East Coast; Western United States. Mimeo. Inst. of Communications Research. University of Illinois. Urbana, Ill.
Survey of research in progress at various centers and universities.

Murphy, Gardner. Fall 1962. Science and world order. Background, Journal of International Studies Association. 6(1-3): 5-11.
Claims that not just one science created our predicament today, and so not just one (e. g. , nuclear physics) bears the responsibility of working toward peace. Appeals to the individual sciences to turn to a generalized science, and to heed the challenge of basic research (using methods of science) that can be of use to our society in working toward peace.

Nerlich, Uwe. 1963. Krieg und Frieden. (War and Peace.) C. Bertelsmann Verlag, Gütersloh, West Germany.
Series of publications on problems of international politics, including translations of work relevant to peace research.

North, Robert C. , Ole R. Holsti, M. George Zaninovich, and Dina A. Zinnes. 1963. Content Analysis: A Handbook with Application for the Study of International Crisis. Northwestern University Press. Evanston, Ill.

North, Robert C. 1962. International Conflict and Integration: Problems of Research. In Muzafer Sherif, Ed: Intergroup Relations and Leadership. Wiley. New York, N. Y.

Oppenheimer, Martin. October 1963. Peace research: a criticism. The American Behavioral Scientist. Spring 1964. The peace research game. Dissent (with a rebuttal by Arthur Waskow, Institute for Policy Studies).

While those engaged in peace research form a useful counterweight to the "New Civilian Militarists" on the campus, they still share many of the assumptions of the academic establishment, and tend to view society as a functioning whole beset from time to time with minor dysfunctions. Hence peace researchers see problems as involving adjustments rather than basic changes in society, and focus their research upon decision-making by elites, communication among elites, and the construction of utopian models. The two articles review different aspects of current research and its assumptions and conclude that scientists need to grapple with the quality of social change necessary before peace can be achieved.

Russell, Roger. 1960. Roles for the psychologist in the maintenance of peace. Am. Psychol. 15(2): 95-109.
    The roles are in research and education.

Singer, J. David. April, 1961. Raising the sights of research on peace. Amer. Behavioral Scientist. 4(8): 11-13.
    Contemporary problems of international relations demand a sharp revision of our present research techniques. This involves filling in the gap between two fields: the psychology of group behavior, which may not be applicable without modification to the behavior of states; and traditional political science, which usually limits itself to compiling random historical "facts" or to armchair speculation. The nature of the linkage between individual and state behavior needs to be elucidated.

Van der Lely. 1963. Peace as a Problem and a Challenge. (In Dutch.) Stichting Vredesopbouw, Amsterdam, Holland.
    Discussion of economic, psychological and political aspects of the war-peace problem, and suggested research projects. (From International Newsletter on Peace Research. Vol. 2, No. 1.)

Wuesthoff, Freda. 1963. Working Programme for a Lasting Peace. Society for the Scientific Study of Peace. c/o Mme. Henriette Jaquet, Quispel, 8 Quai des Arenières, Geneva, Switzerland.
    Outlines a research program in the fields of psychology, sociology, history, politics, economics, jurisprudence, pedagogy, theology, and philosophy.

Defining the social problem of war and peace. March/April 1963. Wetenschap and Samenleving. (Science and Society.) (In Dutch.) Amsterdam, Holland.
    Report on papers and discussions at a conference of the Alliance of Scientific Researchers and the Netherlands Pubwash Committee, Jan. 1963.

ATTITUDES AND IMAGES

The following reported investigations represent one variety of peace research, which is used to learn what people think about such issues as conflict and world government.

Levy, Sheldon G., and Robert Hefner. Nov. 1, 1962. Multidimensional Scaling of International Attitudes. Working Paper #201. Center for Research and Conflict Resolution. Ann Arbor, Mich.
    The purpose of this research is to obtain a census of international attitudes which would serve as a tension indicator and eventually contribute to the resolution of conflicts.

Buchanan, William and Hadley Cantril. 1953. How Nations See Each Other. A Study in Public Opinion. University of Illinois Press. Urbana, Illinois.
    A UNESCO-sponsored report of a cross-cultural survey. A questionnaire

was given to respondents in nine countries to ascertain attitudes and stereotypes about their own and other countries. The authors found that stereotypes are symptoms rather than determiners of international tensions.

Canadian Attitudes — Here Are Some of Them. Feb. 20, 1963. Canadian Peace Research Institute. Dundas, Ontario, Canada.

Some results of the opinion survey of Canadian attitudes toward disarmament and related subjects are given. Four out of five wanted a strong U. N. army. At least half had no economic fears of disarmament. Seven out of ten favored disarmament even if it meant a loss of income or job.

Christiansen, Bjorn. 1959. Attitudes Toward Foreign Affairs as a Function of Personality. Oslo University Press, Oslo, Norway.

In a comprehensive description of the attitudes of 167 students in Norwegian Military Schools, reactions are classified on 2 scales: threat- versus problem-oriented, and outward- versus inward-directed. Highest correlation between reactions to interpersonal and international situations were found for the threat-oriented responses. For threat-oriented, outward-directed individuals these correlations varied widely and consistently, depending on the person's position on a "nationalism" scale; the more nationalistic, the higher the correlation. Passive reactions were less well correlated (between the international and interpersonal sphere) than aggressive reactions.

Cory, Robert H., Jr. October 1963. Images of United States disarmament negotiating system. J. of Arms Control. 1(4): 654-662.

Confidential interviews and informal group discussions with individual diplomats were used to help formulate images of the United States disarmament policy. The Soviet-bloc delegates are best informed. The sophisticated level of their private views of U. S. policy contrasts with the oversimplified stereotype they present in public. The eight "new" nations at the disarmament table have representatives somewhat less well informed, backed by inadequate depth of staff. Diplomats of the nations taking part only at the U. N. level are poorly supplied with technical advice. They lack military and political articulation. Their image of Russia and the U. S. is of two giants, each capable of destroying civilization. Representatives are aware of difficulties in the way of disarmament and pressures against it in the United States. Further studies of this type could be useful in helping guide successful steps toward disarmament.

Deutsch, Karl W. and Lewis J. Edinger. 1959. Germany Rejoins the Powers. Mass opinion, interest groups, and elites in contemporary German foreign policy. Stanford University Press. Stanford, California. 320 pp. $6.50.

This book was intended to analyze the making of German foreign policy and to assess her reliability as an ally. The writers use a complex five-point method of analysis. History shows that the German people have always been Jekyll and Hyde and they still are. Only 25 per cent are fully committed to popular government (as shown in polls), although the younger people seem to be more democratic. About 25 per cent still hold a favorable opinion of Hitler and believe that no one who resisted Hitler should be in the government. Apart from the pro-Nazis, 41 per cent of Germans think they were better off before 1939. The political hero is Bismarck. The constitution is designed to prevent weakness and thus a takeover, but it has never been tested. Although the top politicians are anti-Nazi, 20 per cent of the cabinet ministers were Nazis, and many civil groups (except trade unions) have a poor anti-Nazi record.

Laulicht, Jerome and John Paul. Attitudes of the general public: Internal constraints to negotiated agreements. Canadian Peace Research Institute, Dundas, Ontario, Canada. Paper given at International Arms Control and Disarmament Symposium. University of Michigan. Ann Arbor, Michigan. 12 pp. plus 4 pp. of tables. Jan. 1964.

Public opinion studies can act as guides to governments in formulating foreign policy. In the absence of knowledge about what is acceptable to the electorate, national leaders might hesitate to adopt radically new or long-range policies, even if they consider them desirable. Reports results of a study with a national Canadian sample. One implication of the findings is that people hold less coherent views on foreign policy than is generally thought, and, therefore, it should be relatively easy to change attitudes· on particular issues if the national leaders wish to do so.

Scott, William A. and Stephen B. Whitney. 1958. The United States and the
   United Nations: The Public View, 1945-55. Manhattan Publishing Company.
   New York, N. Y.
   The purpose of the book is to mirror the United States public view of the United Nations, to determine the extent to which the public is giving and can be expected to give informed and stable support to the U. N. The data presented by the authors were derived from more than one hundred surveys conducted by five national polling agencies from 1945 through 1954.

GAME THEORY IN PEACE RESEARCH

This mathematical theory regards action in a conflict situation as a game in which each player tries to maximize his own gains and his opponents' losses. One assumption is that the players are wholly rational in their calculations.

Rapoport, Anatol. 1960. Fights, Games and Debates. University of Michigan
   Press. Ann Arbor, Mich.
   The application of game theory to the understanding of conflict and the recognition of the blind and irrational forces that block reconcilation.

Schelling, Thomas. 1960. The Strategy of Conflict. Harvard University Press.
   Cambridge, Massachusetts. 309 pages.
   When game theory is applied to international politics and strategy, the "mixed-motive" game, in which the antagonists have a common interest as well as conflicting interests (like labor and management) is more applicable than the usual "zero-sum" game.

Schelling, Thomas C. and Morton H. Halperin. 1961. Strategy and Arms Control.
   The Twentieth Century Fund. New York, N. Y. 148 pp.
   One of four books published as a result of a disarmament study group of the American Association for the Advancement of Science in 1960. Recommends stable deterrence. Emphasizes the same game-theoretical viewpoint as Schelling's Strategy of Conflict, namely, that the protagonists have common interests as well as conflicting interests.

Shubik, Martin. 1963. Some reflections on the design of game theoretic models
   for the study of negotiation and threats. J. of Conflict Resolution. 7(1): 1-12.
   It must be understood that models are not representations of reality, but only aids to understanding and guides to further research. The type of model used in game theory is that of a self-policing system, with built-in enforcement of the redistribution of benefits. It is an oversimplification to represent the relations between two countries as a two-person game, since there are many groups, sometimes in conflict, within each country; it is really an n-person game with coalitions.

ECONOMICS OF DISARMAMENT AND DEFENSE

Here are analyses about the economic consequences of disarmament in the United States and several other countries.

Baade, Fritz. 1961. Disarmament and the Economy (Abrustung und Wirtschaft). Atomzeitalter, Frankfurt a. M. booklet 8. pp. 180-182.
How would radical disarmament affect the economy? Does a shut-down of the armament industry lead to a shrinkage of the market and mass unemployment? Leading economists of West and East had discussions about these problems in Kiel and decided to hold other conferences. Preliminary results are reported.

Barber, Arthur. Oct. 1963. Some industrial aspects of arms control. J. of Arms Control. I(4): 585-588.
Arms control should be not an isolated discipline, but an inherent function of industry as well as of government and universities. Consider some fallacies in present discussions.

Benoit, Emile, et al. 1962. Economic Impacts of Disarmament. U. S. Arms Control and Disarmament Agency Publication No. 2. U. S. Government Printing Office, Washington 25, D. C. 15 cents.

Benoit, Emile and Kenneth Boulding, Eds. 1963. Disarmament and the Economy. Harper and Row. New York, N. Y.

Chase, Stuart. 1959. Live and Let Live; A Program for Americans. Harper. New York, N. Y.
The author outlines the major changes which have brought the U. S. and the world to the present impasse and explains why the threats of the nuclear age are not faced squarely by most people. He describes the world's three main problems (preventing war, checking population growth, and raising living standards) and proposes solutions.

Gilmore, John S. Proposed State and Local Preparation for Curtailment of Defense Spending in Colorado. Statement presented Nov. 8, 1963, to the Manpower and Employment Subcommittee. Mimeo, 25 pp. Prof. Gilmore, University of Denver, Denver, Colorado.
The Colorado economy is more dependent on defense spending that that of other sections of the U. S.; it is especially involved with offensive (retaliatory) nuclear weapons and their carriers. Defense spending in 1962 is estimated as 29 per cent of total personal income. The problems in reconversion and their solutions are examined.

Herring, Frances W. July-Sept. 1962. Economic and social impacts of disarmament. Pax et Libertas. Pp. 1-3.
The article, which is written largely from the U. S. standpoint, points out that the purely economic tasks fall into two classes: those involved in maintaining an over-all rate of national production and employment sufficient to absorb the released manpower, and those involved in dealing with regions and industries wholly engaged in military production. An outline is made of the different situations to be met by Communist and by private enterprise countries, because of the different attitudes toward planning.

Humphrey, Hubert H. The Economic Effects of Disarmament. Speech excerpts. Available from Nat. Com. for SANE Nuclear Policy. 17 E. 45th Street, New York 17, N. Y. 4 pp. 5 cents.

Ivanov, K., M. Kalugin and B. Bazanov. Economic programme for disarmament. International Affairs, Moscow, December 1962 and January 1963. (Reported in Disarmament and Arms Control 1(1).)
Part One describes the reasons for having an economic program to use the resources freed by disarmament and outlines the ways these resources could be put to best effect. Part Two gives details of the ways underdeveloped countries

in Asia, Africa, and South America would be aided and the benefits to mankind of developing these parts of the world.

Khan, A. A. October 1962. Economic and social consequences of disarmament. Pakistan Horizon, Karachi. (Reported in Disarmament and Arms Control. 1(1).)

Reports on U. N. Expert Group, of which Khan was a member. Statistical breakdown of world arms expenditure. Emphasizes need for radical change in governmental attitudes toward economics and toward aid to underdeveloped countries. Discusses use of released resources.

Melman, Seymour, Ed. 1962. Disarmament: Its Politics and Economics. American Academy of Arts and Sciences. Boston, Mass.

Piel, Gerald. February 3, 1962. On the feasibility of peace. Science. 144: 648-652.

This includes information drawn from a special study by the U. S. Bureau of the Budget of the probable effects of a disarmament agreement on the economy and the federal budget.

Rosenbluth, Gideon. May 1964. The Economic Consequences of Disarmament. Canadian Peace Research Institute. Dundas, Ontario, Canada. 23 pp.

Considers both the American and the Soviet plans.

Rosenbluth, Gideon. November 1963. The Effect of Disarmament on the Canadian Economy. Canadian Peace Research Institute. Dundas, Ontario, Canada. 15 pp.

This is a preliminary report of a continuing study on the major problems in the economics of disarmament; namely, maintenance of aggregate demand and mobility.

DECISION-MAKING AND FOREIGN POLICY FORMULATION

Some of the political, economic, and psychological forces at work to shape a nation's foreign policy are discussed.

Cook, Fred J. 1962. The Warfare State. Macmillan. New York, N. Y. $4.95.

Described by Bertrand Russell in the Foreword as one of the most important and terrifying documents he has ever read, the book defines the military-industrial complex that has, in Cook's opinion, fostered the warfare state. He explains the origin of this power alliance within the country, its role in perpetuating the Cold War, and, in general, its effect upon both domestic and international affairs of the nation.

Frankel, Joseph. 1963. The Making of Foreign Policy: An Analysis of Decision-Making. Oxford University Press, Oxford, England.

The book deals with the way in which modern national states reach their decisions in the realm of international politics. After a theoretical model of decision-making, he gives illustrations of recent practice in the U. S. A. , U. S. S. R. , England, and to a lesser degree, Germany, France, and India.

Fromm, Erich. 1961. May Man Prevail. Doubleday Anchor Book. New York, N. Y. 252 pp.

Subtitled "An Inquiry into the Fact and Fiction of Foreign Policy," the book challenges many of the assumptions underlying American foreign policy.

Horowitz, Irving Louis. 1963. Games, Strategies and Peace. Beyond Deterrence Series, American Friends Service Committee, 160 N. 15th Street, Philadelphia, Pa. 64 pp.

The alternative to annihilation is disarmament; but a body of experts, the new civilian militarists, stand in the way. Such experts treat policies in terms of military strategy and frequently reduce the balance of terror to the level of games.

Jacobson, Harold Karan, Ed. 1960. America's Foreign Policy. Random House, New York, N. Y. 756 pp.

An anthology which, after presenting selections dealing with the framework of policy-making and the contemporary environment of world politics, juxtaposes contrasting and sometimes conflicting analyses of some of the principal problems of present foreign policy.

Knorr, Klaus and Sidney Verba, Eds. 1961. The International System: Theoretical Essays. Princeton University Press. From a Symposium at the Center of International Studies, Princeton University, Princeton, N. J.

Includes essays on such subjects as the application of game theory to international relations, distinctions between agrarian and industrial international systems, system interaction analysis in the international crisis, role of international law in three concrete situations, and distinction between the international and national level of analysis.

Nieburg, H. L. 1963. Uses of violence. J. of Conflict Resolution 7(1): 43-54.

The theme developed is the following: the threat of violence, and the occasional outbreak of real violence which gives the threat credibility, are elements in conflict resolution, not only in international, but also in national communities, and even in sub-national units.

Northrop, F. G. C. 1960. Philosophical Anthropology and Practical Politics; A Prelude to War or Just Law. Macmillan, New York, N. Y.

To avoid war, politicans must perceive and understand the diverse "goal values" of other countries; they should seek an anthropological and sociological approach to politics.

Rosenau, James N. , Ed. 1961. International Politics and Foreign Policy: A Reader in Research and Theory. Free Press of Glencoe Inc. New York, N. Y.

TOWARD A WARLESS WORLD

The authors of these publications sketch out the possible world of the future, its government and its economy, and they discuss some of the means of achieving it.

Baade, Fritz. 1962. The Race to the Year 2000. Doubleday, New York, N. Y. 246 pp.

An optimistic estimate of the near future of the human race. Assuming no nuclear war and not too much economic waste in preparing for one, the world can support a much greater population (predicted total for 2000: 6.5 billion) by fully exploiting the oceans as well as all land for food production; all parts of the world can enjoy the same high standard of living, and this will remove any rational incentive to war.

Bernal, J. D. 1959. World Without War. Marzani & Munsell. New York, N. Y. 308 pp.

The author, a British scientist and science historian, analyzes the prospects for raising the standard of life throughout the world if disarmament were to be realized and if needed resources were diverted from war production.

Larson, Arthur, Ed. 1964. A Warless World. McGraw Hill, New York, N.Y.
Larson, head of the World Rule of Law Center at Duke University, asked a formidable array of thinkers about how the world might operate after disarmament. Twelve authors contributed essays, among them Hubert Humphrey, Arnold Toynbee and Margaret Mead.

Millis, Walter, Reinhold Neibuhr, Harrison Brown, James Real and William O. Douglas. 1961. A World Without War. Washington Square Press. New York, N.Y. 45 cents.
Composed of materials originally appearing in four pamphlets published by the Center for the Study of Democratic Institutions, the book deals with the following issues: the status and future of the arms race, the practicability of a warless world, deciding power disputes in a warless world, and the role of law in world affairs.

MORAL ISSUES

Since the fateful day in August, 1945, when the bomb was dropped on Hiroshima, a new set of ethical problems has arisen.

Bennett, John C., Ed. 1962. Nuclear Weapons and the Conflict of Conscience. Chas. Scribner's Sons. New York, N.Y. Luttenworth Press, London. 190 pp.
Seven leading Americans—three Protestant theologians, a scientist, a psychoanalyst, a political scientist, and an educator—discuss nuclear war from the point of view of the conscience of the individuals who must take part in it. They discuss how the U.S. can preserve itself without surrendering all moral norms in the process.

Eatherly, Claude and Gunther Anders. 1962. Burning Conscience. Monthly Review Press. New York, N.Y. 139 pp. $4.00.
This is a record of a correspondence between two persons different in almost every conceivable respect, except in their expressed determination to prevent another war. Eatherly, pilot of the lead plane over Hiroshima, was at the time of the correspondence a patient in a mental hospital to which he had been committed after having engaged in several antisocial acts. Anders, a German phenomenologist, once a student of Husserl, interprets Eatherly's behavior as the refusal to accept the hero's role and guiltlessness, and as the expression of his need to draw attention to the crime of Hiroshima. The book is of interest to behavioral scientists, not only because of the provocative discussion of ethical issues, but also because it raises questions relevant to the psychopathology of the nuclear age.

Pope John XXIII. 1963. Pacem in Terris (Peace on Earth). Fellowship Publications. Nyack, N.Y.
The significant and influential encyclical of the late Pope.

SIGNIFICANT JOURNALS

These three publications are frequent contributors to the literature on human survival.

1. Bulletin of Atomic Scientists. A consistent source of information on policy and proposals regarding war and peace. Its editor is a renowned scientist, Eugene Rabinowitch, and its authors are both physical scientists (e.g., the late Leo Szilard, "Are we on the road to war?" April 1962) and behavioral scientists (e.g., Charles A. Osgood, "A case for graduated unilateral disarmament," April

264

1960). Of special interest is the September 1962 issue which in its entirety was
devoted to disarmament.

2. Journal of Conflict Resolution. This journal is an essential source of
information on the psychological, sociological, economic, and interdisciplinary
literature on survival. Sample of its content follow:

Kelman, H. , et al. , a series of papers primarily sociological-psychological in
orientation. Entire issue 2(1).

Deutsch, Morton, Trust and suspicion, 2(4): 263-79.

Rinde, E. , S. Rokkan, et al. Toward an international program of research on
the handling of conflicts 3(1): 1-84. A series of 5 papers that grew out of a
seminar on conflict research at the University of Oslo, Norway.

Bauer, R.A. Problems of perception and the relations between the United States
and the Soviet Union. 5(3): 223-229.

Brady, R.A. Deterrence strategies: an annotated bibliography. 4(4): 441-457.

Kuhn, H. W. , et al. Game theory bargaining and international relations. Entire
issue. 6(1).

North, R. C. , et al. Case studies in conflict. Entire issue. 6(3).

Le Vine, R.A. , et al. The anthropology of conflict. (The range of approaches
and data which anthropologists bring to bear on the study of social conflict
and ethnocentrism.)

3. Journal of Social Issues. The quarterly publication of the Society for the
Psychological Study of Social Issues, it is used by the society to communicate
scientific findings and interpretations, in a nontechnical manner, "on human
problems of the group, the community, and the nation as well as the increasingly
important ones that have no national boundaries." One example is: Psychology
and policy in a nuclear age. 1961. 17(3).
This important issue, edited by Roger W. Russell, brought together the
application of psychological data, analysis, and research proposals to problems
of survival. Some of the topics are the Cold War mentality, the emotional and
motivational aspects of the disarmament problem, the mirror image in Soviet-
American relations, psychological considerations relevant to national policy,
and current and needed research in international relations. Previous issues on
survival include Supplement Series No. 9, The Role of the Psychologist in International Affairs, edited by Otto Klineberg.

PEACE RESEARCH ORGANIZATIONS

Activities in many nations have already been reported by Dr. Galtung.
Further description is given in Mrs. Boulding's paper which is abstracted below.
Then follows a list of organizations.

Boulding, Elise. International Newsletter on Peace Research. Winter 1963.
1(1): International Consultative Committee on Peace Research, Women's International League for Peace and Freedom. Ann Arbor, Mich. 22 pp.
Describes the role of WILPF in Peace Research and then presents a very
complete listing of peace research centers around the world and in the U.S. ,
with a brief outline of the programs and activities of each. Information on: Australia, Belgium, Canada, Czechoslovakia, England, France, Germany, Ghana,

265

Holland, India, Japan, Poland, Denmark, Norway, Sweden, Spain, Switzerland, U. S. S. R. , Yugoslavia. In the United States, besides the Arms Control and Disarmament Agency and small groups in the Departments of Defense and State, thirty-eight private institutes, professional associations, university research centers, student groups, and associations and foundations are listed as active in the peace research field.

Arms Control and Disarmament Agency. 1710 H. Street, N. W. , Washington, D. C.
Boston Area Faculty Group on Public Issues. C/o Professor William Schreiber, Massachusetts Institute of Technology, Cambridge, Mass.
Canadian Peace Research Institute. Dundas, Ontario, Canada.
Carnegie Endowment for International Peace. United Nations Plaza at 46th Street, New York, N. Y.
Center for Research on Conflict Resolution. University of Michigan, Ann Arbor, Mich.
Center for International Affairs. Harvard University, Cambridge, Mass.
Center of International Studies. Princeton University, Princeton, N. J.
Center for Peace Research. Creighton University, Omaha, Neb.
Center for the Study of Democratic Institutions. Box 4068, Santa Barbara, Calif.
Committee on Research in International Conflict and Peace. Washington University, St. Louis, Mo.
Conferences on Science and World Affairs (Pugwash Conferences). C/o Dr. Eugene Rabinowitch, 935 East 60th Street, Chicago 37, Ill.
Council for Correspondence. 218 East 18th Street, New York, N. Y.
Hudson Institute. Grasslands Road, Eastview, N. Y.
Institute for Defense Analyses. Washington, D. C.
Institute for International Order. 11 West 42nd Street, New York, N. Y.
Institute for International Studies. Massachusetts Institute of Technology, Cambridge, Mass.
Institute for Social Research. Oslo, Norway.
Institute for Strategic Studies. 18 Adam Street, London WC 2, England.
Institute for War and Peace Studies. Columbia University, New York 16, N. Y.
Peace Research Institute. 1329 18th Street, N. W. , Washington 6, D. C.
RAND Corporation, Santa Monica, Calif.
Scientists' Committee for Radiation Information. C/o New York Academy of Sciences, 2 East 63rd St. , New York 21, N. Y.
Society for the Psychological Study of Social Issues. 1333 16th Street, N. W. , Washington 6, D. C.

MISCELLANEOUS SOURCE MATERIALS

Peace Research Abstracts. Canadian Peace Research Institute. 25 Dundana Ave. , Dundas, Ontario, Canada.
As of April 1964 PRA had 9000 references, of which 6500 were abstracted. Over 600 journals are represented, and several languages. The abstracts are subdivided into 350 categories and are available through a photostat process to scholars who request them. PRA are available also in journal form, 12 issues per year with approximately 1000 abstracts per issue.

Political Behavior. A List of Current Studies. External Research Staff, Bureau of Intelligence and Research. United States Department of State, Washington, D. C. Spring, 1963. 60 pp.
The second in a series of annotated bibliographies of behavioral science research on political processes and international relations. Published and unpublished, completed and ongoing studies are reported. The work is current, for even among the completed studies, most were not finished until 1963. The

studies are categorized; some headings are: change, cognition, decision-making methodology, and motivation. The External Research Staff also publishes ten lists in its Social Science Series. Nine of these are area studies; one is on international affairs.

The Poor Man's Guide to War/Peace Literature. 1964, Spring-Summer edition. New York Peace Information Center. 218 East 18th St., New York 3, N. Y. 21 pp. 25 cents.
     Lists 271 selected titles covering the whole gamut of literature. Special emphasis on inexpensive publications, and paperback editions when these are available.

Science Information Exchange, Smithsonian Institution. 1730 M Street, N. W., Washington, D. C.
     In the area of human survival, as in others, the Exchange will supply scholars and scientists with notices of research projects of current studies. The notices are copies of those submitted by investigators.

Where in the World. . . ? An Annual Index of War/Peace Information, Aids and Services. June 1964. New York Peace Information Center. 218 East 18th Street, New York 3, N. Y. 19 pp. 50 cents.
     An invaluable aid for those interested in the diverse and sometimes obscure sources of information on the many topics related to peace activity and research: directories, organizations, libraries.

Current Thought on War and Peace. Box 4847, Duke Station, Durham, N. C. $7.00 per year.
     This is a quarterly publication of abstracts of the books, articles, and research in progress in the broad field of international relations.

The Balance of Fear.
     A series of 17 half-hour programs on disarmament. Office of Radio and Television. Wayne State University, Detroit 2, Mich.